CD BPO 372
3 2528 06300 3281

Issues in Aging
Vol. 3

SERVICES TO THE AGING AND AGED

Garland Reference Library
of Social Science
Vol. 802

Issues in Aging

DIANA K. HARRIS
Series Editor

THE REMAINDER OF THEIR DAYS
Domestic Policy and Older Families in the United States and Canada
edited by Jon Hendricks and Carolyn J. Rosenthal

HOUSING AND THE AGING POPULATION
Options for the New Century
edited by W. Edward Folts and Dale E. Yeatts

SERVICES TO THE AGING AND AGED
Public Policies and Programs
edited by Paul K.H. Kim

THE POLITICAL BEHAVIOR OF OLDER AMERICANS
edited by Steven A. Peterson and Albert Somit

SERVICES TO THE AGING AND AGED

Public Policies and Programs

edited by

Paul K.H. Kim

GARLAND PUBLISHING, INC.
New York & London / 1994

Library of Congress Cataloging-in-Publication Data

Services to the aging and aged : public policies and programs / edited by Paul K.H. Kim
p. cm. — (Garland reference library of social science ; v. 802. Issues in aging ; v. 3)
Includes bibliographical references and index.
ISBN 0-8153-0611-3
1. Aged—Services for—United States. I. Kim, Paul K. H. II. Series: Garland reference library of social science ; v. 802. III. Series: Garland reference library of social science. Issues in aging ; v. 3.
HQ1064.U5S468 1994
362.6'0973—dc20 94-28668
CIP

Printed on acid-free, 250-year-life paper
Manufactured in the United States of America

Dedicated to
all friends who have helped me to grow

Contents

Series Editor's Foreword

This series attempts to address the topic of aging from a wide variety of perspectives and to make available some of the best gerontological thought and writings to researchers, professional practitioners, and students in the field of aging as well as in other related areas. All the volumes in the series are written and/or edited by outstanding scholars and leading specialists on current issues of considerable interest.

This volume is an invaluable resource for those persons seeking a broad, comprehensive coverage of current public policies and service programs for the elderly. Besides dealing with present gerontological services, it also explores the emerging challenges that these services must face in the future. One of the outstanding features of the book is that its contributors include some of the most prominent authorities in the field of gerontology. This is an exceptionally important and timely volume and is a much needed addition to the literature on aging.

Diana K. Harris
University of Tennessee

Preface

The graying world calls for gerontological human service workers who are dedicated to the welfare of the aged in an increasingly complex society. This awareness is reshaping the reality of needs in training and research. As scientific knowledge develops, symbiotic relationships should sprout in a field otherwise isolated in the academic domain.

This book is designed to discuss selective gerontological services, including public policies and service programs, and to suggest a proactive service model from an international perspective. The intent of the book is to critically review current public policies and service programs with a futuristic perspective. Beginning from an overview of the U.S. policy ventures, the Older Americans Act and such policies as retirement, housing, and health care are discussed. For the service programs, six areas relevant to social services, income security, retirement planning, housing, health, and mental health care are detailed. In conclusion, a unified approach to gerontological human services is introduced, which may be characterized by a synthesis of Eastern and Western values, as well as by joint effort among family, community, and government of the respective country. Albeit modest, it is hoped that this book serves as a building block leading to a perfected welfare state for the aging and aged at home and abroad.

It is indeed a great honor to bring to this effort a number of established colleagues in the field of gerontological human services. The editor is profoundly indebted to the contributing authors who, independently or jointly, enriched the depth and scope of varied analyses. On behalf of these authorities and myself, I extend sincere gratitude to Diana K. Harris of the University of Tennessee for her words of confidence.

Paul K.H. Kim
1994

PART I

Introduction

CHAPTER 1

The Demography of Aging

Jerome L. Blakemore
Robert O. Washington
R.L. McNeely

The aging of America represents a myriad of political, economic, and services delivery problems for the nation. The growth of the elderly population has increased, making the elderly a topic of concern and discussion for health and social services planners. The concerns of the elderly are of major importance to politicians, in part because of the increasing numbers of the elderly, but also because of their active involvement in the voting and political process.

The status of the elderly has changed dramatically since the turn of the century. At the beginning of this century the elderly (persons 65 and older) accounted for only 4.1 percent of the total U.S. population, therefore constituting only one of every 25 Americans. The number of elderly, by 1987, had increased to approximately 29.8 million or 12.3 percent of the total U.S. population. Table 1 indicates the growth of the elderly population (65 and older) from the turn of the century through 1990 as compared to total population figures. As the table reflects, the elderly population has increased threefold since the beginning of the century. The status of the elderly has even greater potential for change as we approach the beginning of the next century during which their numbers are expected to more than double.

The elderly population has more than doubled since the 1950s. The aging of America will continue through the next century largely due to the number of "baby boomers" who will be maturing at that time. The first cohort of "boomers" will reach the age of 65 beginning in 2010, increasing still further the proportion of persons who are elderly during the 21st century.

Table 1: Distribution of the Population by Year 1900–1990 in Thousands

Year	Population All Ages	Population 65+	Percent
1900	76,303	3,084	4.0
1910	91,972	3,950	4.3
1920	105,711	4,933	4.7
1930	122,755	6,634	5.4
1940	131,669	9,019	6.8
1950	150,967	12,270	8.1
1960	179,323	16,560	9.2
1970	203,302	19,980	9.8
1980	226,505	25,544	11.3
1990	248,709	31,241	12.7

Source: U.S. Bureau of the Census, 1989. *Projections of the Population of the United States, by Age, Sex, and Race: 1988–2080*. Current Population Estimates Projections Series P-25, No. 1018. Washington, DC: U.S. Government Printing Office.

Overall life expectancy rates have gradually risen throughout the century. In 1900 the overall life expectancy for Americans was 47.3 years. The average present-day life expectancy rate has increased to an even 75 years, an increase in longevity of more than 50 percent. Given advances in medical technology, the trend toward longer life expectancy rates will increase. This increase will place more of a burden on an already taxed health and social service system because personal maintenance requires greater use of public resources and services (Stone and Fletcher,

1988). The elderly are the fastest growing population group in America.

Age Groups

The U.S. population figures for 1990 reflect continuing trends toward advancing age of Americans. Forty-one million Americans are 55 years old or older. The vast majority of the elderly are women and this trend increases as persons mature into the higher age categories. Moreover, the median age of U.S. citizens is also increasing. The median age of people in the United States reached a peak of 32.1 years in 1987. By the turn of the century, the median age of the country will be 36.8 and will increase to 46.4 by 2050.

The aging of America is illustrated in the number of advanced elderly who reside in the United States. While the overall population in the United States is becoming increasingly older, the average age of the elderly population is also increasing (U.S. Bureau of the Census, 1989). Table 2 details the estimated percentages of the elderly by age group and projections for the elderly through 2050.

Currently the elderly population 85 years of age or older totals approximately 2.9 million. The number of elderly persons of this age group is expected to reach 4.6 million and then increase to 8 million in 2030 (U.S. Bureau of the Census, 1989). It is important to note that this increase in the number of elderly persons 85 and over will occur before the surviving members of the "baby boomer" population reach the age of 85.

The projected population figures for the turn of the century, now less than a decade away, indicate that there will be nearly 35 million Americans 65 years or older and nearly half of this number will be at least 75 years of age (Berry, 1990). Further projections by the U.S. Bureau of the Census indicate that there will be nearly 70 million Americans over the age of 65 by the year 2050. This represents more than a doubling of the elderly

Table 2: Actual and Projected Percent of 65+ Population by Age Group (1960–2050)

Year	65–74 Age Group	75–84 Age Group	85 + Age Group	Median age of the Elderly
1960	66.3	28.1	5.6	71.9
1965	64.1	29.7	5.9	72.3
1970	62.1	30.7	7.1	72.6
1975	61.3	30.7	8.0	72.5
1980	60.9	30.3	8.8	72.8
1985	59.6	31.0	9.4	70.0
1987	59.2	31.2	9.6	73.1
1990	58.2	31.5	10.3	73.3
1995	56.1	32.3	11.6	73.8
2000	52.3	34.4	13.3	74.5
2005	50.8	34.5	14.7	74.2
2010	53.4	31.0	15.5	74.2
2020	59.5	27.7	12.8	73.0
2030	54.9	32.8	12.4	74.0
2040	45.2	36.8	18.0	76.1
2050	46.1	31.6	22.3	76.1

Source: U.S. Bureau of the Census, 1989. *Projections of the Population of the United States, by Age, Sex, and Race: 1988–2080*. Current Population Estimates Projections Series P-25, No. 1018. Washington, DC: U.S. Government Printing Office.

population from 31 million in 1990 to 67 million by the middle point of the 21st century. This trend toward an increase in the elderly population is expected to continue through the remainder of the 20th century through midpoint of the next century. The figures are detailed in Table 3.

As Table 3 indicates, the elderly will continue to increase in total numbers throughout the next century. The midpoint of the next century will arrive with one of every five persons being 65 years of age or older. While the 65 and over cohort of the elderly is increasing, the over 85 group is also increasing in dramatic fashion. There will be 57 million elderly persons 65 and over by the year 2020. Nearly nine million of this number will be persons 85 or older. This age group is expected to triple by

2020. The total number of persons 85 and older is projected to nearly double between the years 2040 and 2060 (Soldo and Manton, 1985).

Table 3: Aging Trends 2000–2050 in Thousands

Year	Population All Ages	Population 65 +	Percent over 65
2000	267,955	34,921	13.0
2010	283,238	39,195	13.8
2020	296,597	51,422	17.3
2030	304,807	64,581	21.2
2040	308,559	66,988	21.7
2050	309,488	67,411	21.8

Source: U.S. Bureau of the Census, 1989. *Projections of the Population of the United States, by Age, Sex, and Race: 1988–2080*. Current Population Estimates Projections Series P-25, No. 1018. Washington, DC: U.S. Government Printing Office.

The projected increase in the number of elderly population raises a number of concerns relative to the care of the elderly. Three primary concerns include the following (Krout, 1991):

- Medicare costs are projected to more than double by the year 2020 with the greatest proportional increase serving the oldest age groups.
- The number of nursing home residents age 85 and above will increase by 2040 to a level two to three times the current number of person 65 and older currently in nursing homes.
- There will be between 6.1 and 9.8 million Americans with moderate to severe dementia requiring 92 to 149 billion dollars annually for their care.

People of Color

Persons of color currently represent a small portion of the elderly population as compared to whites. Projections indicate that while the size of the elderly population is expected to grow, the elderly minority population is also expected to increase dramatically through 2050. This increase in the non-white group is due in part to higher fertility resulting in a 247 percent increase of African-American elderly and a 395 percent increase in the Hispanic elderly population. These figures compare with a 92 percent rate of increase in the white elderly population for the period between 1930 and 1990. Currently the minority elderly population is 14 percent of the total population of people 65 and older. People of color will constitute 32 percent of the total elderly population by the year 2050. While the total white population of elderly is higher and will remain higher throughout the next century, the rate of increase of the minority elderly will occur at a faster rate than the rate of increase for whites. Table 4 reflects the percentage of the minority population as compared to the white population for 1990 and as projected through the year 2050.

Table 4: Ethnic Minority Population Projections (1990–2050)

Year	Percent of Minority Population
1990	14%
2000	16%
2010	20%
2020	22%
2030	25%
2040	28%
2050	32%

Source: U.S. Bureau of the Census, 1989. *Projections of the Population of the United States, by Age, Sex, and Race: 1988–2080*. Current Population Estimates Projections Series P-25, No. 1018. Washington, DC: U.S. Government Printing Office.

In 1990, African Americans represented 8 percent of the total elderly population. Projections indicate that by 2050 African Americans will constitute 14 percent of the elderly population. Hispanics, who are projected to be the fastest growing population during the next century, currently represent 5 percent of the elderly population. The percentage of the Hispanic elderly as compared to the total elderly population is expected to triple by the year 2050 representing 12 percent of the total elderly population. The overall minority population will increase from 14 percent in 1985 to 33 percent in the year 2050 (U.S. Bureau of the Census, 1989).

Economics and the Minority Elderly

The increase in the number of minority elderly is significant because of their economic status. Poverty increases with age. Persons of color have higher poverty rates than European Americans. In 1987 the poverty rate for elderly African Americans was 31 percent and the rate for Hispanics was 22.5 percent, as compared to a 10.7 percent poverty rate for European Americans. The economic status of the elderly, particularly minority elderly, is also influenced by whether or not the elderly person resides alone or with others. Currently, of those African-American elderly who live alone, more than half (57 percent) live below the poverty level. For Hispanic elderly, nearly two of every three (approximately 60 percent) of those who live alone live at a level which is 125 percent of the poverty level, a level generally considered "near poverty." Less than one of every five elderly European Americans lives below the poverty level and 32 percent of all elderly European Americans who live alone live at a level which is 125 percent of the poverty level. A reality of aging is that as the age increases so does the possibility of living at or near the poverty level.

Gender

In 1989, there were more men than women in all ethnic groups under the age of 35. The trend of men outnumbering women begins to change, however, as the population grows older. Women 65 and older outnumber men in the same age group by nearly 6 million (U.S. Senate Special Committee on Aging, 1991). The sex ratio of women to men is even higher as the elderly population becomes increasingly older. Based on 1989 data in the 65–69 age category, there are 84 men for every 100 women. In the 70–74 age group, there are 76 men for every 100 women; for the group in the age range of 85 and older, there are only 39 men for every 100 women (Miranda and Morales, 1992). This results in women living out their later years alone and having longer periods of retirement. This disparity will continue in part because of the life expectancy differences between men and women.

Geographic Distribution

The majority of the elderly population (52 percent) resides in nine states. The states with the highest number of elderly citizens are California, New York, Florida, Pennsylvania, Texas, Illinois, Ohio, Michigan, and New Jersey. These states are also the nine most populated states in terms of total population for all

Table 5: Rank Order of States by Number of People 65+ (1989)

State	Rank	Elderly Population
California	1	3,071,000
New York	2	2,341,000
Florida	3	2,277,000
Pennsylvania	4	1,819,000
Texas	5	1,714,000

Source: Bureau of the Census, 1989. State Population and Household Estimates. Current Population Estimates Projections Series P-25, No. 1018. Washington, DC: U.S. Government Printing Office.

age groups in the United States. The states with the largest elderly population and their national rank are shown in Table 5.

Illinois, Ohio, Michigan, and New Jersey are currently the only other states to have an elderly population of more than one million persons. While these states have the highest actual numbers of elderly persons, they are not necessarily the states that have the highest proportion of elderly persons. The states with the highest percentage of elderly are shown below in Table 6.

Table 6: People 65 and over as Percent of State's Population (1989)

State	Rank	Percent
Florida	1	18.0
Pennsylvania	2	15.1
Iowa	3	15.1
Rhode Island	4	14.8
Arkansas	5	14.8

Source: Bureau of the Census, 1989. State Population and Household Estimates, Current Population Estimates Projections Series P-25, No. 1018. Washington, DC: U.S. Government Printing Office.

The United States Bureau of the Census projects that by the year 2010 California and Florida will have the nation's largest number of older citizens (U.S. Senate Special Committee on Aging, 1991). California will have more than four million older citizens who will constitute 12.3 percent of the state's population. Florida's elderly population is projected to increase some 72 percent between 1989 and 2010. The elderly population in Florida will constitute "approximately twenty percent" of that state's total population.

The changes in the aging population will also be reflected by where the elderly live. For the first time a greater number of the elderly will live in the suburbs rather than in the city (U.S. Senate Special Committee on Aging, 1991).

Rural Elderly

In 1980, individuals living in rural areas comprised nearly one-third of the nation's elderly population (Watson, 1983). While the rural elderly do not constitute a majority, their needs present unique and special concerns for health and human service planners and providers. The problems of the rural elderly are largely a function of interrelated circumstances. Typically these circumstances include the fact that a disproportionate number of persons living in rural areas require help in the conduct of everyday life, and the limitations of rural transportation systems often result in lessened access to human services.

The problems of the rural elderly are complicated by the inequitable distribution of health and human service personnel for rural areas as compared to urban areas. This situation includes inequities in federal funding which exist between rural and non-rural areas of the country. Rural areas receive $9.04 per capita in federal spending. Non-rural areas receive $19.18 (more than double this amount). It has been suggested that the inter- and intra-state funding formulas of the Older Americans Act should be changed to provide a greater share of federal dollars to the rural elderly because of the unique problems they face (Krout, 1991). These problems, which include transportation and access, are compounded for the rural elderly because poverty rates for nonfarm rural areas are considerably higher than the rates for urban dwellers.

Implications

While these forecasts indicate that the aging population will continue to increase, they do not indicate the potential problems associated with having such a large cohort of the elderly in America. The elderly are the heaviest users of health services. The elderly have three more visits to physicians per year than younger patients and are hospitalized three times more often. When hospitalized on average the elderly stay about

50 percent longer than younger patients (National Center for Health Statistics, 1987).

A by-product of an increasing elderly cohort is the added potential for health problems which are associated with aging. Alzheimer's disease is a major condition associated with aging. There are approximately four million people who suffer from Alzheimer's disease in the United States. Current projections suggest that Alzheimer's disease will have a major effect on the economic status and the quality of life of the elderly. Miranda and Morales (1992) indicates that 14 million Americans will be directly affected by this disease. The incidence of Alzheimer's tends to increase as a person ages. Evans (1989) in a study of elderly living in community residences found that 10 percent of persons up to the age of 65 had probable Alzheimer's disease. The incidence of Alzheimer's disease nearly doubles for persons between the ages of 75 to 84 and jumps to approximately 47 percent for persons age 85 and older. If these patterns are consistent, the "graying of America" will obviously mean an increased demand on scarce medical resources.

While Alzheimer's disease is of major concern to public health officials, there are other age-related ailments that may also increase as the elderly population grows. Heart disease, cancer, and stroke are currently responsible for three-fourths of all deaths among the elderly (Miranda and Morales, 1992). These conditions are very costly because generally they require long term care. The economic costs of these few age-related infirmities provide cause for concern for social service and health care planners in particular.

Implications for Caregivers

The demographics of aging mandate increased attention to a variety of factors and concerns. Key among these is the role that caregiving plays in the provision of basic and necessary social and human services. There has been increased concern expressed in the human services literature about the role of informal helping networks (Biegel and Blum, 1990). These informal networks tend to include family and/or friends who provide some form of caregiving for persons who have physical limitations, chronic illnesses, or age-related conditions.

In 1987, the U.S. Senate Select Committee on Aging (1991) estimated that the vast majority (72 percent) of caregivers are women. A major change in the nation's labor force, however, has been the increasing number of women entering the work force, resulting in a decrease in the availability of women to assume the caregiving burden.

Declining Youth Population

While the aging population is increasing, the youthful population is on the decline. The Older Women's League estimates that during the current decade the total number of births will decline by 9.2 percent while the elderly population will increase by 10 percent during the decade of the 1990s. This pattern of decline is further exacerbated by a marked decrease in the fertility rates during the period of 1955 through 1975. Given the potential for age-related physical disability and illness, the potential stresses for caregivers are great and may require a more focused response from policy makers and health and human service planners, particularly given the fact that proportionately there will be more elderly individuals but fewer family members of caregiving age.

While there is an obvious need for human services systems to develop new age-specific programs targeting the elderly, it should also be noted that the plight of the elderly also includes concerns not generally associated with aging. For example, among these concerns is the increasing number of homeless elderly persons. Kurtza and Keigher (1992) view homelessness as a rediscovered, but not new, social problem which now affects an increasing number of elderly persons. They indicate that while the elderly homeless are a small percentage of the homeless, their needs are unique largely because their advanced age renders them particularly vulnerable.

Summary

Society has made a number of assumptions about the elderly. Two of those assumptions have been brought into question by this review of the demographic trends of the elderly. One of the most pervasive assumptions about the elderly is that there is a singular elderly population. Cockerham (1991) indicates that the elderly population of the next century will be healthier, better educated, and more affluent than any comparable cohort of the elderly in the past. This summation of the elderly suggests that there is an "elderly group" whose needs are similar and consistent. Given the differences in income and social status reported here it should be clear that "the elderly" are not a homogenous group whose status, access to resources, and needs are similar. The elderly, perhaps more than any group in this country, are an ever-increasing population with needs that are complex, unique, and diverse. The diversity of the elderly is evidenced in a number of areas including income, resources, health status, and general welfare. Assuming that the elderly are a homogenous group is particularly harmful because it allows health and human service systems to plan without a thorough understanding or appreciation for the needs of the various elderly groups.

A popular view of many Americans that older age represents a time of carefree existence full of fun and enjoyment is also a major assumption related to the elderly. This assumption, which is generally referred to as the golden years, is inaccurate because for an increasing number of elderly citizens, particularly rural and minority elderly, these years are not "golden" at all but are wrought with poverty, poor health, and uncertainty. The implications of having such a phenomenal increase in the cohort of the elderly are varied and complex. Identifying the complexity of needs for this growing population represents a major challenge for public policies and human services.

REFERENCES

Berry, J. 1990. Planning for the 21st century. *Journal of Aging and Social Policy*, 2, 9–12.

Biegel, D. & Blum, D. 1990. *Aging and Caregiving: Theory, Research and Policy*. Beverly Hills, CA: Sage.

Cockerham, W. 1991. *This Aging Society*. Englewood Cliffs, NJ: Prentice Hall.

Evans, D. 1989. Prevalence of disease in a community population of older persons. *Journal of the American Medical Association*, 262.

Krout, J. 1991. Rural advocates must raise their voices. *Perspectives on Aging*, 20, 4–9.

Kurtza, E. & Keigher, S. 1992. The elderly "new homeless": An emerging population at risk. *Social Work*, 36, 273–364.

Miranda, M. & Morales, A. 1992. "Social Work Practice with the Elderly." In A. Morales & B. Sheafor, eds., *Social Work: A Profession of Many Faces* (pp. 383–417), Boston, MA: Allyn & Bacon.

National Center for Health Statistics. 1987. Washington, DC: U.S. Government Printing Office.

Schneider, E. & Guralnik, J. 1990. Aging in America. *Journal of the American Medical Association*, 263, 2335–2340.

Soldo, B.J. & Manton, K. 1985. Health status and service needs of the oldest old: Current patterns and future trends. *The Millbank Memorial Fund Quarterly*, 63, 286–319.

Stone, L. & Fletcher, S. 1988. "Demographic Variations in North America." In E. Rathbone-McCuan & B. Havans, eds., *North American Elders: United States and Canadian Perspective* (pp. 3–36), Westport, CT: Greenwood.

U.S. Bureau of the Census. 1989. *Current population estimates projections series* P-25, No.1018. Washington, DC: U.S. Government Printing Office.

U.S. Senate Special Committee on Aging. 1991. *Aging America trends and projections*. Washington, DC: U.S. Government Printing Office.

Watson, W. 1983. "Selected Demographics and Social Aspects of Older Blacks." In R.L. McNeely & J. Colen, eds., *Aging in Minority Groups*. Beverly Hills, CA: Sage.

PART II

Public Policies for the Elderly

CHAPTER 2

Public Policy and Aging
An Overview

Robert H. Binstock

Public policies have substantially improved the well-being of older Americans in the last half of this century. But we are now approaching an important set of crossroads.

There are still many urgent needs within our growing elderly population. Yet our political system may not respond to these needs. After many decades of expansion in benefits to older persons, the present climate of American politics and public discourse is increasingly hostile to the elderly, in general.

In the early 1990s American public resources are perceived as scarce. The need to "reduce the deficit" of the federal government is a rhetorical mainstay of domestic politics. "Containing health care costs" is widely considered to be one of the major problems of our society.

Population aging is commonly viewed as worsening each of these problems and others as well. More than a quarter of the annual federal budget is expended on benefits to the aging (U.S. Senate, 1989). One-third of all American health care expenditures is on older persons (U.S. House of Representatives, 1989). The present 32 million Americans aged 65 and over, 12.5 percent of our population, is projected to more than double—to 69 million—by the middle of the next century. As early as the year 2030, fully 20 percent of Americans are expected to be aged 65 and over (Taueber, 1990). Accordingly, there is much anxiety about costs of governmental benefits to the aging, now and in the future. Already, a great many issues of domestic policy portray "the aged" as in conflict with other groupings of Americans, and as a growing and unsustainable burden that will undermine our national well-being. How did this political context of hostility to older persons develop? What are some of the urgent needs that remain within the older population? And what are the prospects and strategies for a satisfactory response to those needs through public policy?

1935–1978: Compassionate Ageism and the "Old Age Welfare State"

American policies toward older persons have been adopted and amended in substantially different social, economic, and political contexts during the past half century. And the reasons why each policy was originally enacted and subsequently altered can be, and have been, subjected to widely variant interpretations (Achenbaum, 1983; Achenbaum, 1986; Bernstein and Bernstein, 1989; Campion, 1984; Cohen, 1985; David, 1985; Derthick, 1979; Graebner, 1980; Harris, 1966; Holtzman, 1963; Light, 1985; Marmor, 1970; Marmor and Mashaw, 1988; Myles, 1989; Rich and Baum, 1984).

In 1935, nearly a quarter of a century later than all other western industrialized nations (King, 1971), the United States first enacted a Social Security program of public retirement benefits. Since then American society has adopted and financed many old age programs and tax and price subsidies for which eligibility is determined by age, and not by need. Through Social Security, Medicare, the Older Americans Act, and a variety of other policies, older persons have frequently been exempted from income and asset tests that are customarily applied to other Americans in order to determine whether they are worthy of public help.

The assumption that some citizens should receive special attention by virtue of old age was strengthened by a number of old-age based interest groups that began to develop a national presence in the 1960s (see Binstock, 1972; Pratt, 1976). These groups articulated compassionate stereotypes of older persons, telling us repeatedly that the elderly are poor, frail, socially dependent, objects of discrimination, and above all deserving (see Kalish, 1979).

Through this compassionate ageism—the attribution of the same characteristics, status, and just deserts to the elderly—advocates managed to artificially homogenize, package, label, and market a heterogenous group of older persons as "the aged." But ageism, in contrast with racism, has provided many benefits to older persons.

During the 1960s and 1970s just about any issue or problem affecting some older persons that could be identified by advocates for the aging became a governmental responsibility: nutritional, supportive, and leisure services; housing; home repair; energy assistance; transportation; help in getting jobs; protection against being fired from jobs; special mental health programs; a separate National Institute on Aging; and on, and on, and on (Estes, 1979; Kutza, 1981). By the late 1970s, if not earlier, American society had learned the catechism of compassionate ageism very well and had expressed it through a variety of governmental programs and objectives that constituted an "old age welfare state" (Myles, 1983). We had rejected proposals for universal national health insurance, for example, but—through Medicare—we were willing to establish national health insurance for the elderly (see Marmor, 1970).

The Emergence of the Aged as Scapegoat

Since 1978, however, the long-standing compassionate stereotypes of older persons have been undergoing an extraordinary reversal (see Binstock, 1983). Older persons have come to be portrayed as one of the more flourishing and powerful groups in American society, and attacked as a burdensome responsibility. These new stereotypes, devoid of compassion, are:

1. The aged are relatively well-off, not poor, but in great economic shape.
2. The aged are a potent political force because there are so many of them and they all vote in their self-

interest; this "senior power" explains why more than one-quarter of the annual federal budget is spent on benefits to the aged.

3. Because of demographic changes, the aged are becoming more numerous and politically powerful and will claim even more benefits and substantially larger proportions of the federal budget. They are already costing too much and in the future will pose an unsustainable burden for the American economy.

Even as the earlier compassionate stereotypes concerning older persons were partially unwarranted, so are these current stereotypes. They are generated by applying simplistic assumptions and aggregate statistics to a grouping called "the aged" in order to gloss over complexities.

If one chooses to compare changes in the median or average income of all older persons with changes in the income of other groupings, one can conclude that the aged are relatively well off and ignore millions of older persons who are in dire economic circumstances (Smeeding, 1990). If one wishes to ignore abundant evidence to the contrary (see Hudson and Strate, 1985; Binstock, 1990a; Jacobs, 1990), one can assume that the votes of older persons are determined by issues—particularly one issue above all others: that they will respond to that one issue self-interestedly, and that they will all perceive their self-interests to be the same. If one pretends that outlays for Social Security, Medicare, and other policies are mechanistically determined by demographics rather than by legislative and administrative decisions, one can conclude that benefits to the aged constitute an unsustainable burden for the American economy. But as the enactment of an amendment to Medicare in 1988 and its speedy repeal in 1989 (Atkins, 1990; Binstock, 1990b; Findlay, 1989; Tolchin, 1989) have reminded us, extrapolation from existing policies and institutional arrangements is a poor mode of prediction.

Two fundamental elements seem to account importantly for the reversal of stereotypes. One was a tremendous growth in the amount of federal funds expended on benefits to the aging, which journalists (e.g., Samuelson, 1978) and academicians (e.g., Hudson, 1978) began to notice and publicize in the late 1970s.

The proportion of the annual federal budget being spent on benefits to the aging had reached 26 percent. It has remained this high for more than a decade (U.S. Senate, 1989), and is now widely recognized as one of the few large expenditure categories in the budget.

Another element in the reversal of old-age stereotypes was dramatic improvement in the aggregate status of older Americans, in large measure due to the impact of federal benefit programs. Social Security, for example, helped to reduce the proportion of elderly persons in poverty from about 35 percent three decades ago (Clark, 1990) to 12.2 percent today (U.S. Senate, 1989). Federal benefit programs have improved the average economic status of the aged to the point where journalists can now accurately depict older persons, in the aggregate, as "more prosperous than the general population" (Tolchin, 1988).

Regardless of specific causes, the reversal of stereotypes has continued to the point where the new stereotypes can be readily observed in popular culture. Typical of contemporary depictions of older persons was a *Time* "cover story" entitled "Grays on the Go" (Gibbs, 1988), filled with pictures of senior surfers, senior softball players, and senior "swingers." Older persons were pictured as America's new elite—healthy, wealthy, powerful, and "staging history's biggest retirement party." A dominant theme in such portrayals of older persons is that their selfishness is ruining the nation. The *New Republic* highlighted this motif in 1988 with a cover story displaying "Greedy Geezers." It announced that "The real me generation isn't the yuppies, it's America's growing ranks of prosperous elderly" (Fairlie, 1988). Or, as a *New York Times* Op-Ed essay headline expressed it: "Elderly, Affluent—and Selfish" (Longman, 1989).

In serious forums of public discourse these new stereotypes of the prosperous, hedonistic, and selfish elderly have laid a foundation upon which the aged have emerged as a scapegoat for an impressive list of American problems. As social psychologist Gordon Allport observed in his classic work, *ABC's of Scapegoating*: "An issue seems nicely simplified if we blame a group or class of people rather than the complex course of social and historical forces" (1959, pp. 13–14).

Advocates for children (e.g., Carballo, 1981) and demographers (e.g., Preston, 1984) have blamed the political power of the elderly for the plight of youngsters who have inadequate nutrition, health care, education, and supportive family environments. A former Secretary of Commerce (Peterson, 1987) has suggested that a prerequisite for the United States to regain its stature as a first-class power in the world economy is a sharp reduction in programs benefiting older Americans.

Perhaps the most serious scapegoating of the aged—in terms of vulnerability for older persons and, perhaps, vulnerability for all persons in American society—has been with respect to health care. A widespread concern about high rates of inflation in health care costs has been refocused in the past few years from health care providers, suppliers, administrators, and insurers—the parties that are responsible for setting the prices of care—to the elderly patients for whom health care is provided and who pay for more than 40 percent of their aggregate care through supplemental private insurance premiums and out-of-pocket (U.S. House of Representatives, 1989, p. 8).

Because the elderly population is growing, absolutely and proportionately, health care costs for older persons have been depicted as an unsustainable burden, or as a biomedical ethicist, Daniel Callahan, has put it, "a great fiscal black hole" that will absorb an unlimited amount of our national resources (1987, p. 17).

Concerns about health care expenditures on older persons are laden with misperceptions. Frequently-quoted statistics concerning costs are often misunderstood and/or unexamined with respect to their significance; decision processes through which American physicians actually decide whether and how to treat elderly patients are not widely known (see Binstock and Post, in press).

Nonetheless, because of concerns about health care costs of the old, in 1984 a Governor of Colorado, Richard Lamm, was widely reported to have pronounced that terminally ill old people have a "duty to die and get out of the way" (Slater, 1984). And Callahan (1987; 1990) has urged that life-saving care be denied to older persons, categorically, without regard to clinical conditions. Such proposals have received a great deal of attention from the media, and may not represent the climax of a process through which the aged have become scapegoats for health care expenditures in the U.S.

Scapegoating the aged seems to have had a cumulative impact of leading some elites and social observers to the assumption that an appropriate, axiomatic means of financing social policy initiatives in the 1990s is through elimination and redistribution of public benefits to older persons.

A notable instance of this trend took place in 1989 when a distinguished "Executive Panel" of American leaders convened by the Ford Foundation designated older persons as the only group of citizens responsible for financing a broad range of social programs for persons of all ages, including infants. In a report called *The Common Good: Social Welfare and the American Future,* the Panel recommended a series of such programs costing a total of $29 billion, to be financed solely by revenues gained from new taxes on Social Security benefits. Indeed, the only alternative financing options that the Panel considered were other ways of reducing Social Security benefits: "turning Social Security into a means-tested program . . . " and "freeze or cut cost-of-living adjustments in benefits" (Ford Foundation, p. 81). Similarly, an analyst (Beatty, 1990) of the "peace dividend" that might be reaped from the crumbling of Communism in the Soviet Union and Warsaw Pact nations at the end of the last decade recently proposed a substantial wish list of domestic policy initiatives that might be included in "A Post-Cold War Budget." But his only discussion of programs for older persons was as a source of financing for this list of initiatives (p. 81).

Equity as an "Intergenerational" Construct

Although scapegoating of the aged began in the late 1970s, an interest group formed in 1984, Americans for Generational Equity (AGE), has effectively reinforced and disseminated images of the elderly as a prosperous and selfish group responsible for a number of problems in our society. Established to propound issues of what it terms "intergenerational equity," AGE appears to have solid backing from the corporate sector as well as a handful of Congressmen who lead it. According to its annual reports, most of its funding comes from insurance companies, health care corporations, banks, and other private sector businesses and organizations that are in competition with Medicare and Social Security (Quadagno, 1989).

Central to AGE's credo is the proposition that the large aggregate of public transfers of income and other benefits to today's cohorts of older persons, financed through unfairly burdensome taxes on the contemporary labor force, is unlikely to be available in the future as old age benefits (e.g., Social Security and Medicare) when the present cohort of workers, commonly termed the "baby boomers," becomes elderly retirees starting in the year 2010 and continuing through several decades (see Longman, 1987). Moreover, AGE frequently contrasts the relatively prosperous average circumstances of the elderly with those of other groups such as disadvantaged children and an estimated 37 million Americans who lack health insurance.

As the self-designated representative of generational equity AGE disseminates its views from its Washington office through press releases, media interviews, and the *Generational Journal*, a quarterly publication. It also convenes several conferences a year focused on themes suggesting that public expenditures on older persons are wasteful and should be reallocated to younger age groups. At a conference on "Medicare and the Baby Boom Generation," for example, one of the organization's prominent board members espoused the view that "In the interest of doing the greatest good for the greatest number, some forms of medical intervention should be denied, as a matter of government policy, to elderly or terminally-ill patients" (Lamm, 1987).

Every indication suggests that this organization will persist in adding to the rhetoric that pits the young and the middle-aged against an artificially homogenized group of older Americans, as exemplified by the title of one of AGE's recent conferences—"Children at Risk: Who Will Support Our Aging Society?"

Although some members of Congress are among the founding members of Americans for Generational Equity, they have yet to inject into legislative proposals their view that inequities represented by programs benefiting the aging should be redressed through drastic policy changes. So far they have confined their efforts to conferences, speeches, and publications. No bills have been introduced to curtail drastically Social Security or Medicare benefits; reallocate funds from programs for the aged to programs for children; or officially deny medical care for older persons whose lives are in danger.

Nonetheless, AGE's basic approach—framing public policy questions as issues of intergenerational conflict—seems to reflect and/or have captured successfully the mind-set of the media and of powerful members of Congress as well. For example, as the U.S. Congress ended its 1989 session, Congressman Dan Rostenkowski, Chairman of the House Ways and Means Committee, observed: "One of the most unhappy results of our ongoing budget gridlock has been an uneven contest between the very young and the very old . . . " He said "the sad story of the 1980s," was that "the old have gotten more while the young have gotten less" (Tolchin, 1989). The record does not bear out Congressman Rostenkowski. There were no legislative choices or contests during the decade between "the very young and the very old," and the old did not get "more." But the very fact that he was willing to characterize Congressional activity in the 1980s in these terms reflects the general contemporary context through which the aged have become a political scapegoat.

The Unfinished Agenda: Some Illustrations

With contemporary issues framed as matters of intergenerational conflict, and the American political economy dominated by concerns for deficit reduction and health care cost containment, policies to expand public benefits for older persons seem unlikely in the near future. The umbrella of compassionate ageism that nurtured development of the old age welfare state has eroded. Yet there are still urgent needs to be met within the elderly population, discussed in chapters throughout this volume. Two such needs—income maintenance and the financing of long-term care—are briefly outlined here as important illustrations of the unfinished policy agenda on aging, and the types of fundamental political issues that will have to be dealt with if government is going to respond in a major fashion to meet additional needs of older persons.

Income Maintenance

Even though our national government now distributes about $300 billion annually in benefits to the aging, some 3.6 million older persons have an annual income that is below the government's official poverty line; an additional 4.4 million persons aged 65 and over are in families that have annual incomes that are between the poverty level and 150 percent of that level—in other words, within a few hundred to a few thousand dollars of poverty. Altogether, about one-third of older Americans either live in poverty as officially defined, or very near to it—highly vulnerable economically to unexpected health care bills and sudden inflation in housing costs (Smeeding, 1990).

Particularly vulnerable are older women and Black, Hispanic, Asian\Pacific, and Native American minorities (U.S. Senate, 1989), who, in addition to problems of income, confront gender and racial barriers throughout many dimensions of their everyday lives. For instance, among older persons living as "unrelated individuals" the percentage of black females in poverty is 60 percent compared with 24 percent for white females and 17 percent for white males (U.S. Senate, 1988, pp. 6–7).

Unless national policies are changed substantially in the years immediately ahead, such clusters of older persons who are extremely vulnerable with respect to income will not disappear. The eligibility and benefit structures of the Old Age Insurance (OAI) program of Social Security are based upon the labor force record of potential recipients. Persons who do not have a long and stable history of employment, or who work in jobs not included in the Social Security taxation system, receive very low OAI benefits or do not qualify for them at all. Still others receive benefits that are not sufficient for an adequate income in retirement (see Schulz, 1988). Consequently, although Social Security has saved tens of millions of older Americans from poverty, and can continue to do so in the years ahead, its program structure is such that millions more older persons will remain vulnerable to poverty because of their limited work histories within the Social Security system.

While the Supplemental Security Income Program (SSI) provides a minimum guaranteed income through payments averaging $280 per month to older persons who qualify through means-tests (Social Security Administration, 1989), most estimates are that only 40 to 60 percent of those who are eligible for it apply. Reasons for this lack of participation are not precisely clear, but researchers have suggested a variety of possible factors. These include ignorance of the program; distaste for the stigmatization of being a welfare recipient; the severity of asset and income tests that are applied to determine eligibility; and the small marginal value of the income to be obtained through SSI payments (Schulz and Leavitt, 1988; U.S. Senate, 1988; Commonwealth Fund Commission on Elderly People Living Alone, 1987; Zedlewski and Meyer, 1987). For most of those who do receive SSI payments the amount is not sufficient to bring their Social Security income up to the poverty line even in communities where the state government supplements the federal payment (Quadagno, 1989).

Reforming OAI and SSI to achieve an adequate income for all older persons is not a difficult technical problem. Practical proposals for changing these policies so as to target income maintenance programs to the most economically vulnerable elderly have been put forward for years (see, e.g., Pechman et al., 1968; Cohen and Friedman, 1972; Munnell, 1977; Commonwealth Fund Commission on Elderly People Living Alone, 1987). But they have not been strongly supported politically, either by Congress or by the organizations in the field of aging. And adequate political support for such reforms will probably not be forthcoming unless American society accepts the fundamental notion that adequate public income support for older persons should be made available on the basis of need rather than work history. In doing so, however, the principle that all persons of any age deserve adequate public income support on the basis of need probably would have to be politically supported through widespread public acceptance.

Public Long-Term Care Insurance

Another issue that has been prominent on the agenda of old age policy in the past few years is the expansion of public insurance for health and social care of persons with long-term illnesses and disabling conditions. Two factors have combined to bring this issue to the fore. First, the distribution of age groupings within the population aged 65 and over is rapidly becoming markedly older. And second, the need for long-term care increases dramatically among population cohorts as they advance into the age range of mid-70s and older (Committee on an Aging Society, 1985).

The Aged Population Is Growing Older

The number and proportions of older Americans who are living into their mid-70s and 80s have been increasing markedly and will continue to do so. In 1980, for example, persons aged 85 and over constituted only 8.8 percent of the American older population; in 1990 they are 10.3 percent, and in the year 2000 they will be over 13 percent of the group. Similarly, in 1980 persons aged 75 and older constituted 39 percent of the older population; in 1990 they are 42 percent, and by 2000 they will be about half of it (U.S. Senate, 1989). Viewed another way, by the end of this century the median person in the 65-plus age group will be 75 years of age.

High Rates of Care at Older Old Ages

Older age groupings within the aged 65 and over population use substantially more long-term care than younger elderly persons. Presently, about 1 percent of Americans aged 65 to 74 years are in nursing homes; this compares with 6 percent of persons 75–84 years of age, and 22 percent of persons aged 85 and older (Hing, 1987). The greater numbers of persons who soon will be in the older old-age categories is a major factor in projections that the current nursing home population of 1.5 million persons will increase to 2 million by the year 2000, and reach 4.4 million some 40 years later (U.S. Senate, 1989).

For every older person in a nursing home there are more than twice as many (71 percent of the long-term care older population) residing at home or in age-segregated communities who, because of functional limitations in their activities of daily living, need home health and social care services from paid professionals or from their families or friends on an in-kind basis (Gornick et al., 1985). Among contemporary cohorts of older persons residing in the community there are dramatic increases, by five-year old age intervals, in the percentage having limitations in activities of daily living (e.g., feeding, toileting, bathing, dressing, and getting in and out of bed). The proportion needing help rises from 7.7 percent in the 65–69 year old category to 26.6 percent in the aged 85 and over group, with the largest percentage increase occurring between the 70–74 and 75–79-year-old categories (Jahnigen and Binstock, in press).

As suggested by these comparisons among older groups, the age-specific prevalence of many acute and long-term chronic diseases and other disabling conditions rises exponentially among populations aged in their late 70s and in their 80s (Manton, 1990). It is possible, of course, that advances could be made in preventing and treating urinary incontinence, osteoporosis, stroke, dementia, and other "geriatric conditions." Such breakthroughs would have substantial impact in delaying the onset of chronic illness and disability to older ages than at present, thereby reducing both the prevalence and duration of illness near the end of the life span, and the health care it requires.

A few biomedical researchers and physicians have written about the possibility of such a "compression of morbidity" at the end of life, painting a scenario in which we are all relatively healthy until shortly before we die (Fries, 1987). There is no epidemiological evidence to date that would support this paradigm (Schneider and Guralnik, 1987). But recent reports of successful clinical trials in treating osteoporosis in women (Watts et al., 1990), and in promoting the growth of bone mass and lean body mass in older men (Rudman et al., 1990) provide some hints of a basis for long-run optimism.

In the absence of breakthroughs in preventing and treating disabilities and diseases associated with old age, the aging of our older population provides a foundation for dramatic estimates of the need for long-term care in the future. One projection, for example, suggests that by the year 2040 the cost of nursing home care could increase nearly five-fold, reaching $139 billion annually (in inflation-adjusted dollars), with as many as 3.8 million nursing home residents aged 85 and older—or about 3 times as many as today's total of individuals aged 65 and over in nursing homes (Schneider and Guralnik, 1990).

Paying for Long-Term Care

The national expenditure for long-term care was estimated at $40 billion in 1989. Older persons and their families paid out-of-pocket for 57 percent of this total, with their incomes and assets. Medicaid, the federal-state insurance program for the "medically indigent," paid for 40 percent (Wiener, 1990).

The annual cost of a year's care in a nursing home averages $24,000 (U.S. Senate, 1989) and ranges as high as $80,000. Although nursing homes originally developed as an alternative to home care, their financial costs have redirected great attention during the past 15 years to home care as a cheaper alternative. But numerous demonstrations and studies have concluded that home care is not a cost-effective substitute for nursing home care (Kane and Kane, 1987; Weissert, 1990).

The Medicare health insurance program does not reimburse patients for long-term care, either in nursing homes or at home. Private long-term care insurance, in an early stage of development as a product, is very expensive for the majority of persons, and its benefits are limited in scope and duration. Only 3 percent of older persons have any private long-term care insurance, and only about 1 percent of nursing home costs are paid for by private insurance (Wiener, 1990). Even when the product matures, it is unlikely to prove helpful to most older persons. A recent Brookings Institution study suggested that even when all the "bugs" are worked out, only 25 to 40 percent of older persons will be able to afford the premiums (Rivlin and Wiener, 1988).

Medicaid, available to persons of all ages who qualify through classification as economically poor, does pay for long-term care in nursing homes, but not for home care that will be effective in most cases. Most state Medicaid programs provide reimbursement only for the most "medicalized" components of the full range of health and social services that are necessary to maintain a long-term care patient in a home environment; rarely reimbursed are supports such as chore services, assistance with food shopping and meal preparation, transportation, companionship, periodic monitoring, and respite programs for family and other unpaid caregivers.

As an alternative to public and private insurance coverage for the full range of formal home care services, many have looked to the family as a source for supportive care. But estimates are that about 85 percent of the various elements of the continuum of care necessary for living in the community is presently provided by family members on a voluntary basis (U.S. Senate, 1989). In short, there is no reason to expect that families can be looked to as a greater source of in-kind financing that will meet the growing need for long term care. Changing patterns of family structure and a persistent upward trend labor force participation by middle-aged women who have traditionally provided much of this care (Brody, 1990) suggest that the current rate of informal care giving could even decline.

The Politics of Expanding Public Insurance

The fear of living long enough to experience a need for long-term care, the threat of impoverishment through paying for it, and the increasing pervasiveness of family contact with the issues and experiences of providing it or arranging for it (see Brody, 1985) have made the expansion of public long-term care insurance coverage an issue on the agenda of national politics. Opinion polls seem to indicate that Americans fear the financial, familial, psychological, and social consequences of long-term care (McConnell, 1990).

A half-dozen major bills and several dozen minor ones have been introduced in Congress in the last several years to provide some form of federal coverage for home care and/or nursing home care (OMB Watch, 1990). But none of them may be passed for at least several years. The enactment and repeal of the Medicare Catastrophic Coverage Act of 1988 has made members of Congress more aware than they were of the high cost of insuring long term care and, particularly, the political risks involved in levying new taxes to pay for it (Atkins, 1990).

A clear lesson from the Catastrophic Coverage Act is that a broad supportive political constituency needs to be developed in order to sustain any attempt to finance a major new health program. Opponents of the Catastrophic Coverage Act, those who had to pay the most taxes and who perceived that they already had the coverage to be provided through the law, were a small numerical minority (Findlay, 1989; Tolchin, 1989). But they were dispersed through every Congressional district. When they protested vociferously against the Act, Congress received no evidence of popular support for the bill (despite the fact that it had been endorsed by the American Association of Retired Persons). Indeed, it appeared that many older persons were under the impression that the bill was going to cover the catastrophic costs of long-term care, rather than catastrophically expensive hospital and physician bills stemming from extended acute care.

Although it seems clear that long-term care financing will stay on the agenda of Congress in the immediate future, it is not at all clear that a bill will be enacted, and what form it would take. A sentiment has crystallized favoring the general principle of expanded coverage. But many complex ideological issues are masked by the broad label "public long-term care insurance," and such issues have just begun to surface in public debate (Eckholm, 1990; Tolchin, 1990). A number of different technical approaches to financing and determining eligibility for expanded long-term care insurance have been set forth (see Spence and Hanley, 1990), but they are too technical to serve in mobilizing broad political support.

Widespread public debate of ideological issues will be required if constituents as well as Congress are to understand the implications of any legislation that is to be enacted. Vague sloganeering for long-term care insurance will not be adequate; otherwise, even if enacted, such legislation could quickly be repealed as was the poorly-understood 1988 amendment to Medicare.

Serious debate on this topic will have to start with the fact that the United States already has public long-term care insurance, in the form of Medicaid, for nursing homes. That is, any older person who becomes sufficiently impoverished to be unable to pay for long-term care out of income and assets becomes eligible for Medicaid reimbursement of services; the spouse is protected by law (Medicare, 1988) from complete impoverishment. Because home care services reimbursed by Medicaid do not usually include all of the continuum that is necessary in a home setting, the Medicaid-financed patient usually ends up as a nursing home resident. So part of the long-term care agenda is public insurance that can provide a genuine choice of home care poor elderly patients for whom it will suffice.

Most of the current interest in additional public insurance, however, is apparently generated by the possibility of becoming poor through "spending down" assets on long-term care. There is a distinct middle-class fear—both economic and psychological—of using savings and selling a home to finance one's own health care. This fear reflects a widespread desire to protect inheritances, as well as the psychological intertwining of personal self-esteem with material worth and independence.

Despite this interest, we will need to confront and resolve many fundamental issues if we are to achieve an effective, enduring government program of expanded public long-term care insurance. Among these issues are:

- Assuming that spouses can be effectively protected from impoverishment, why shouldn't people spend their assets and income on their health care?
- Is it government's responsibility to preserve estates?
- Should government take a more active role than at present in preserving economic status inequalities from generation to generation?
- On what basis should some persons be taxed to preserve the estates and inheritances of others?
- Is it government's role to preserve the psychological sense of self-esteem that for so many persons is bound up on their accumulated material worth?
- Should an age cut-off be used for eligibility, or should public funds be available for long-term care patients of all ages? Presently there are more than twice as many severely disabled adults, aged 18 to 64, who live

> outside institutions than all of the chronically-ill and severely disabled persons aged 65 and older who reside in nursing homes and elsewhere (Gornick et al., 1985, pp. 22–23).

These are some of the issues that must inevitably surface, in one form or another, if expanded national long-term care insurance is to become a serious legislative proposition. And they will be accompanied by extended debate as to whether the financing of such a measure will take place through a "social insurance" payroll tax, through general revenues, or through direct premiums from older persons themselves, such as those that now finance a part of Medicare. Estimates for present annual financing of such public insurance range from $30 million to $60 billion, depending upon proposals for services covered and the age categories for eligible patients.

Strategies and Prospects

The United States is presently at a critical juncture in its social policies toward aging. Through a half century of compassionate ageism we created an old-age welfare state.

But with a shrinking of available public resources has come a shrinking of compassion. In the present context of concerns for fiscal deficit reduction and health care cost containment, the aged have become a scapegoat for a variety of problems in American life. Domestic policy problems now tend to be framed as issues of intergenerational conflict between older and younger citizens. There are many strong proponents of limiting or drastically reducing public resources now devoted to programs for the aging.

Yet many urgent needs within the aged population still remain. About one-third of older persons are still extraordinarily poor. And the growth and aging of the older population is generating—for older persons, and their families as well—urgent needs for financing good quality care for long-term illnesses and disabling conditions.

Dealing with these and other ongoing issues affecting older persons will be difficult in the present political context. What sorts of strategies are likely to evoke an effective response to the unfinished policy agenda on aging?

One approach suggested has been to emphasize the argument that public benefits to older persons also are of indirect value to persons of all ages through "ties that bind," particularly in a family context (Kingson et al., 1986). In a similar vein it has been argued that issues of intergenerational equity can be defused and diffused through new public policies providing benefits that can be shared directly by persons of all ages (Wisensale, 1988), and that programs based on age should be "played down" rather than "played up" (Neugarten & Neugarten, 1986). Another suggestion has been that old-age advocacy organizations—in order to demonstrate that they are not selfish—form coalitions with other interest groups (Kingson, 1988). And still another approach has been to argue that issues of intergenerational equity are spurious, masking issues of inequities among persons of all ages that should be confronted head on (Binstock, 1985).

Whatever strategy is employed, policies for eliminating the problems of the most severely disadvantaged aged will probably not emerge unless the special place that older persons have had in American health and welfare policy gives way to a broader focus on vulnerable persons of all ages. Such a focus would require an ideological consensus that our government should provide effective help to all persons who are not in a position to help themselves, regardless of age.

Ironically, the development of such a broadened American welfare consensus could be fostered through a preoccupation with the problems of old age and an understanding of the life course experiences that lead to them. The persons who are most vulnerable in childhood and throughout their working years are the ones most likely to be vulnerable in their old age, if they live that long.

More than twenty years ago United States President Lyndon B. Johnson presented a very open-ended charge to a White House Task Force on Older Americans: "What are the most important things that can be done for the well-being of the most older Americans?" The Task Force members well understood that vulnerability in old age is the product of a life course of experiences. Their priority statement to the President was that "economic and social opportunities for current generations of the young and middle-aged are the most effective measures for ensuring opportunities for future generations of older Americans" (President's Task Force on Older Americans, 1968, p. 1). Such a perspective on our common human vulnerability will need to be widely accepted before American public policy toward the aging and other constituencies develops a priority focus on helping our most disadvantaged citizens.

REFERENCES

Achenbaum, W.A. 1983. *Shades of Gray: Old Age, American Values, and Federal Policies Since 1920.* Boston: Little Brown.

———. 1986. *Social Security: Visions and Revisions.* New York: Cambridge University Press.

Allport, G.W. 1959. *ABC's of Scapegoating.* New York: Anti-Defamation League of B'nai B'rith.

Atkins, G.L. 1990. The politics of financing long-term care. *Generations, XIV,* 2:19–22.

Austin, C.D. 1990. Yes, but who will deliver the care? *The Gerontologist,* 30: 134–135.

Beatty, J. 1990. "A Post-Cold War Budget." *The Atlantic,* 256: 74–82.

Bernstein, M.C., and Bernstein, J.B. 1989. *Social Security: The System That Works.* New York: Basic Books.

Binstock, R.H. 1972. Interest-group liberalism and the politics of aging. *The Gerontologist,* 12:265–280.

———. 1983. The aged as scapegoat. *The Gerontologist,* 23:136–143.

———. 1985. The oldest-old: a fresh perspective or compassionate ageism revisited? *Milbank Memorial Fund Quarterly/Health and Society,* 63:420–451.

———. 1990a. The politics and economics of aging and diversity. In S.A. Bass, E.A. Kutza, and F.M. Torres-Gil, eds., *Diversity in Aging: Challenges Facing Planners and Policy Makers in the 1990s,* 73–99. Glenview, IL: Scott, Foresman and Company.

———. 1990b. The "catastrophic" catastrophe: Elitist politics, poor strategy. *The Aging Connection,* XI, 1:9.

Binstock, R.H., and Post, S.G. eds. In press. *"Too Old" for Health Care?: Controversies in Medicine, Law, Economics, and Ethics.* Baltimore: The Johns Hopkins University Press.

Brody, E.M. 1985. Parent care as a normative family stress. *The Gerontologist,* 25:19–29.

———. *Women in the Middle: Their Parent Care Years.* New York: Springer.

Callahan, D. 1987. *Setting Limits: Medical Goals in an Aging Society.* New York: Simon and Schuster.

———. 1990. *What Kind of Life: The Limits of Medical Progress.* New York: Simon and Schuster.

Campion, F.D. 1984. *The AMA and U.S. Health Policy Since 1941.* Chicago: Chicago Review Press.

Carballo, M. 1981. "Extra Votes for Parents?" *The Boston Globe* (Dec. 17):3.

Clark, R.L. 1990. Income maintenance policies in the United States. In R.H. Binstock and L.K. George, eds., *Handbook of Aging and the Social Sciences,* third edition, 382–397. San Diego: Academic Press.

Cohen, W.J. 1985. Reflections on the enactment of medicare and medicaid. *Health Care Financing Review Annual Supplement:* 3–11.

Cohen, W.J. and Friedman, M. 1972. *Social Security: Universal or Selective?* Washington, DC: American Enterprise Institute.

Committee on an Aging Society/Institute of Medicine and National Research Council. 1985. *Health in an Older Society.* Washington: National Academy Press.

Commonwealth Fund Commission on Elderly People Living Alone. 1987. *Old, Alone and Poor: A Plan for Reducing Poverty Among Elderly People Living Alone.* Baltimore: Commonwealth Fund Commission on Elderly People Living Alone.

David, S.I. 1985. *With Dignity, the Search for Medicare and Medicaid.* Westport, CT: Greenwood.

Derthick, M. 1979. *Policy Making for Social Security.* Washington: The Brookings Institution.

Eckholm, E. 1990. Haunting issue for U.S.: Caring for the elderly ill. *The New York Times* (March 27):1.

Estes, C.L. 1979. *The Aging Enterprise.* San Francisco: Jossey-Bass.

Fairlie, H. 1988. 'Talkin' 'bout My Generation." *The New Republic, 198* (13):19–22.

Findlay, S. 1989. "The Short Life of Catastrophic Care." *U.S. News and World Report* (December 11):72–73.

Ford Foundation. Project on Social Welfare and the American Future, Executive Panel. 1989. *The Common Good: Social Welfare and the American Future.* New York: Ford Foundation.

Fries, J.F. 1987. An introduction to the compression of morbidity. *Gerontological Perspecta,* 1:5–8.

Gibbs, N.R. 1988. Grays on the go. *Time, 131* (8):66–75.

Gornick, M., Greenberg, J.N., Eggers, P.W., and Dobson, A. 1985. Twenty years of medicare and medicaid: Covered populations, use of benefits, and program expenditures. *Health Care Financing Review Annual Supplement:* 13–59.

Graebner, W. 1980. *A History of Retirement: The Meanings and Functions of an American Institution, 1885–1978.* New Haven, CT: Yale University Press.

Harris, R. 1966. *A Sacred Trust.* New York: The American Library.

Hing, E. 1987. *Use of Nursing Homes by the Elderly: Preliminary Data from the 1985 National Nursing Home Survey, Advance Data No. 135.* Hyattsville, MD: National Center for Health Statistics (May 14).

Holtzman, A. 1963. *The Townsend Movement: A Political Study.* New York: Bookman.

Hudson, R.B. 1978. The "graying" of the federal budget and its consequences for old age policy. *The Gerontologist,* 18:428–440.

Hudson, R.B., and Strate, J. 1985. "Aging and Political Systems." In R.H. Binstock and E. Shanas, eds., *Handbook of Aging and the Social Sciences,* second edition, 554–585. New York: Van Nostrand Reinhold.

Jacobs, B. 1990. "Aging in Politics." In R.H. Binstock and L.K. George, eds., *Handbook of Aging and the Social Sciences,* third edition, 349–361. San Diego: Academic Press.

Jahnigen, D.W., and Binstock, R.H. In press. "Economic and Clinical Realities: Health Care for the Old." In R.H. Binstock, and S.G. Post, eds., *"Too Old" for Health Care?: Controversies in Medicine,*

Law, Economics, and Ethics. Baltimore: The Johns Hopkins University Press.

Kalish, R.A. 1979. The new ageism and the failure models: A polemic. *The Gerontologist,* 19: 398–407.

Kane, R.A., and Kane, R.L. 1987. *Long-Term Care: Principles, Programs, and Policies.* New York: Springer.

King, A. 1971. *Ideologies as Predictors of Public Policy Patterns: A Comparative Analysis.* Paper delivered at the 1971 annual meeting of the American Political Science Association, New York.

Kingson, E.R., Hirshorn, B.A., and Cornman, J.M. 1986. *Ties That Bind: The Interdependence of Generations.* Washington: Seven Locks.

Kingson, E.R. 1988. Generational equity: An unexpected opportunity to broaden the politics of aging. *The Gerontologist,* 28: 765–772.

Kutza, E.A. 1981. *The Benefits of Old Age.* Chicago: University of Chicago Press.

Lamm, R.D. 1987. "A Debate: Medicare in 2020." In *Medicare Reform and the Baby Boom Generation,* edited proceedings of the second annual conference of Americans for Generational Equity, April 30–May 1, 1987, 77–88. Washington: Americans for Generational Equity.

Light, P. 1985. *Artful Work: The Politics of Social Security Reform.* New York: Random House.

Longman, P. 1987. *Born to Pay: The New Politics of Aging in America.* Boston: Houghton Mifflin.

———. 1989. "Elderly, Affluent—and Selfish." *The New York Times* (October 10):27.

Manton, K.G. 1990. "Mortality and Morbidity." In R.H. Binstock and L.K. George, eds., *Handbook of Aging and the Social Sciences,* third edition, 64–90. San Diego: Academic Press, Inc.

Marmor, T.R. 1970. *The Politics of Medicare.* London: Routledge and Kegan Paul.

Marmor, T.R., and Mashaw, J.C., eds. 1988. *Social Security: Beyond the Rhetoric of Crisis.* Princeton, NJ: Princeton University Press.

McConnell, S. 1990. Who cares about long-term care? *Generations, XIV,* 2:15–18.

Medicare. 1988. *Catastrophic Coverage Act of 1988,* Title III, Section 303.

Munnell, A.H. 1977. *The Future of Social Security.* Washington: The Brookings Institution.

Myles, J.F. 1983. Conflict, crisis, and the future of old age security. *Milbank Memorial Fund Quarterly/Health and Society, 61:* 462–472.

Myles, J. 1989. *Old Age in the Welfare State: The Political Economy of Pensions.* Lawrence, KS: University of Kansas Press.

Neugarten, B.L., and Neugarten, D.A. 1986. "Age in the aging society." *Daedalus, 115*(1): 31–49.

OMB Watch, 1990. *Long-Term Care Policy: Where Are We Going?* Boston: Gerontology Institute, University of Massachusetts at Boston.

Pechman, J.A., Aaron, H.J., and Taussig, M.K. 1968. *Social Security: Perspectives for Reform.* Washington: The Brookings Institution.

Peterson, P. 1987. "The Morning After." *The Atlantic,* 260(4): 43–69.

Pratt, H.J. 1976. *The Gray Lobby.* Chicago: University of Chicago Press.

President's Task Force on Older Americans. 1968. *Report of the President's Task Force on Older Americans.* Washington: Executive Office of the President of the United States.

Preston, S.H. 1984. "Children and the Elderly in the U.S." *Scientific American,* 251(6): 44–49.

Rich, B.M., and Baum, M. 1984. *The Aging: A Guide to Public Policy.* Pittsburgh, PA: University of Pittsburgh Press.

Quadagno, J. 1989. Generational equity and the politics of the welfare state. *Politics and Society,* 17, 3:353–376.

Rivlin, A.M., and Wiener, J.M. 1988. *Caring for the Disabled Elderly: Who Will Pay?* Washington: The Brookings Institution.

Rudman, D., Feller, A.G., Nagraj, H.S., Gergans, G.A., Lalitha, P.Y., Goldberg, A.F., Schlenker, R.A., Cohn, L., Rudman, I.W., and Mattson, D.E. 1990. Effects of human growth hormone in men over 60 years old. *New England Journal of Medicine,* 3: 1–6.

Samuelson, R.J. 1978. Aging America: Who will shoulder the growing burden? *National Journal,* 10:1712–1717.

Schneider, E.L., and Guralnik, J.M. 1987. The compression of morbidity: a dream which may come true, someday! *Gerontological Perspecta,* 1: 8–14.

———. 1990. The aging of America: Impact on health care costs. *Journal of the American Medical Association,* 263: 2335–2340.

Schulz, J.H. 1988. *The Economics of Aging,* fourth edition. Dover, MA: Auburn House.

Schulz, J.H., and Leavitt, T.D. 1988. *Time to Reform the SSI Asset Test?* Washington: American Association of Retired Persons.

Slater, W. 1984. "Latest Lamm Remark Angers the Elderly." *Arizona Daily Star* (March 29):1.

Smeeding, T.M. 1990. "Economic Status of the Elderly." In R.H. Binstock and L.K. George, eds., *Handbook of Aging and the Social Sciences,* third edition, 362–381. San Diego, CA: Academic Press.

Social Security Administration, 1989. *Social Security Bulletin, Annual Statistical Supplement,* 1989. Washington: U.S. Department of Health and Human Services.

Spence, D.A., and Hanley, R.J. 1990. Public insurance options for financing long-term care. *Generations, XIV,* 2:28–31.

Taueber, C. 1990. "Diversity: The Dramatic Reality." In S. Bass, E. Kutza, and F. Torres-Gil, eds., *Diversity in Aging: Challenges Facing Planners and Policy Makers in the 1990s,* 1–45. Glenview, IL: Scott, Foresman and Company.

Tolchin, M. 1989. "Lawmakers Tell the Elderly: 'Next Year' on Health Care." *The New York Times* (November 23):10Y.

———. 1988. "New Health Insurance Plan Provokes Outcry Over Costs." *The New York Times* (November 2):1.

———. 1990. "Paying for Long-Term Care: The Struggle for Lawmakers." *The New York Times* (March 29):1.

U.S. House of Representatives. Select Committee on Aging. 1989. *Health Care Costs For America's Elderly 1977–88.* Washington: U.S. Government Printing Office.

U.S. Senate. Special Committee on Aging. 1988. *Developments in Aging: 1987*—Volume I. Washington: U.S. Government Printing Office.

U.S. Senate. Special Committee on Aging. 1989. *Aging America: Trends and Projections.* Washington: U.S. Government Printing Office.

Watts, N.B., Harris, S.T., Genant, H.K. Wasnich, R.D., Miller, P.D., Jackson, R.D., Licata, A.A., Ross, P., Woodson, G.D., III, Yannover, M.J., Mysiw, W.J., Kohse, L., Rao, M.B., Steiger, P., Richmond, B., and Chesnut, C.H., III. 1990. Intermittent cyclical etidronate treatment of postmenopausal osteoporosis. *New England Journal of Medicine,* 323: 73–79.

Weissert, W.G. 1990. Strategies for reducing home care expenditures. *Generations, XIV,* 2: 42–44.

Wiener, J.M. 1990. Which way for long-term care financing? *Generations, X,* 2: 4–9.

Wisensale, S.M. 1988. Generational equity and intergenerational policies. *The Gerontologist,* 28:773–778.

Zedlewski, S.R., and Meyer, J.A. 1987. *Toward Ending Poverty Among the Elderly and Disabled: Policy and Financing Options.* Washington: The Urban Institute.

CHAPTER 3

The Older Americans Act and the Defederalization of Community-Based Care

Robert B. Hudson

Since its inception in 1965, the Older Americans Act (OAA) has been marked by lofty goals, mixed mandates, and uneven accomplishments. Defenders of the Act and its legacy point to the development of elder services and to the creation and growth of an "aging network" of planning and service agencies that have provided elders with a policy presence at the state and substate levels that they otherwise would never have had. Critics have long seen the OAA as a piece of hopelessly ambitious legislation, one that is internally inconsistent and more about politically recognizing older persons than in seriously addressing problems that elders face.

Experiences under the Older Americans Act are also instructive from a much broader point of view. As will be shown in this chapter, the successes and shortcomings of OAA programs have mirrored and in some ways symbolized the changing policy presence and needs of older Americans over the past quarter century. The aged and their legislative allies fought for recognition and funding in the Great Society era, and succeeded in attaining a major policy presence by the mid-1970s as new legislation was enacted and appropriations under existing programs were dramatically increased.

The 1980s brought unprecedented fiscal pressure and program choices to the OAA and aging policy more generally. The diversity among America's elders—long heralded by gerontologists—quite suddenly and unexpectedly came to center stage politically. An increasing proportion of elders had private pensions, personal savings, and medical insurance. Yet growing numbers of elders were clearly vulnerable by virtue of physical or mental frailty, inadequate housing, and social isolation, problems often reinforced by patterns of discrimination based on race and gender as well as age.

These changes had increasingly profound effects on the OAA and the aging network during the 1980s. Tensions arose around whom to serve (and not serve), what benefits should be provided, how the network should be oriented and structured, and how to stretch limited dollars. But, by the end of the 1980s, many network agencies had accepted the challenges posed, taking a central role in the development of broad-based and indigenous service systems at the state level. Such developments are precisely what the OAA framers always had in mind but which were frustrated for most of the OAA's first twenty years.

Philosophy and Context

The Formal Rationale

Since passage of the Older Americans Act there has been a widespread belief that the formal language of mission, goals, and objectives has been so encompassing as to provide little guidance to those charged with its administration. The ten initial objectives in Title I include assuring adequate income, the best possible physical and mental health, suitable housing, opportunities for employment, retirement in health, honor, and dignity, and efficient community services, among others. The statutory and monetary resources ever available under the Act—or conceivable under any piece of legislation—are so dwarfed by these lofty objectives as to make them essentially irrelevant to implementation activities.

The more relevant provisions of the Act are found in its major operational titles. Principal among these are Title III, which authorizes grants for state and community programs, and Title V, which authorizes a community service employment program for the elderly. (The latter is discussed elsewhere in this volume in the chapter dealing with senior employment programs.) Title II establishes the Administration on Aging (AoA) to administer the OAA at the federal level, Title IV authorizes training, research, and demonstration grants, and Title VI authorizes services to Native Americans.

Title III lies at the heart of the OAA in that it initially established the state and substate aging agencies operating under the Act and authorizes them to allocate funds appropriated under the Title, now totaling $720 million. Those agencies are charged with assuring the development and provision of social and allied services designed to maximize the ability of community-based elders to maintain their independence. The Older Americans Act is based on a *services approach*—as contrasted with an income or voucher approach—to the resolution of social problems. As such, it reveals itself to be very much a part of the Great Society initiatives of the 1960s. Other major services legislation of this period includes Medicare, Medicaid, the Elementary and Secondary Education Act, and the Manpower Development and Training Act.

Since 1969, the state and later the area agencies have also been charged with *planning and advocacy* functions under the Act. Through the development of state plans, they are to assess the availability of services in their jurisdictions and propose ways in which the services network can be enhanced. The results of state and local planning processes are designed to tailor federal mandates to local conditions, but, as is often found in federal/state programs, there can be tension between federal directives and local preferences.

As advocates, network agencies—AoA in Washington, the State Units on Aging (SUA), and, since 1973, the substate Area Agencies on Aging—are charged with bringing the needs and abilities of older Americans to the attention of elected officials, government agencies, the private sector, and the public at large. In theory, were the OAA and the network successful in these efforts, they could put themselves out of a business, having completed a job well done.

The Older Americans Act is an age-based categorical federal grant-in-aid program. As contrasted with so-called block grants, categorical grants place considerable limits on how states and localities can spend federal dollars. The boundaries between categories of the OAA have become somewhat looser—even as new client and service categories have been added—but as the legislation's name makes clear, program activities must be confined to older persons. In fact, even the appropriateness of this age-60-and-above designation is becoming a topic of debate in some policy circles in light of the growing diversity within the older population and growing areas of common concern among older and younger populations.

The formal rationale behind the Older Americans Act holds that a comprehensive array of service interventions can effectively help elders remain in community settings. Not only is this an outcome that is unquestionably desired by older persons, but it is one which may, as well, be cost-effective from a public finance perspective.

The Political Context

Understood politically, passage of the initial Older Americans Act is less about services and advocacy than it is about interest groups and symbolism. A series of political interests—organized labor, social welfare professionals, senior citizen groups—had come together in the 1960s, primarily concerned with enactment of Medicare. That battle won, two questions of political recognition moved to center stage.

First, there was a desire to recognize older Americans as a singular and legitimate program constituency, much as the poor, the unemployed, the young, and the sick had been recognized in other Great Society programs (Sundquist, 1968). Interest in aging had slowly grown throughout the post-World War II period, and pressures were building to create a federal program and a federal agency that would bring formal recognition to the standing of America's growing older population (Pratt, 1976). Second, a number of the interests which had pushed for Medicare had professional concerns and affiliations that extended beyond medicine and health. These groups, too, wished to see legislation in place that could both fund their efforts and be designed in accordance with their interests. An account of these actors and their concerns is found in Binstock's classic article (1972) on interest groups and aging policy.

The passage and early years of the OAA are a classic case of what Lowi (1964) refers to as "distributive politics." Legislation is passed benefiting a large number of actors, yet at the same time the legislation's enactment is perceived as bringing few or no costs to anyone else. No one was opposed to the OAA, and the early appropriations were so low—$7.5 million in the first year—as to be virtually invisible in a broader policy context.

Over time, a symbiotic relationship developed among supporters of the OAA. Aging-related interest groups favored expansion of the Act in order that they might design and build new service programs; the Administration on Aging, brought into existence by passage and funding of the OAA, had its future completely tied to that of the legislation; and members of Congress, especially those serving on aging-related Congressional committees, garnered considerable political support at home for championing the cause of older Americans.

Thus each of the actors involved could offer to the others the political capital they most valued—funding for the provider groups, legitimacy for the administering agency, and voting support for the elected officials. Where it can exist, political symbiosis is highly valued politically because it brings credit without conflict or in many cases even compromise.

A *Wall Street Journal* (1973) editorial critiquing passage of the 1973 Amendments to the OAA is very much in this vein:

> The Older Americans Act, pocket vetoed last fall, passed the Senate February 20 by a vote of 82 to 9 and passed the House by a vote of 329 to 69. The bill authorizes $1.55 billion over three years to do all kinds of wonderful things for Americans 45 and up, almost all of which involve employing social workers and such to provide "social services" and manpower training. A new bureaucratic empire would be spawned, along with a host of new boards, commissions, and advisory councils. Almost all the mea-

> sure duplicates programs already being run by HEW, Labor, and other agencies. (Wall Street Journal, p. 58)

Legislative opposition to OAA re-authorization has remained essentially non-existent to this day, although voices have been raised in recent years criticizing the OAA's lack of clear focus and the uneven place of the aging network agencies nationwide.

The Early Years

The conditions associated with symbiotic politics were very much present during the first decade of the OAA (1965–74). The extraordinary economic growth of the 1950–1974 quarter century had not yet given way to oil shocks and inflation. Older persons constituted a very legitimate political constituency, based both on the sympathetic attitudes Americans have held toward the old and on the massive data pointing to the economic, social, and physical problems that confronted older Americans (Marmor, 1973; Pratt, 1976). From these factors emerged a "political utility" (Hudson, 1978) of the old that could only work to the advantage of politicians who promoted their interests. It was hardly by accident that the great liberalizations in policies beneficial to the aged occurred during the 1965–74 decade: Medicare, Medicaid, Age Discrimination in Employment Act, Supplemental Security Income, and an 89 percent increase in Social Security benefits (Myers, 1981) culminating in their being tied to a cost-of-living-adjustment (COLA) by the end of the period.

The late 1960s and early 1970s also represented the principal period of expansion in the OAA's history. Between 1966 and 1969, appropriations increased moderately (to $23 million), and 1969 saw modest amendments to the original legislation. Opportunity and serendipity brought major increases in both programming and appropriations during the next four years. At a well-publicized White House Conference on Aging in 1971, President Nixon, as a means of distracting attention from his opposition to a 20 percent increase in Social Security benefits during a Presidential campaign, announced a "five-fold" increased in spending under the Older Americans Act (Hudson,

1973). Impressive as it sounded, this was very small money when compared to Social Security increases, but it resulted in increasing OAA appropriations from $32 million in 1971 to $196 million by 1973.

Major new authorizations quickly followed on the heels of the White House Conference. Partially because of widespread concern that the Administration on Aging and the nascent State Units on Aging could not effectively administer these new monies (Sheppard, 1971), the Administration called for the creation of the Area Agencies on Aging (AAA) as part of the 1973 Amendments. The Administration also agreed to a major new authorization for nutrition programs (originally Title VII, later folded into Title III), gave the state agencies new planning responsibilities, and strengthened language to maximize community independence for elders. Authorization for the ensuing years were given another major upward adjustment, and actual appropriations under Title III rose to $185 million in 1974 and to $222 million in 1975. A period of political liberalism, economic expansion, and political one-upmanship brought the OAA from a minor afterthought to other major legislative enactments to one of the larger social grant programs to the states.

However, economic, political, and demographic changes, beginning in the mid-1970s, have significantly altered these early politics and programmatic concerns associated with the OAA. Economic growth yielded to a decade of "stagflation," the political liberalism of the 1960s yielded to the conservatism of the Reagan and Bush administrations, and distributive politics became re-distributive, with the metaphor shifting from "dipping into the pork barrel" to "whose ox is going to be gored." Largely as a result of these historical shifts, both the politics and programming associated with the OAA were greatly transformed. Those changes can be chronicled in turn along each of the four key dimensions of public programs—client eligibility, program benefits, delivery structure, and financing mechanisms.

Eligibility: Universal or Targeted?

A major hallmark of the Older Americans Act is that all persons over 60 are eligible to receive service benefits. The original drafters intended to make a statement that all older Americans should be acknowledged and served. More recent events have called this singular and "compassionate" (Binstock, 1983) imagery into question. Emergent critics of U.S. aging policy speak, on the one hand, of the aged's economic and social resources and their individual capabilities and, on the other, of the country's need to allocate limited resources in new and troublesome policy areas, often focused on the young.

The change in political perceptions of the aged is perhaps best captured by shifting emphasis of the decennial White House Conferences on Aging, held since 1961. The small 1961 Conference, confined largely to professionals and academics, was about seeing if something called gerontology could gain more prominent attention. The clarion call of the 1971 Conference was for recognizing the unmet needs of older Americans. In marked contrast, the tone of the 1981 Conference was much more about how to meet "the problem" of having such a large population of elders and especially how to meet the costs associated with their rising needs and numbers (Hudson, 1983b). Because it could be both politically charged and expensive, the White House Conference, scheduled for 1991, is tentative to take place in a later year, if at all.

The Issue of Target Populations

The singularity of the old as a service constituency, a minor question since the Older American Act's passage, moved toward center stage by the mid-1970s. It was increasingly recognized by legislators and program administrators that there would never be sufficient resources to serve all who might come forward and that there were clearly some elders with greater needs than others. The tension, which continues to this day, was about how to avoid formal means-testing of would-be beneficiaries (and thereby reneging on the important symbolism of all elders together and deserving) while concentrating the limited resources on those who might be appropriately deemed most in need.

O'Shaughnessy (1991) reviews the shifting language about population eligibility that has been seen during successive reauthorizations of the OAA. The 1973 Amendments required states to take into consideration the number of low income persons in setting up the new Planning and Service Areas. The 1978 Amendments called on state and area agencies to give preference to elders with "the greatest economic and social needs." The 1984 Amendments further refined that phrase by requiring states to give special attention to low-income minority individuals and by defining low-income to mean below the officially stated poverty level. The 1987 Amendments placed greater emphasis and new requirements on identifying minority elders and documenting prior outreach efforts that had been made. In 1984 and 1987, provisions were also added calling for greater service emphasis on behalf of the "geographically isolated" and rural residents (O'Shaughnessy, 1991). Hasler (1990) lists the shift in emphasis before and after the 1987 Amendments and their implementing regulations:

Pre-1987	Post-1987
Greatest Economic Need	Total participants
Greatest Social Need	American Indians/ Alaskan Natives
Total Minority Persons subdivided into:	Asian/Pacific Islanders
American Indians/Alaskan Natives	Blacks/not Hispanic
Asian/Pacific Islanders	Hispanics
Blacks/not Hispanic	Frail/Disabled
Hispanics	Residents of rural areas
Whites/not Hispanic	Low-income non-minority
	Low-income minority

Targeting based on income inadequacy is theoretically the most straightforward approach to concentrating limited resources, but it is made extremely difficult administratively when there is no direct way to ascertain what are a potential client's economic means. As noted later in the discussion of client cost-sharing, there is currently discussion of mandatory self-declaration of income, but problems emerge here in the definition of what is income and in the accuracy of the self-reported figures.

Nor is targeting based on minority status as self-evident as it might first appear. Data presented during 1987 re-authorization Hearings of the Senate Special Committee on Aging revealed a 21 percent decline in minority participation since 1981; however, data from the Administration on Aging submitted to the House Appropriations Committee in 1987 and again in 1989 reported no decrease (O'Shaughnessy, 1990). As noted by Hasler (1990), issues of client confidentiality, inadequate definitions and knowledge among data recorders, and the wide absence of unduplicated counts of service utilizer make difficult ascertaining the amount of minority-based targeting in fact taking place. As a consequence, the counts nationwide fluctuate a great deal and are thought to be quite unreliable (Hasler, 1990; Skinner, 1990).

Finally, targeting based on being "socially disadvantaged" opens up yet other areas of controversy. Is being over age 70 or 75 to be "socially disadvantaged"? Are, as many advocates suggest, all older women socially disadvantaged? Should individuals whose "activity of daily living" scores are above a certain threshold be so designated? Serving rural elders is important, but what are the criteria that make their needs more pressing than those of urban elders?

Funding Formulas as a Response

One structural attempt to target benefits while avoiding individual means-testing and the reporting problems above has centered on the funding formulas that determine how OAA program dollars are allocated. The interstate funding formula has been and continues to be based solely on the proportion of citizens aged 60 or older residing in each state. Although employing only that criterion fails to acknowledge targeting as a concern, the provision has remained relatively noncontroversial (as well as politically expedient), and it is not likely to be changed soon.

More controversial have been the intrastate funding formulas—determining state-level allocations to the sub-state planning and service areas. Use of such formulas employed different age, economic, and social criteria to allocate funds disproportionately in the name of targeting vulnerable elders. The General Accounting Office reports 45 states using intrastate funding formulas, with 44 employing one or more economic need factors, 41 containing a factor to direct funds to where persons 60 and over live, and 38 containing a specific factor addressing low-income minorities (U.S. General Accounting Office, 1990). Binstock, Grigsby, and Leavitt (1983) review alternative intrastate funding formulas and their likely consequences.

Cases have now gone to court questioning the use of different targeting criteria. A Florida decision (Meek vs. Martinez) found that the state's using age 75 and above as a criterion—the frailty factor—discriminated against minority elders, who have a shorter life expectancy. However, a Virginia decision (Appalachian Agency for Senior Citizens vs. Ferguson), noting that the OAA is not a poverty program, upheld that state's use of social as well as economic targeting criteria (O'Shaughnessy, 1991). Ideological, methodological, and political issues have confronted all three stages of policy-making: legislative, regulative, adjudicative.

Ongoing questions about eligibility strike at the heart of the Older Americans Act, its goals and objectives. The controversies show the legislation to be fundamentally ambivalent, insisting at once on both the singularity and the diversity of the old. There is no secret about this inconsistency in Washington or the states; however, as a matter of politics, it has not been possible to move definitively in one direction or the other.

As the subsequent sections below suggest, changes in benefits, delivery, and financing structures are leading to an ever-increasing emphasis on the needs of demonstrably vulnerable elders. But this trend is resulting more from fiscal pressures at the state level than from modifications to the OAA.

Benefits: What Do Elders Need?

Longstanding controversies of near equal intensity have arisen around what benefits elders should receive through the

OAA. The ambiguity that emerged during the early years between direct services vs. advocacy services has more recently given way to a pressing tension between the merits of social services for a broad spectrum of elders as contrasted with more health-oriented long-term care services directed toward the functionally impaired.

Social Services or Political Advocacy

The services vs. advocacy debate finds its roots in the mindset of the Great Society: while often valuable, services alone will never solve endemic social problems in the absence of advocacy or "institutional change" activities (Armour, Estes, & Noble, 1980). Services may meet pressing individual needs, but they do not bring the catalyzing and multiplicative gains associated with advocacy efforts directed at system-level actors such as the governor, legislature, or media. Having public or publicly supported agencies engaged in lobbying for broader benefits was a cornerstone of Great Society initiatives. Twenty years later, the ascendant critics of the political right have strenuously attacked such activity, viewing the sight of government agencies lobbying each other as nothing short of political incest.

Predictably, the OAA has called and continues to call for both services and advocacy activities. Section 301 states that "it is the purpose of this title to encourage and assist State and area agencies to concentrate resources in order to develop greater capacity and foster the development and implementation of comprehensive and coordinated service systems to serve older adults . . . ," while Section 305 asks the state and area agencies to "serve as an effective and visible advocate for the elderly."

Periodic mandates toward the former orientation have come under the guise of planning, advocacy, and "pooling and tapping." Beginning with the 1969 Amendments, state aging agencies were to move externally within state government to prod the major functional departments—mental health, welfare, vocational rehabilitation, etc.—into paying more attention to elders, whom they were widely viewed as under-serving at the time. There was great variability in how states went about this charge depending largely on their own capacities and the level of interest state leaders had in their existence and potential. Today the advocacy charge has been toned down a good deal, the most recent efforts of the Administration on Aging concentrating on an "elder care initiative" largely directed at families and the private sector to better recognize the needs of community elders.

There has also been an evolution within the narrower "service delivery" orientation. The open-ended list of eligible services has, over time, been consolidated and focused into a three-part functional grouping. Thus the original listing of services which can and have been made available over the years is a lengthy one. Section 321(a) of the Act enumerates eighteen supportive or direct services, including transportation, health, recreation, crime prevention, abuse prevention, pre-retirement counseling, housing, residential repair, ombudsman, and employment, among others, and, in fact, concludes with a nineteenth item permitting "any other services" in keeping with purposes of the program.

Toward giving some direction, service priorities were first mandated in the 1975 Amendments, and, in 1978, these were consolidated into three distinct categories: (1) access services (transportation, outreach, information, and referral); (2) in-home services (homemaker, home health aid, chores, maintenance); and (3) legal services. Moreover, area agencies had to assure that at least 50 percent of their Title III-B funds (social supports) were allocated to these services. While that left 50 percent for other services, this provision was softened in 1981, stating simply that an "adequate proportion" of budgets had to be used for these purposes (National Association of State Units on Aging, 1985).

Social or Health Services

More recent changes in legislative emphasis and in aging network activity reflect demographic trends within the older population. More important here than the aging of the American population is the aging of the older population itself, the "old-old" now constituting the fastest growing age group in the country (see chapter 1). The heightened levels of frailty associated with advanced age are making the long-term care needs of community-based elders a major national concern.

This programmatic concern and, in fact, the very concept of long-term care for community-based elders is of recent origin. Until some time in the 1970s, long-term care was taken to mean institutional care in a chronic care hospital or nursing home. Community services generally referred to socialization, educational or leisure activities, usually located in a community center of some type. In neither theory nor practice was there much evidence of community-based long-term care.

By the mid-80s the concept of community-based long-term care had major currency. Costs associated with institutional long-term care escalated dramatically—especially for nursing home care in the federal-state Medicaid program—and emphasis increasingly came to be placed on presumptively less expensive community-based services. Nor were cost containers the only ones who favored home and community-based services; the community is unquestionably where elders themselves wish to remain and to be served.

The aging network has increasingly been brought into this community-based care/long-term care debate. The state and area agencies blanket the nation geographically and have, by now, been in existence for some twenty years. As state-level policy-makers have come to discover that there is already in place a network of agencies devoted to promoting independent living of community-based elders, community-based long-term care has become a virtual manifest destiny for any aging network agencies in the 1990s.

For the network, the services issues raised by the emergence of long-term care are subtle. In fact, a cursory review would suggest that not a great deal of what the network does has changed. As in the past, the network today is actively involved in planning, oversight, and delivery of services related to community-based living and virtually all of the services enumerated in the OAA are directed toward assisting the non-institutionalized population.

A more careful review, however, finds significant differences both in service mix and in service purpose. The early years of the OAA saw major activities in the areas of recreational services, senior center construction, and efforts to involve older persons in their communities. The focus was largely on well elders and activities to further enhance their lives. But the senior center construction authority has long since lapsed, the 20-item listing of services has evolved into the three-part codification (access, in-home, legal), the in-home nutrition program now constitutes 41 percent of all OAA nutrition spending (up from 21 percent in 1980), and a section specifically authorizing non-medical in-home services for the frail elderly was added in 1984. In contrast, a section added in 1984 authorizing personal health education—arguably directed primarily toward well elders—was never funded and was dropped during the 1987 reauthorization process.

Each of these changes point to a move toward greater emphasis on allowing frail elders to remain in their homes. This is in contrast with the earlier emphasis on helping older persons in their homes to have access to the community and interesting things to do when they got there. Put differently, the new emphasis is more on keeping persons who might otherwise need institutional care in the community than in easing the lives of persons who it was presumed would be staying in their homes for the foreseeable future. It is in this way that the OAA emphasis has shifted toward health-related long-term care services and away from wellness-related social services.

Strategically placed in this transformed world, network agencies have either chosen or been forced to alter their service mix. For some this new "domain environment" has been threatening, but other network agencies, especially some SUAs, have taken the lead in the design and operation of emergent community-based long-term care systems. Coming to grips with long-term care imperatives is the biggest organizational issue facing network agencies today.

The Delivery System and the Organization of Benefits

What has made the OAA perhaps the most distinctive of the Great Society programs is the singular network of agencies that are identified with it. As with the OAA itself, the network in its early years served as recognition of the place and standing of older Americans and of the nation's willingness to acknowledge them and their contributions to subsequent generations. Today the network finds itself under scrutiny from many sources, the concerns being no less fundamental than the purpose it should serve and the singularity it should have. A version of "the bureaucratic empire" alluded to in the *Wall Street Journal* (1973) editorial is now in place, but its territorial boundaries are increasingly unclear.

The early years of what was to become "the network" were spent getting the State Units established, making minute grants to community groups, and trying to gain some level of recognition by other agencies and officials within the states. The network rubric followed in the wake of the 1973 Amendments, establishing what are now the 650 Area Agencies on Aging. In the ensuing years, the network agencies grew and consolidated their activities, and, most recently, have come face-to-face with the long-term care needs of community-based elders. The major structural tensions encountered by the network in this period of transition have centered on questions of *accountability* (to whom is the network of state and sub-state agencies brought into existence through federal legislation responsible?), and of *scope* (to what extent should the network remain separate from other community care organizations or be melded into them?).

The Network, Federalism, and Accountability

Many of the accountability issues confronting both the network and those variously charged with overseeing it stem from the ambiguities of federalism itself. Under the OAA as with most federal grant-in-aid legislation, states choose to participate in a federal program and receive federal reimbursement for their activities in exchange for meeting legislative and regulatory requirements. The latitude of states' activity and their eagerness to participate will vary depending on the requirements (ranging from narrowly categorical to broadly permissive) and the rate of "federal financial participation" (rates generally ranging from as little as one-third to as much as 90 percent).

The grant-in-aid mechanism inherently creates multiple sources of accountability. In the case of the OAA, there are at least three. First, the state and area agencies must abide by the

OAA and the regulations and directives coming from the Administration on Aging. Second, they are accountable to state and local officials. At the state level, the SUA may report to the governor, the secretary of a human services department, or to commissioners appointed by the governor and/or legislature. At the area level, the AAA may be a unit of general purpose government reporting to the mayor or county commissioners or may be a private non-profit organization with its own board of directors. Third, the OAA planning process calls for the development of plans based on the needs and preferences of elders as determined through public hearings, needs assessments, and advisory board input.

Thus the network agencies have found themselves taking cues from multiple sources. Noting in addition that the agencies themselves have different priorities and capacities makes clear why aging network activities have been much more varied than the network metaphor would suggest. Nonetheless, at least three patterns can be discerned.

In the early years—when the state and area agencies were fledgling organizations and when federal oversight of state activities was more stringent than was later the case (U.S. General Accounting Office, 1991)—many state agencies followed OAA guidelines quite closely and often with relatively little input or interference from local officials. The prevailing view here was that this was essentially "free" federal money and who could object to providing social services to elders. So long as local officials could engage in a modicum of "credit claiming" (Mayhew, 1974), agencies were left largely to their own devices.

As agency budgets grew—both with OAA money and funds from other sources—state and area political officials took increasing interest in the network agencies.

In those cases where the agencies had effective leadership and where that outside interest became strong political support, network agencies emerged as leaders in developing new advocacy efforts and service systems. These agencies were notable for setting and carrying out their own agendas and paying less attention to OAA language than did many of their sister agencies.

Their being able to do so was abetted by the policy of neglect and attrition that the Reagan administration adopted toward the Administration on Aging. AoA lost nearly 40 percent of its professional staff between 1981 and 1989, staff travel funds were cut 81 percent, and the regional offices of AoA were instructed to cease interacting with the SUAs and AAAs (U.S. General Accounting Office, 1991). In the case of the high capacity organizations (Hudson, 1983a; 1986), both the OAA and AoA became less central with the passage of time, just one of many supports and constraints in their operating environment.

A third pattern is found where SUAs with strong internal leadership have been able to convince state political leadership to put aging-related issues on the front burner. This happened occasionally in the early years. Massachusetts set up a network of "home care corporations" even prior to the birth of AAAs and has continued to fund them with nearly $100 million of state funds. In the late 1970s, Pennsylvania established a Department on Aging and dedicated its state lottery proceeds to a prescription drug subsidy program for seniors.

More recently and largely as a result of long-term care pressures, selected state aging agencies (and selected AAAs in different parts of the country) have moved into a new league organizationally. These SUAs have gone well beyond the traditional roles of elder advocacy and oversight of the OAA programs to taking lead roles in the development of community-based long-term care systems statewide. The activities in six of the more innovative states—Arkansas, Maine, Oregon, Wisconsin, Illinois, and Maryland—are discussed by Justice (1988).

The important lesson of these cases is that the SUAs are showing themselves to be major state-level players, working with other agencies and packaging services funded through a number of federal and state sources, not just OAA money. Here the "vertical" federal/state/local orientation associated with the early years of the network has given way to a much more "horizontal" emphasis involving numerous actors at the state level.

The Emerging Network: Out of the Insular Mode

One of the troublesome aspects of the aging network metaphor has been its connoting that there is or should be a separate and unique set of agencies blanketing the country engaging in age-related activities. The presence and especially the growth of the network delivery system has never sat easily with the primary historical charge to agencies operating under the aegis of the OAA to engage other sets of actors into better serving older persons. After years of debate and activity around "service delivery/system building" vs. advocacy and "institutional change" (Hudson, 1974; Armour, et al., 1980; Estes, 1979), more recent events are forcing network agencies out of the insular mode (though not necessarily in the direction of advocacy).

Several factors have led SUAs and AAAs in outward directions. First, the problems of aging are growing and are increasingly recognized by other actors. Governors, mayors, and commissioners are themselves under the gun to deal with aging-related issues and are turning to these agencies for answers. Second, funding levels under the OAA, after the explosive growth during the 1970s, have been flat to down during the 1980s, just the time when these new demands were being made. Third, because of the success of the Reagan Administration in cutting federal domestic expenditures (Bawden and Palmer, 1984), the search for additional resources—especially for the AAAs—has been almost entirely at the state and local levels.

Finally, the passage of time—network agencies are now between 15 and 25 years old—has made them increasingly integral parts of their local environments. That aging issues are important and that OAA funding has been cut substantially less than have other social service agencies has made state and area agencies relatively more prominent locally than has historically been the case. Thus they both need state or locally generated revenues, and, in a growing number of cases, have developed the standing to get it.

The most dramatic case of the new autonomy of network agencies is found in the move toward relations with the for-profit private sector. Agencies that once were almost totally supported by OAA funds and later by public sector funds at the state and local level are now brokering services, usually for a fee, to a host of additional actors: corporations, national "care management" referral networks, hospitals, physicians, and elders and their families.

More than any other issue, these private sector initiatives have brought to a head the relationship of the network—especially the AAAs—with the OAA and AoA. An effort made in 1986–87 by the National Association of Area Agencies on Aging (N4A, 1987), the trade association for the AAAs, to establish a nationwide "care management system" to be sold in the private sector drew the wrath of the Commissioner on Aging. She argued that the care management concept usurped the state level priority setting authority rightly belonging to the SUAs under the OAA. Furthermore, the initiative, by getting the AAAs involved in direct service and thus competing with service agencies with whom they were supposed to plan and coordinate services, undermined the intent of the OAA (Fisk, 1987). For reasons of policy, pressure, and personality, N4A's care management initiative later foundered, but discrete actions of this type are now widespread around the country.

Area Agencies are confronted with tight and shrinking public sector support and see numerous other agencies and individuals marketing their services to elderly and their families. Most galling to these agencies is "losing" the clients they served for so many years now that the private sector has discovered "gold in gray" (Minkler, 1989). They argue that not being able to plan and oversee services for elders outside of the relevant public programs—the OAA, Medicaid, and various state-level programs—not only leaves them on the sidelines but serves to stereotype their clients as public charges or "welfare" recipients. Continuing to serve those clients and those paying or supported privately would not only be helpful to the agencies but would be valuable to older persons as well. Critics contend that the most impoverished and vulnerable will be left behind in moves toward the private sector, but constraints on public sector involvement continue to force many agencies in the private direction.

The move toward AAAs working with locally-based or nationally-referred private sector actors represents a major step in the shift in the OAA delivery system from the "narrow and vertical" of the first decade to the "broad and flat" of today. With the Area Agencies working increasingly in this new domain and many of the state agencies taking lead roles in broad-based and multiply-funded long-term care programs, the centrality of the OAA to the network grows ever more attenuated.

Financing: What Function Follows

Nowhere is this attenuation seen more directly than in agency and program financing. Funds appropriated through the OAA have remained flat as problem awareness has heightened; state dollars appropriated for state-only programs or as state match for Medicaid have grown significantly; private sector dollars, while small in amount, are increasingly spilling into the aging network; and, as noted below, client and family dollars are entering the system. These shifts in financing—from national to local, from public to private, and from formal to informal—have the cumulative effect of diminishing the role and place of the OAA.

OAA and Other Federal Revenues

In the beginning, OAA dollars were essentially all that there were. Put simply, without them there would have been no aging network. As well, virtually all of the social, nutrition al, transportation, and allied community-based programs that emerged prior to the mid-to-late 1970s owe their existence to federal funding through the OAA.

Three fairly distinct Title III funding stages can be seen in the OAA's 27–year history: the near-pittance of the 1966–71 period; the extraordinary expansion of the 1972–81 period; and the roughly level-funding of the 1982–90 period. The breakpoint of these three epochs can be seen below:

Period I		*Period II*		*Period III*	
1966	$ 5.0 mil.	1972	$ 35.0 mil.	1982	$606.6 mil.
1971	$ 13.0 mil.	1981	$624.7 mil.	1990	$719.2 mil.

The standing and status of the network have, not surprisingly, been associated with how much (or little) the network was charged with spending. Progress was so fragile in the first period that the future of the OAA, AoA, and the state agencies, immediately prior to the White House Conference of 1971, was seriously in doubt (Sheppard, 1971). The extraordinary expenditure growth of the 1970s resulted in the network being put in place and taking hold. These funds, of course, helped support the state and area agencies, but because these agencies was largely precluded from providing direct services, the bulk of these monies was contracted out to a variety of service providers, numbering in the thousands.

The advocacy efforts of this period were about money as well as services. A high priority among advocacy activities was "pooling and tapping" the resources of other sectors, agencies, and leaders. Toward showing success in these efforts, the Administration on Aging amassed estimates of state and area agencies as to how many resources they had, in fact, pooled. In 1977 the estimated national total of pooled resources was $440 million, of which $227 million was cash resources and the remainder was in-kind. Of the overall total, $311 million was from federal sources (U.S. Senate Special Committee on Aging, 1978). By the 1980s "pooling and tapping" data were no longer reported in the Administration on Aging's reports to the Senate Committee. This was in part due to a lessening of emphasis on that activity and in part due to the increasing difficulties in locating federal social service dollars subsequent to passage of the 1981 Omnibus Budget and Reconciliation Act, which dramatically cut social services spending (Salamon and Abramson, 1984).

The Growth in State-Level Appropriations

In the early years of the OAA, state-level efforts were minimal. States did little more than meet the very modest matching requirements under the OAA. OAA funds initially reimbursed the states for 75 percent of their administrative and service costs, and the federal figure grew to an extremely generous 90 percent for services in the wake of the 1972 Amendments establishing the AAAs (later reduced to 85 percent). States seldom did more than meet these minimal amounts: in 1969 a federal official complained that almost half the states did not even spend the $25,000 in federal money they were allotted for administrative costs, and Congressman Brademas termed "foul" the revelation that Nebraska had contributed only $16,000 to its state unit, or 9 cents for every older resident (Hudson, 1973). By the 1970s the states were certainly spending all the federal money to which they were entitled, but many continued to contribute little more than was required.

An increasing number of states became both programmatically and fiscally active during the 1980s. The rise of the old-old, earlier hospital discharges under Medicare, and more stringent cost containment efforts in institutional long-term care under Medicaid brought community-based long term care issues and the aging network increasingly to center stage. The table below shows how significant state fiscal activity became in the 1980s:

Table 1. State Spending for Home and Community-Based Care for the Elderly

Pennsylvania	$154 million	Washington	$23 million
Massachusetts	$105 million	New York	$14 million
New Jersey	$ 85 million	Minnesota	$13 million
Illinois	$ 70 million	Colorado	$13 million
Florida	$ 35 million	Wisconsin	$11 million

(Does not include state match for OAA or state match for community-based programs under Medicaid.)

Source: U.S. General Accounting Office, 1991.

The rapid fall-off in dollar amounts, even among these state-level spending leaders, reveals in yet another domain the variability in aging and long-term care effort among the states. The picture is clouded further because some states are now devoting significant levels of Medicaid funding to non-institutional alternatives, yet these states are not necessarily the ones in the list above, e.g., Oregon and Arkansas. Adding differences in administrative arrangements muddies the picture still further. States such as Massachusetts and Pennsylvania have devoted significant state dollars to community-based care and have kept it largely confined within the aging network. Illinois, Oregon, and Arkansas have added major Medicaid dollars and have made efforts to integrate the network with other health and welfare agencies (Justice, 1988). And yet many states have lesser community-based efforts altogether.

Because of the large number of states in the last group, national figures show that the OAA still provides a high proportion of community-based care dollars (U.S. General Accounting Office, 1991). In 1986 Medicaid accounted for 40 percent of state-administered community-based program dollars for the eldery, the OAA 24 percent, state-only programs 19 percent, and the federal social services block grant 17 percent. Among 49 of the 50 states (New York, accounting for over one-half of these Medicaid expenditures nationwide, is often set aside for purposes of these comparisons), OAA funds emerge as the largest single source in 28 states (U.S. General Accounting Office, 1991). But again, where OAA dollars are significant, programs are small.

"Informal" Financing—Contributions and Cost-Sharing

In light of the leveling off in OAA funding and the perception that growing numbers of elders could afford to pay for at least some portion of their services, two new client-oriented funding strategies emerged during the 1980s. One, voluntary contributions, emerged near the beginning of the decade, and the other, client cost-sharing, emerged toward the end. How to determine which clients could and should contribute or share without crossing the line into means-testing was again a central issue.

Beginning in 1981 providers operating under the OAA were required to "provide each older person [receiving services] with a full and free opportunity to contribute toward the cost of the service." This provision has been most utilized at nutrition sites, where elders may make contributions at the door. This provision generated $79 million in 1981, $131 million in 1984, and by 1988 it was generating $168 million annually (U.S. Senate Special Committee on Aging, 1985, 1990). Initial controversy centering on potentially coercive peer pressure and instances of the poor contributing while the well-off did not have waned in recent years.

The more recent controversy has focused on client cost-sharing. Currently cost sharing is prohibited for OAA services, but it is now widely practiced in the state-only financed companion programs often administered by network agencies. As proposed for the OAA—and as often operated under the existing state programs—clients would "self-declare" their income and then be charged a sliding fee dependent on the amount of the declaration.

As a progressive financing mechanism, cost-sharing is the flip-side of targeting as a progressive eligibility mechanism. Its aim is to expand the pool of available resources so that more persons, especially of lower income, could be served by the program. As well, proponents argue that OAA-funded services could be more efficiently integrated with essentially indistinguishable state-funded programs (U.S. General Accounting Office, 1989). Since such activities are already going on in 36 states, this is more than a hypothetical concern. Critics of cost-sharing argue that the poor would, in fact, be discouraged from participation, that the program would come to be understood as a means-tested rather than a universal program, would lead agencies increasingly to serve higher income clients, and would create conceptual confusion around whether network agencies were publicly-supported agencies with private pay clients or were private sector agencies now receiving a public subsidy (National Council of La Raza, 1991; National Caucus and Center on Black Aged, 1991; Hudson, 1991).

Recent studies by the U.S. General Accounting Office and the Inspector General of the Department of Health and Human Services find support among planners, providers, and clients for cost-sharing programs where they have been put in place. The GAO study reports state and area agencies finding that cost-sharing improves service equity, serves more low-income persons, and reduces welfare stigma, and the GAO found no evidence that services were shifted toward higher income persons (U.S. General Accounting Office, 1989). Providers in the Inspector General study also said cost-sharing allowed them to expand service, and clients were reported satisfied with both the cost and quality of services received (Kassner, 1991). Yet after strenuous debate during the 1991 reauthorization process, cost-sharing language was ultimately dropped from the completed legislation.

Conclusion

The OAA and the aging network are far different from what they were in their early years. Shifts in the aging policy terrain have generated pressures and brought about changes that were nonexistent or unanticipated in the 1960s. Addressing those changes has tested the mettle of network agencies, and many are stronger for it by reasons of both necessity and choice. The language and emphases of the OAA have moved with the times as well, but events at the subnational level have placed the role and influence of the legislation increasingly in doubt.

The Substantive Issues

Collating the eligibility, benefits, delivery system, and financing discussions above places the trends reviewed in each area into sharper relief. Eligibility pressures have been in the direction of targeting; benefits are moving in the direction of home and community-based long-term care; delivery systems are, in many areas, becoming integrated into or subsumed under larger service systems; and financial support is moving from reliance on the federal government to the states and, to a lesser extent, from public sources to private and informal ones.

The composite of these trends shows an increasingly state-based health-oriented delivery system focused on increasingly frail or vulnerable clients most of whom continue to be publicly supported. But an increasing number of frail clients are also economically comfortable, and are being served by network agencies as private-pay or cost-sharing clients. A service system that was once vertical, narrow, and heavily focused on so-called well-elders has become horizontally-based, more functionally integrated, and targeted on identifiably vulnerable populations.

The Organizational Success

Today, after years of abandoned hope, perhaps the major organizational goal of the original 1965 Older Americans Act is being accomplished as a growing number of network agencies are gaining heightened standing and acceptance. Not only has this led to advocacy and service successes, but the agencies' growing capacity has also rendered them increasingly independent of the OAA.

This new autonomy might appear to be a mixed blessing to those for whom the ultimate success of the OAA was seen as being a Washington-oriented national social services network. But independence of the OAA and integration into sub-national delivery systems is very much in keeping with the founding OAA philosophy. According to that vision, services and service functions fully incorporating the needs of elders would be taken up by other human service agencies at the state and substate level. In fact, until 1970 OAA allocations to providers were based on a declining federal participation formula—from 75 percent/25 percent to 60 percent/40 percent to 50 percent/50 percent to zero—the intent being to wean providers of OAA support as their efforts were increasingly valued and assumed locally. Those formulas were abandoned when it became clear by the early 1970s that no one was going to jump in so long as "the feds" were paying.

The situation today, however, is in many places remarkably different. In the face of growing long-term care needs, despite the continued inadequacy of OAA funds, and because of the presence of several high capacity SUAs and AAAs, several state and substate delivery systems are in place and succeeding largely independent of current OAA funding support. That this has happened in a network long dismissed by outsiders as politically popular and functionally marginal is a truly extraordinary development.

The Political Dilemma

In light of trends and developments detailed above, the political dilemmas faced by those involved with the OAA continue to grow. To what extent should the Congress try to define and design interventions network agencies make at the sub-national level? Should the Administration on Aging—continuing to face major staffing shortages—devote its energies to guiding network activities, or should it move in a more policy analytic direction, addressing broad issues of aging and the respective place in their resolution of the public and private sectors (Gerontological Society of America, 1988)? Can SUAs and AAAs continue to play an advocacy role for elders at large as they are increasingly drawn into long-term care systems functions?

The transformation of the place of the OAA and the roles of the agencies it brought into existence has taken place along three policy continua: public and private; formal and informal; national and local. The original OAA was a prototypical example of a public, national, formal program. Emergent trends increasing the importance of state and sub-state decision-making, involving proprietary private sector actors, and asking clients and families to assume some of the burdens are pressing the OAA in new directions along each of these continua. As programs move toward the local, private, informal—albeit still with many exceptions—federal policy-makers will need to decide if they wish to accommodate themselves to such trends or to renew efforts to maintain distinctive policy space for the OAA in Washington and around the country. The latter may well be about turning the clock back in ways that are no longer possible and, to many, are no longer necessary or desirable.

REFERENCES

Armour, P.K.; Estes, C.L.; and Noble, M.L. 1980. "Implementing the Older Americans Act." In R.B. Hudson, ed., *The Aging in Politics: Process and Policy*. Springfield, IL: Charles C. Thomas.

Bawden, D.L. and Palmer, J.L. 1984. "Social Policy: Challenging the Welfare State." In J.L. Palmer and I.V. Sawhill, eds., *The Reagan Record* (177–216), Cambridge, MA: Ballinger.

Binstock, R.H. 1983. The aged as scapegoat. *Gerontologist, 23*, 136–143.

———. 1972. Interest group liberalism and the politics of aging. *Gerontologist, 12*, 265–280.

Binstock, R.H.; Grigsby, J.; and Leavitt, T.D. 1983. *An Analysis of "Targeting" Policy Options under Title III of the Older Americans Act*. Waltham, MA: Brandeis University.

Estes, C.L. 1979. *The Aging Enterprise*. San Francisco, CA: Jossey-Bass Publishers.

Fisk, C.F. 1987. *Letter to Nancy Peace*. Washington: National Association of Area Agencies on Aging.

Gerontological Society of America. 1988. *The Aging Society: Opportunities for the New Administration*. (Washington: Author mimeo.).

Hasler, B.S. 1990. *Reporting of Minority Participation under Title III of the Older Americans Act*. Washington, DC: American Association of Retired Persons.

Hudson, Robert B. 1991. *Administration on aging: More federal action needed to promote service coordination for the elderly*. Washington: U.S. General Accounting Office.

———. 1986. "Capacity-building in an Intergovernmental Context: The Case of the Aging Network." In A.M. Howitt and B.W. Honadle, eds., *Perspectives on Management Capacity Building*. Albany, NY: State University of New York Press.

———. 1973. "Client Politics and Federalism: The Case of the Older Americans Act." Paper presented to the 1973 Annual Meeting of the American Political Science Association, New Orleans.

———. 1978. The "graying" of the federal budget and its consequences for old age policy. *Gerontologist, 18*, 428–440.

———. 1974. Rational planning and organizational imperatives: Prospects for area planning in aging. *Annals of the American*

Academy of Political and Social Science, 415 (September, 1974), 41–54.

———. 1991. "Re-authorization of the Older Americans Act." Testimony before the U.S. House of Representatives Committee on Education and Labor, Washington, DC, May, 1991.

———. 1983a. (Review of) final report of the 1981 White House conference on aging. *Gerontologist, 23,* 216–217.

———. 1983b. "Strategies for Capacity-Building in the Aging Network." Project Report submitted to Department of Health and Human Services, Administration on Aging.

Justice, D. 1988. *State Long Term Care Reform: Development of Community Care Systems in Six States.* Washington, DC: National Governors' Association.

Kassner, E. 1991. "Cost-sharing under Title III of the Older Americans Act." *AARP Issue Brief #6.* Washington, DC: American Association of Retired Persons.

Lowi, T.J. 1964. American business, public policy, case-studies, and political theory. *World Politics, 16* (December 1964), 677–715.

Marmor, T.J. 1973. *The Politics of Medicare.* New York: Aldine.

Mayhew, D.R. 1974. *Congress: The Electoral Connection.* New Haven, CT: Yale University Press.

Minkler, M. 1989. Gold in gray: Reflections on business discovery of the elderly market. *Gerontologist, 29,* 24–31.

Myers, R.J. 1981. *Summary of the provisions of the old-age, survivors, and disability insurance system, the hospital system, and the supplemental medical insurance system.* (mimeo).

National Association of Area Agencies on Aging. 1987. *Establishing the Area Agency Network as Elder Care Managers.* (mimeo. Washington, DC: Author).

National Association of State Units on Aging. 1985. *An Orientation to the Older Americans Act.* Washington, DC: Author.

National Caucus and Center on Black Aged. 1991. *Older Americans Act Reauthorization.* Washington, DC: Author.

National Council of La Raza. 1991. *NCLR policy initiative for the 1991 re-authorization of the Older Americans Act.* (February).

O'Shaughnessy, C. 1990. *Older Americans Act: 1991 Re-Authorization Issues.* Washington, DC: Congressional Research Service.

———. 1991. *Targeting Services to Older Persons under Title III of the Older Americans Act.* Washington, DC: Congressional Research Service.

Pratt, H.J. 1976. *The Gray Lobby*. Chicago: University of Chicago Press.

Salamon, L.M. and Abramson, A.J. 1984. "Governance: The politics of retrenchment." In J.L. Palmer and I.V. Sawhill, eds., *The Reagan Record* (31–68). Cambridge, MA: Ballinger.

Sheppard, H. 1971. *The Administration on Aging—Or a Successor?* Washington, DC: U.S. Government Printing Office.

Skinner, J.H. 1990. *Cost sharing amendments to the Older Americans Act and their potential impact on the black aged*. Washington, DC: National Caucus and Center for the Black Aged.

Sundquist, J.L. 1968. *Politics and Policy*. Washington, DC: Brookings Institution.

U.S. General Accounting Office. 1991. *Administration on aging: More federal action needed to promote service coordination for the elderly.* Washington: Author.

U.S. General Accounting Office. 1989. *In-home services for the elderly: Cost sharing expands range of services provided and population served.* Washington: Author.

U.S. General Accounting Office. 1990. *Older Americans Act: Administration on aging does not approve intrastate funding formulas.* Washington: Author.

U.S. Senate Special Committee on Aging. 1978. *Developments in aging: 1977*. Washington: U.S. Government Printing Office.

U.S. Senate Special Committee on Aging. 1985. *Developments in Aging: 1984 volume II*. Washington, DC: U.S. Government Printing Office.

U.S. Senate Special Committee on Aging. 1990. *Developments in Aging: 1989 volume II*. Washington, DC: U.S. Government Printing Office.

Wall Street Journal. 1973. "Santa Claus Lives on Capitol Hill." March 15, p. 58.

CHAPTER 4

Public and Private Retirement Policies
Inequities in Income Support among the Elderly

Laura Katz Olson

Introduction

Similar to other industrialized nations, the United States continues to experience steady demographic changes in its age structure. Rising from 3.1 million people aged 65 and over in 1900, and representing only 4 percent of the population, this age group accounted for 32 million people by 1990, or over 12 percent of the total. It is projected that by the year 2030 the number of elderly will double to approximately 65 million; at that time nearly one-fifth of the population will be 65 years of age or older (Stone and Fletcher, 1988). (See chapter 1, The Demography of Aging.)

Moreover, the elderly population itself is growing older; the extreme age group constitutes the fastest growing sector, a trend that began as early as the 1940s and has accelerated since the 1960s. Currently there are 2.8 million people aged 85 and over, or 1 percent of the population. In 10 years this number is expected to reach 4.9 million, and by the year 2030 to extend to 8.6 million or more people, or 3 percent of the total population (Stone and Fletcher, 1988) . The average life expectancy at birth is now 71.3 for men and 78.3 for women.

At the same time, there has been a steady decline in the percentage of older workers. By 1990 only about 17 percent of the 65-and-over male population participated in the labor force, compared to nearly half in 1950. Moreover, their numbers are projected to drop to less than 10 percent by the year 2000. Retirement has occurred at increasingly earlier ages, as well; the number of working males aged 55 to 59 has dropped to 79 percent (U.S. Senate Special Committee on Aging, 1990b). While there is a growing number of older women workers, especially among those aged 55 to 64, the vast majority remains outside the labor force. In addition, most older workers are employed in part-time and/or low-paying jobs.

Federal Income-Support Programs

As suggested above, the elderly rely increasingly, and for longer periods of time, on public and private income support systems to meet their economic needs. Concomitantly, both population aging and older people's greater economic dependency confront an escalating American fiscal crisis.

Income support programs for the elderly comprise a significant and rapidly growing percentage of total federal spending. In 1990 outlays for Social Security Old-age and Survivors Insurance (OASI) accounted for $223.4 billion or 17.8 percent of the budget. The Railroad Retirement System ($4.3 billion), the Federal Retirement System ($31.5 billion), the Military Retirement System ($21.6 billion), Veterans Pensions ($3.6 billion), and Supplementary Security Income (SSI) ($12.7 billion) together represented an additional $73.7 billion, or 5.9 percent of the budget. Moreover, expenditures for other special programs for older people, such as Medicare ($66.7 billion), housing for the elderly ($.3 billion), Older Americans Employment ($.4 billion), and Medicaid (approximately $17 billion), totaled $84.4 billion, or 6.7 percent of federal spending. (Total federal spending for Medicaid in 1990 amounted to $41.1 billion. Approximately 40 percent of that figure, or $17 billion, accrues to the elderly poor, primarily for nursing home care.) In other words, nearly one-third of the national budget accrues to an age group that represents only twelve percent of the population (see Table 1).

Table 1. Federal Outlays for Old Age Income Support and Related Programs, 1990, in Billions of Dollars

Program	Cost	Percent of Budget
Social Security (OASI)	$ 223.4	17.8
Railroad Retirement System	4.3	*
Federal Retirement System	31.5	2.5
Military Retirement System	21.6	1.7
Veterans Pensions	3.6	*
SSI	12.7	1.0
Medicare	66.7	5.3
Elderly Housing	.3	*
Older Americans Employment	.4	*
Medicaid	17.0	1.4
Total Outlays	$ 1,251.7	29.7

Source: U.S. Government Budget, 1992. Washington, DC: U.S. Government Printing Office.

A growing number of policy-makers attribute the burgeoning federal deficit, which reached $220 billion for 1990 alone, to rising costs for old age programs, particularly Social Security and Medicare. As Minkler (1991) points out, such officials infer that "the costly elderly are a central part of our economic crisis. . . . The scapegoating of Social Security and Medicare as primary causes of the fiscal crisis has served to deflect attention from the more compelling and deep-seated roots of the current economic crisis" (pp. 75–77). It also has encouraged cost controls that tend to worsen program inequities.

Moreover, in an effort to cut public costs, political leaders have been attempting to privatize an increasing number of social programs, including income support for the elderly. Since the 1980s these officials have advocated the growth of Individual Retirement Accounts (IRAs), 401(k)s, and Keogh Plans, as well as enhanced coverage under employer-sponsored private retirement systems. The assumption has been that the private sector should, and would, shoulder greater economic responsibility for retirement. Karen Ferguson, Director of the Pension Rights Center, has sardonically labeled these efforts over the last decade as a "do it yourself retirement" (U.S. House Select Committee on Aging 1991, pp. 76–77).

Privatization efforts, however, have engendered escalating public costs without improving the economic situation of older people, especially the condition of disadvantaged groups. In 1990 Federal outlay equivalents through tax expenditures represent an additional $104 billion for old age support programs. In fact, tax credits for private retirement plans, which include Employer Pension Plans ($60.5 billion), Individual Retirement Accounts ($8.7 billion), and Keogh plans ($1.9 billion) represent the single largest deduction in taxes (U.S. House Select Committee on Aging, 1991). Other exclusions encompass capital gains for those persons age 55 and over selling their home ($4.3 billion); untaxed Medicare premiums ($7.3 billion); Railroad Retirement System Benefits ($305 million); additional tax deduction for the elderly ($1.9 billion); Social Security benefits for retired workers and their survivors ($19 billion); and Veterans Pensions ($80 million) (see Table 2).

Table 2. Federal Tax Credits for Old Age Income Support and Related Programs, 1990, in Billions of Dollars

Program	Cost
Employer Pension Plans	$60.5
Individual Retirement Accounts	8.7
Keogh Plans	1.9
Capital Gains Exclusion on Homes	4.3
Special Tax Deduction for Elderly	1.9
Untaxed Medicare Premiums	7.3
Untaxed Railroad Retirement Pensions	.3
Untaxed Social Security Pensions	19.0
Untaxed Veterans Pensions	.3
Total Credits	$ 104.2

Source: U.S. Government Budget, 1992. Washington, DC: U.S. Government Printing Office.

Income Adequacy

The economic situation of older people has a greater variability than that of other age groups. In addition, over the last several decades there has been an increasing transfer of wealth between economic classes rather than among the generations. There has been greater concentration of income at the top as well as growing poverty. According to a recent government report, the share of aggregate income received by the highest quintile of households has increased over the last 20 years, reaching 47 percent of the total in 1990; and at the same time, the number of people living under the official poverty line reached 13.5 percent of the population (U.S. Dept. of Commerce, 1990).

There also has been a feminization of poverty over the years, including single mothers and their children as well as single older women. As noted by Rodgers (1986), female-headed households have always had a high rate of poverty; what has changed dramatically over the last several decades is the number of such households. Increasing rates of divorce, separation, and single parenting are among the primary factors contributing to the growth of female-headed households among younger women; greater female longevity relative to men, coupled with the rapid expansion of the 75-and-over age group, has engendered a large single older female population.

Female heads of households represented 17 percent of all families in 1990 but 53 percent of those that are poor (U.S. Dept. of Commerce, 1990). The median income of families with a female householder was $16,932 as compared with $39,895 for married-couple families (U.S. Dept. of Commerce, 1991). Inadequate social welfare programs and child support, high unemployment, and low wages account for much of the economic problems experienced by female-headed younger families. For example, in 1990 the earnings of full-time working women averaged $19,816, as compared with $27,866 for men (U.S. Dept. of Commerce, 1991).

Poverty and low incomes among these younger women not only continue into old age but their economic situation tends to worsen, especially as a result of widowhood or divorce. Income inequalities during the working years tend to be exacerbated by the structures of old age income support systems in the U.S. As pointed out by Arendell and Estes (1991), "Women's poverty in old age is significantly related to their marital status and to the cumulative effects of unpaid work in the family and wage discrimination in the employment sector" (p. 212). These are significant factors in the computation of public and private retirement benefits.

Approximately 41 percent of single older women are poor or near-poor (U.S. House Select Committee on Aging, 1990a), and an even larger percentage has sorely inadequate economic resources. As Margolis (1990) observes, "census tabulations of poverty for the elderly . . . are based on the federal government's somewhat tortured definition of poverty, which both underestimates the number of poor overall and discriminates against the elderly poor in particular" (pp. 9–10).

Significantly, many previously economically secure wives fall into low and poverty income conditions when they become widowed. Almost four times more single older women live in poverty conditions than do wives of the same age; half of these widows were not poor prior to their husband's death (U.S. House Select Committee on Aging, 1990a).

Social Security

As Baum (see chapter 8) explains, the Social Security System initially was expected to be just one component of retirement income; architects of the programs expected that private pensions and individual savings would comprise a significant portion of the elderly's income needs. However, most workers have not been able to save substantially for their own old age. Only those older people at the top of the income scale have amassed significant economic assets. Schulz (1990) concludes that home equity accounts for the bulk of most older people's wealth and "these assets are not readily converted to spendable funds" (p. 253). As will be shown later, receipt of decent private pensions is concentrated among the economic elite. Significantly, 70 percent of older women depend on Social Security for their sole support (U.S. House Select Committee on Aging, 1990a).

Concern over the burgeoning national debt has thrust the Social Security System into the foreground of public debate. A number of policy-makers argue not only that the program has become an economic burden but also that benefit levels have become increasingly excessive. Political efforts thus aim at controlling costs rather than at restructuring the program to meet the real income needs of economically disadvantaged groups of older people.

At the upper end of the income scale, a worker who retired at age 65, and who had worked steadily in covered employment at the maximum wage level, would earn a monthly benefit of $1,023 or $12,276 annually in 1991. A couple in that situation would receive $18,408 annually if the spouse received her initial benefit at age 65 as well.

In contrast, despite the redistributive features of its benefit formula, the structure of the Social Security system is not well-suited to serve the income needs of most women, blacks, Hispanics, the chronically unemployed, and low-wage earners in general. The program reinforces and even exacerbates income inequalities between the classes and the genders. Although the program is credited with lifting a significant number of older people out of poverty, it has done so, as Minkler (1991) notes, "only to a few hundred dollars or so above the poverty line" (p. 69).

Due to unemployment, poor health, and other factors, low-income workers are more likely to receive their initial Social Security pension prior to age 65. At age 62, such "retirees" receive a permanent 20 percent reduction in their benefit amount; in the years 2005 and 2022 these cuts will be increased to 25 percent and 30 percent respectively. On the other hand, workers who remain in the labor force from ages 65 to 70, the vast majority of whom are high wage earners, receive progressively larger increases in their base amount each year. This percentage will be increased from 3 percent annually in 1990 to 8 percent in 2009.

Moreover, a woman's benefit averages only about 70 percent of the average man's benefit, a percentage that has not improved over the last two decades. In 1990 there were 39 million people receiving Social Security, with an average monthly benefit of $627 for men and $458 for women (U.S. House Select Committee on Aging, 1990a).

Despite the entrance of growing numbers of women into the labor force, they continue to earn substantially lower wages than men on which to base their Social Security benefits. (By 1990 nearly 70 percent of all women worked as compared to 46 percent in 1965.) The program assumes a continuous labor force participation rate and allows only three years of earnings to be dropped from benefit calculations. This provision penalizes women with intermittent work histories who have been the primary caretakers of their young children, or, increasingly, the primary caretakers of their older parents and parents-in-law.

Most married older women rely on the dependency allowance (50 percent of the primary benefit), which tends to be greater than their own pension. The couple thus receives 150 percent of the husband's pension. However, after the death of her spouse, the female is forced to rely on the primary pension alone; almost 90 percent of women over the age of 75 are widows. Widowers are more likely to remarry, at which time the 150 percent benefit is restored. In fact only 16 percent of all men aged 65 and over live alone, as compared to 41 percent of women (U.S. Senate Special Committee on Aging, 1990b).

A divorced woman now is entitled to receive a benefit whether or not her ex-husband, aged 62 or over, has retired. However, she receives only half of his benefit, an amount which provides poverty level conditions for those relying on the pension exclusively.

The regressivity of Social Security's taxation structure also disproportionately burdens the low-income labor force, which tends to consist of minorities and women. Just as important, the program has neutralized the progressive features of the national tax system. In addition it has allowed a significant source of personal economic resources to remain unavailable for social welfare needs. Unlike other federal programs, taxes for Social Security exclude all non-wage income and wages over an annual ceiling amount ($53,400 in 1991) as well as impose a uniform rate, regardless of income. In 1992 this was 7.65 percent for both employers and workers.

At the same time those retirees with relatively high wealth and income are taxed on only a portion of their Social Security benefits. As of 1992, individuals who need to supplement insufficient benefit levels by working are subject to an "earnings" test; benefits are reduced if the worker earns wages greater than $7,080 for those under age 65 and $9,720 for those aged 65 and over.

Since 1975 annual Social Security benefits have increased automatically with the Consumer Price Index (CPI). Although this has benefitted the elderly overall, it also has heightened income gaps among the economic classes. For example, CPI-based benefit growth coincides with upward adjustments in the tax rate, broadening the program's regressive taxation structure. Such across-the-board pension increases also widen steadily the dollar income gap among beneficiary groups (Olson, 1982, pp. 71–72).

Private Retirement System

Over the last several decades the U.S. has lost steadily its world economic hegemony. By the 1980s productivity growth lingered behind nearly all of the industrialized nations. The U.S. increasingly lost its world-wide market shares to other countries in nearly every industry, from traditional manufacturing to high-technology electronics. Faced with such international competition and declining profits, American companies have responded by demanding wage and benefit reductions, re-locating firms in countries where labor is cheap, and merging with or taking over other companies. Jobs in the manufacturing sector declined to 28 percent of total private-sector employment while those in the service sector rose to 72 percent (U.S. Senate Special Committee on Aging, 1990b). Small firms engendered most of the new jobs, employing about 41 percent of the labor force by the 1990s. Such businesses tend to be comprised of low paid workers; only 19 percent of people employed at firms with 25 or fewer workers earned over $20,000 annually in 1988 (U.S. House Select Committee on Aging, 1991).

The real wages of the working population declined, as did both pension coverage and benefit levels. While about half of the full-time private sector work force had pension coverage in 1981, ten years later this was reduced to 44 percent. One primary reason for the reduction in plan participation is that the service and retail industries, as well as small firms, are less likely than the manufacturing sector to offer private pension plans (U.S. House Select Committee on Aging, 1991). Currently there are approximately 870,350 employer-sponsored pension plans covering 76.6 million participants (U.S. Senate Special Committee on Aging, 1990a).

There also has been a trend away from defined benefit plans and toward defined contribution plans 401(k), especially among smaller businesses. Defined contribution plans, which represent 78 percent of all private plans, accounted for 86 percent of all new plans in 1990. Moreover, according to Karen Ferguson, larger companies are freezing existing plans and putting retirement money into 401(k)s (U.S. House Select Committee on Aging, 1991).

As noted in a recent government report, the former type of scheme is less suited for serving the needs of active and retired workers since it: 1) places the risk of adverse economic conditions on the employee rather than on the employer; and 2) retreats from efforts to replace a certain percentage of wages, thus engendering lower benefit levels. A survey by a consulting firm, Wyatt Company, found that:

> The annual defined contribution pension for a retiree earning $15,000 per year averaged about 19% of income. Under a defined benefit plan, the average pension for the same retiree averaged about 28% of income. (U.S. House Select Committee on Aging, 1991, p. 5).

In fact the defined contribution plan often provides a lump-sum payment to workers upon termination of their jobs. In 1988 about 8.5 million workers received lump-sum cash-out, averaging $6,800; about 34 percent spent the entire amount. It has been estimated that about two-thirds of lump-sum payments overall are spent prior to retirement (U.S. House Select Committee on Aging, 1991).

Defined contribution plans also are not guaranteed by the Pension Benefit Guaranty Corporation (PBGC), the federal agency set up to protect workers, to some extent, against plan terminations. Moreover the large number of plant closing, mergers, and takeovers over the last several decades has engendered a rapid rate of plan terminations among defined benefit plan sponsors. As a result the PBGC has a large and growing deficit which reached over 1 billion dollars by 1990.

Private pension coverage and receipt of adequate benefits has always been concentrated among high wage earners. Increasingly, employees must contribute toward the plan if they are to receive any benefits at all. With the growth of voluntary plans in lieu of employer-paid ones, there has been a decrease in participation among low wage earners who cannot afford them. About one-third of all retired private-sector workers currently receive a pension, lump-sum distribution, or other type of annuity.

Women, who tend to be concentrated in the service and retail industries, are less likely to receive a pension based on their own employment. Their more intermittent work histories because of "caring" roles also lower their vesting opportunities and benefit levels. In 1989 16 percent of single women, 28 percent of single men, and 38 percent of married couples received a private pension. The median benefit was $3,800 for men and $1,940 for women (U.S. House Select Committee on Aging, 1990a).

As retirees age, the value of their pension dollars declines steadily since very few plans include protection for inflation. According to a recent Congressional report, only 4 percent of workers participating in medium and large firm plans have automatic increases and these are capped at 3 percent annually. Another 25 percent of retirees receive periodic ad hoc adjustments. Critically, between 1980 and 1988 less than 50 percent of all plans had any cost-of-living increases. During that period the benefits lost about one-third of their purchasing power (U.S. House Select Committee on Aging, 1990b).

Despite an interest among political leaders in privatizing economic support of older people, there have been only limited efforts to improve the effectiveness of the private pension system since the Employee Retirement Income Security Act (ERISA) of

1974. Although women workers, and especially wives, continue to be disadvantaged under the private pension system, the Retirement Equity Act of 1984 improved two of the more conspicuous gender inequities: a worker is allowed five years away from the job without forfeiting benefits; and the joint and survivor annuity is automatic for a vested worker who dies before or after retirement, unless it is specifically waived by the worker and his spouse. On the other hand, pension rules require that plans provide widows only up to 50 percent of the primary benefit. Moreover, only about 3 percent of wives currently receive any benefits earned by spouses who died prior to retirement (U.S. House Select Committee on Aging, 1990a).

In addition, as a result of the Tax Reform Act of 1986, the vesting period for single-employer pension plans was shortened from ten to five years, effective in 1989 (multi-employer plans tend to require ten years before vesting). Moreover, when integrating a pension with Social Security, an employer is allowed to reduce the worker's benefit only by a maximum of 50 percent.

Supplementary Security Income Program

In 1990 4.6 million elderly and disabled poor received benefits under Supplementary Security Income (SSI). Eligibility for the program is based on a stringent "means" test aimed at providing proof of destitution. As pointed out by Margolis (1990, p. 42), the program continues to be beset by numerous problems, including burdensome reporting requirements; stringent regulations; an annual eligibility determination process; low visibility; insufficient outreach; and a welfare stigma. As a result, only about half of those people eligible participate in the program.

Arendell and Estes (1991) conclude that:

> The eligibility rules for public entitlement programs reflect men's patterns of labor force participation and the male model of work. The non-means-tested entitlement programs, such as Social Security, provide men greater access to and higher levels of benefits, rewarding continuous participation in the primary labor force. The means-tested

> entitlement programs . . . including Supplementary Security Income, are set at penurious levels and primarily support women (p. 213).

Maximum federal annual benefits, which in 1990 amounted to $4,632 for a single person and $6,948 for a couple, fell below the poverty lines of $6,280 and $8,420 respectively. Twenty-six states provide supplementary benefits, with the amounts varying considerably.

Conclusion

American society is experiencing rapid population aging along with declining labor force participation among the aged. Thus increasingly larger numbers of people have become dependent on public income-support systems, especially Social Security. The latter program alone represented nearly 18 percent of the total national budget in 1990. At the same time the U.S. is confronting unprecedented, serious economic problems, including an escalating federal budget deficit; growing international trade imbalances; plant closing, mergers, and acquisitions that engender increased unemployment; and movement from a manufacturing to a service economy, a process that has fostered declining real wages and pension coverage.

Rather than address the root causes of our economic predicament, political leaders have attempted to cut social welfare programs. There also have been efforts to privatize such plans, including those serving the elderly. Both of these strategies have worsened economic inequities among income groups; overall, public policy since the late 1970s has fostered a greater transfer of wealth among the classes than between generations.

The pension elite, who have received high wages and have accumulated significant savings and other forms of wealth during their younger years, continue to receive large and multiple pension incomes. Concomitantly, growing numbers of the elderly, especially single women, minorities, the chronically unemployed, and other low wage earners, are forced to live in dire economic conditions. In particular there has been a feminization of poverty among younger female heads of households. Such poverty and low incomes among younger women not only continue into old age but their economic situation tends to worsen. Moreover, population aging has produced an increasing number of single elderly women; many experience poverty conditions for the first time when their spouse dies.

Over the next several decades these trends will continue, and probably worsen, unless political leaders address the fundamental causes of the economic morass we are in. At the same time social welfare programs, including those serving the elderly, must be restructured to better meet the needs of disadvantaged groups.

REFERENCES

Arendell, T. & Estes, C. 1991. "Older women in the post-Reagan era." In M. Minkler and C.L. Estes, eds., *Critical Perspectives on Aging: The Political and Moral Economy of Growing Old* (pp. 209–226). Amityville, NY: Baywood.

Margolis, R.J. 1990. *Risking Old Age in America*. Boulder, CO: Westview.

Minkler, M. 1991. "Generational equity and the new victim blaming." In M. Minkler and C.L. Estes, eds., *Critical Perspectives on Aging: The Political and Moral Economy of Growing Old* (pp. 67–80). Amityville, NY: Baywood.

Olson, L.K. 1982. *The Political Economy of Aging: The State, Private Power, and Social Welfare*. New York: Columbia University Press.

Rodgers, H.R., Jr. 1986. *Poor Women, Poor Families: The Economic Plight of America's Female-Headed Households*. Armonk, NY: M.E. Sharpe.

Schulz, J.H. 1990. *The Economics of Aging*. Dover, MA: Auburn House.

Stone, L. & Fletcher, S. 1988. "Demographic Variations in North America." In E. Rathbone-McCuan & B. Havans, eds., *North American Elders: United States and Canadian Perspective* (pp. 3–36), Westport, CT: Greenwood.

U.S. Department of Commerce, Bureau of the Census. 1991. Money income of households, families, and persons in the United States.

Current Population Reports, Series P-60, No. 174. Washington: U.S. Government Printing Office.

U.S. Department of Commerce, Bureau of the Census. 1990. Poverty in the U.S. *Current Population Reports*, Series P-60, No. 175. Washington: U.S. Government Printing Office.

U.S. House Select Committee on Aging. 1991. *The illusory promise of retirement security*. Hearings before the Select Committee on Aging, Subcommittee on Retirement Income and Employment, 1st session, 102nd Congress, July 10. Washington: U.S. Government Printing Office.

U.S. House Select Committee on Aging. 1990a. *Retirement income for women*. Hearings before the Select Committee on Aging, Subcommittee on Retirement Income and Employment, 2nd session, 101st Congress, July 2. Washington: U.S. Government Printing Office.

U.S. House Select Committee on Aging. 1990b. *Private pensions and retiree health benefits: Under-serving today's retirees, retreating from tomorrow's?* Hearings before the Select Committee on Aging, Subcommittee on Retirement Income and Employment, 2nd session, 101st Congress, July 27. Washington: U.S. Government Printing Office.

U.S. Senate Special Committee on Aging. 1990a. *President Bush's proposed fiscal year 1991 budget for aging programs*. Information paper to the Senate Special Committee on Aging, 1st session, 101st Congress, March. Washington: U.S. Government Printing Office.

U.S. Senate Special Committee on Aging. 1990b. *Aging America: trends and projections* (Annotated). Information paper to the Senate Special Committee on Aging, 2nd session, 101st Congress, February. Washington: U.S. Government Printing Office.

CHAPTER 5

Housing Policy for the Elderly
Problems, Programs, and Politics

Jon Pynoos

Older persons have long been major beneficiaries of federal housing policy. This has occurred because the government's tax policy has favored homeowners, and supply-side housing programs have singled out the elderly as a particular subgroup both worthy and in need of special housing assistance. Over the last decade, however, housing conditions of the elderly have improved, demand-side approaches have replaced many supply-side programs, HUD's overall budget has been reduced, and competition has increased from other needy groups for scarce public funds. In this environment advocates of housing for the elderly have begun to focus their efforts on preserving existing programs and meeting the needs of the growing number of frail older persons who need supportive housing environments linked with services.

Housing Problems of the Elderly

Kingdon (1984) has suggested that policy is influenced by whether a problem is perceived as increasing in magnitude or diminishing. In addition policy can be affected by changes in the nature of the problems, their relative importance to each other, and how problems of one group are viewed in relationship to other groups. Analysts have identified five types of housing related problems: the physical condition of the dwelling unit, crowdedness, affordability, suitability, and linkages with services. Over the last thirty years, significant shifts have occurred in what have been perceived as the magnitude and type of these problems, their relationship to each other,and how the situation of the elderly compares to other groups. While there have been significant lags and gaps, federal policies have begun to shift in response to changing needs by focusing programs on frail older persons.

Housing Conditions Have Been Improving

Throughout the first half of the twentieth century, improving housing conditions was a major focus of housing policy. The large percentage of dilapidated, unsafe, and inadequate units (e.g., those lacking basic features such as hot and cold running water, private toilets, bathing facilities, and complete kitchens) put housing on the top rung of social problems that needed to be addressed. Over time the housing conditions in the United States have generally improved for the great majority of Americans as new housing has been built and older stock upgraded. While it is difficult to exactly determine the magnitude of changes because of differences over time in how and what are considered housing condition problems, housing quality has continued to improve. By 1988 the percentage of elderly households living in dwelling units with problems was 6.3 percent, a percentage similar to that experienced by non-elderly heads of household.

Because the general stock of housing has been improving over time, housing conditions of the elderly have receded on the policy agenda. However, housing conditions remain a problem for particular segments of the elderly population whose dwelling units are in need of substantial structural repair and maintenance. Problems of inadequate housing conditions are concentrated among rural older persons, members of minority groups, renters, and older persons with low incomes. For example, according to the Annual Housing Survey, in 1985 rural-dwelling older households were almost three times as likely to be living in moderately to severely inadequate housing (11.4 percent) compared to their city-dwelling counterparts (4.8 percent). Approximately 4 percent of elderly white owner-households lived in moderately to severely inadequate housing compared to 23 percent of elderly black and 12.5 percent of elderly Hispanic owner-households. Similarly, 5.8 percent of white elderly renter-households, compared to 21.1 percent of black and 16.6 percent of Hispanic elderly renter-households, lived in moderately to severely inadequate housing. Dramatic differences are also found when comparing the housing conditions of different income groups among the elderly. For example, of elderly households with incomes between $10–15,000, 4.4 percent lived in moderately to severely inadequate housing. Those with incomes between $5–10,000 were almost twice as likely (8.7 percent) and those with incomes below $5,000 more than three times as likely (17.4 percent) to be living in conditions of inadequacy. The most common defects, in order of magnitude starting with the most prevalent, were: heating breakdowns, cracks in walls, water source breakdowns, signs of rats, no access to telephones, exposed wiring, public sewer breakdowns, incomplete plumbing, and holes in the floor (Mikelsons and Turner, 1991).

Overcrowding Is Not Considered a Problem for the Elderly

Public health officials and psychologists have been concerned about over-crowding because it can contribute to poor physical and mental health. While it continues to be a problem for younger families, according to the standard used by the Census (1.01 persons per room), overcrowding is an almost insignificant problem for older persons. This is understandable given that the overwhelming majority of older persons live alone or with a spouse and over 70 percent of elderly households own their own homes. In fact from a policy perspective it has been suggested that the elderly under-utilize the space that they occupy. For example, according to the American Housing Survey, in 1987 83 percent of elderly households lived in dwelling units with two or more bedrooms (Mikelsons and Turner, 1991). This seeming under-utilization of the housing stock has led some analysts to suggest that public policy should encourage older persons to move and free up units for younger families with children (Welfeld, 1988). Others have noted that, while the housing occupied by older persons may be somewhat under-utilized, much of it is composed of smaller homes, suggesting that better use of this housing stock can be made through home modification and repair, the addition of accessory units, and home sharing (Hare and Ostler, 1987; Horne and Baldwin, 1988).

Excessive Housing Expenditures Have Become an Increasing Concern

Housing analysts have concluded that excessive housing costs, especially high rents, have replaced housing condition and overcrowding as the major housing problem for the general population and elderly in particular. Excessive housing costs can prevent persons from maintaining their place of residence and result in inadequate funds for other necessities of life such as food, medical care, and transportation.

Large debates have occurred over the past two decades concerning the appropriate standard by which to judge excessive housing costs. In the 1960s federal housing policy was based on the assumption that persons should not spend more than 25 percent of their income on housing. In 1968, when analysts pointed out that many tenants of federally assisted programs such as public housing were spending a higher percentage of their income on rent, Congress passed the Brooke amendment which capped housing expenditures for programs serving lower income persons at 25 percent. During the Reagan administration, however, the percentage of income that tenants were expected to pay was raised to 30 percent, based on the rationale that most tenants were receiving other forms of public subsidies (e.g. food stamps). In addition the administration hoped that such an increase would reduce the amount of subsidy that the government had to provide for its housing programs.

The standard related to how much older persons, in particular, should be required to pay for housing has itself been the subject of much debate. Some analysts have argued that lower-income older persons can actually afford to pay even more than 30 percent because not only do they benefit from publicly subsidized programs such as Medicare and Medicaid, but their overall expenditures are reduced because they do not incur job-related costs such as transportation to work. Other analysts have argued, however, that policy should not simply be based on an arbitrary percentage but adjusted for family size and actual income (Stone, 1990).

Obviously, the standard that is chosen by which to judge excessive housing costs is critical in determining both the dimensions of the problem and the amount of assistance that is needed to address it. Data from the 1985 American Housing Survey indicated that 45 percent of elderly households paid more than the conventional standard of 25 percent of their income for housing. Based on the assumption that low-income persons can pay less for housing than middle- or upper-income persons, Stone (1990) found that a significant proportion—31 percent of the elderly—are shelter poor, with the most serious problems occurring among the lowest income persons.

Similar to housing condition, excessive housing costs differentially impact segments of the elderly population. For example, older single elderly women living alone experience the most severe housing affordability problems: in 1985, 48 percent of the elderly paying 25 percent or more of their income for housing were single elderly women. A similar affordability problem was faced by elderly renters: 62 percent paid more than 25 percent of their income for housing (45 percent were shelter poor according to Stone's analysis). While homeowners are somewhat better off than renters with regard to affordability, in 1985 3.5 million of the 5.8 million shelter poor elderly were homeowners.

Housing Suitability Has Recently Gained Attention

Housing suitability refers to how well a unit fits the needs of its residents with particular concern to those persons with disabilities. When persons become more frail, their living environment needs to be more supportive to compensate for their limitations or disabilities. A significant number of the elderly, however, live in housing that lacks supportive features or presents barriers to mobility. Large scale research in this area began in the mid-1980s. Initial studies suggested that a substantial number of frail older persons required environmental modifications and features (e.g. grab bars, railings) that did not exist in their current dwelling units in order to safely carry out activities and maintain their independence. For example, Struyk (1988) found that 6.6 percent of dwellings occupied by elderly-headed households with health problems or mobility limitations had special features such as handrails or grab bars; the study estimated that an additional 885,000 elderly were in need of at least one such feature. Another study found that approximately two-thirds of all elderly headed households with members having one or more activity limitations lived in units lacking features such as a ramp, grab bar, raised toilet, elevator, or stair lift (Soldo and Longino, 1988).

Linking Housing and Services Has Emerged as a High Priority

Linking housing and services, like suitable housing, emerged on the federal agenda in the late 1980s as evidence began to accumulate suggesting that most housing lacked the long-term care services necessary to support the increasing number of older persons requiring assistance to function in their own apartments or homes (Pynoos, 1992b). For example, Struyk, et al., (1989) found that approximately 7 percent of the 1.6 million elderly in federally assisted housing needed help with at least one Activity of Daily Living (ADL) and 12–17 percent needed assistance with at least one Instrumental Activity of Daily Living (IADL)—about 350,000 overall. In another study of public housing tenants, Holshouser and Waltman (1988) found that approximately one-third expressed unmet needs for assistance in transportation, shopping, housekeeping, and meals.

Because almost two-thirds of these elderly residents lived alone, compared to one-third of elderly who lived in the community (Congressional Budget Office, 1988; Kasper, 1988), they were considered more reliant on formal services to maintain their independence.

The responsibility for providing services to tenants of federally assisted housing has been indeterminate (Heumann, 1988). For example, studies suggest that managers, the first line of defense in identifying problems, making referrals, and coordinating services, generally had limited knowledge, experience, and available time to perform such tasks (Brice and Gorey, 1990). It has also been unclear who will pay for the addition of service coordinators/case managers or the actual services that residents require: owners, residents, and/or other private and public sources. Particular concern has been expressed about tenants in private apartments who may be even more in need of assistance because owners of such properties are even less likely to be aware of their older tenants' needs or to view services as part of their management responsibility.

Housing Policy and Programs

Over time the federal government has developed a range of housing policies and programs that have assisted older persons. Foremost is the policy allowing homeowners to deduct the interest on their mortgage from their federal taxes, an "indirect" housing subsidy that has benefited a large number of older persons who have been homeowners. Older persons have disproportionately occupied units in "direct" housing programs (e.g. public and Section 8 housing) which, although not initially developed with them in mind, have served them disproportionately because they were considered "needy" and desirable tenants. Older persons have also benefited from Section 202, the only housing program especially developed for the elderly. Several major problems, however, have plagued "direct" housing programs. First, because housing has not been considered an entitlement, they have always been limited, meeting the needs of only a relatively small number of persons. Second, large cuts in

HUD's budget during the 1980s resulted in the curtailment of many housing programs. Third, policy has been shifting away from supply-side programs that build new units towards demand-side approaches that use certificates or vouchers for existing housing. Fourth, policy has only recently been developing to encourage the development of supportive housing for frail older persons; for many years housing programs of the federal government focused instead on active, independent older persons.

Federal Tax Policy and Supply-Side Programs Have Been Major Thrusts of Government

Housing Policy

Although tax policy is not a component of housing legislation, Dolbeare (1986) has argued that tax policy allowing home owners to deduct mortgage interest from income taxes is the largest housing subsidy program. In 1984 she estimated that income deductions from home mortgages amounted to over $39.4 billion compared to $8.5 billion of housing assistance payments. This tax benefit accrued primarily to middle- and upper-middle-income homeowners. Given that over 70 percent of elderly heads of household are homeowners, many older persons have been major beneficiaries of this policy. When discussions periodically arise about the amount of this subsidy and its inequities, powerful organizations such as the National Association of Realtors and the National Association of Home Builders have successfully come to its defense.

While supply-side programs have assisted many fewer persons than overall tax policy, they have been more targeted towards low- and moderate-income persons. The largest supply-side program has been public housing. As a program emanating out of the depression, public housing had as its major goals the provision of jobs, the elimination of slums, and the housing of temporarily poor families. It was not until the 1960s when public housing began to be viewed as permanent housing for low-income, primarily minority, residents that the elderly, viewed as the "deserving poor" and a group in need of better housing, became a major constituency of the program. This shift allowed many projects primarily serving the elderly to be built in more suburban locations that would not have supported the building of family oriented public housing.

While public housing for the elderly and disabled had some special features (e.g. emergency call buttons), it, like its parent program, did not include services and was targeted to active, mobile older persons. By the early 1990s over 40 percent of the public housing stock of 1.4 million units was occupied by the elderly, with about 300,000 older persons living in public housing units designated for the elderly and handicapped.

The Section 202 program for the elderly and the handicapped, begun in 1959, was viewed as public housing with a difference. Sponsors were non-profit and tenants originally of moderate income who would not be eligible for public housing. Section 202 housing was also intended for the active elderly although some space for services and common activities was considered an allowable cost. Services, however, were not guaranteed and residents or sponsors were responsible for funding meals and programs. In the 1980s Section 202 housing became much more targeted to lower-income persons who were eligible for Section 8 Rental Certificates. By 1990 the Section 202 program had approximately 200,000 units.

Older persons have also benefited from several other supply side programs. Although not directly targeted to the elderly, programs such as Section 221 d3 and Section 8 new construction have over time housed substantial numbers of older persons. Section 221 d3, like the 202 program, was originally targeted to moderate-income persons who were not eligible for public housing. While few of the tenants were elderly when they moved in, many "aged in place" and by the 1990s were in their 60s and 70s. The Section 8 new construction program was targeted at lower-income persons. Owing to the needs of older persons and the view that elderly would present few problems, many Section 8 projects were built for the elderly.

While supply-side programs such as public housing for the elderly and Section 202 were judged relatively successful in terms of absence of serious management problems and high tenant satisfaction, they were never very large in magnitude. Public housing, in particular, suffered from the overall negative image of "bare bones" subsidized housing, a lack of funds for routine maintenance, and many poor locations. Their problems began to be compounded during the 1970s, when policy analysts began to suggest that providing persons with vouchers or certificates that could be used in existing housing was two to three times less expensive than building new units. During the 1980s and early 1990s these arguments were used by the Reagan and Bush administrations, which philosophically did not want the federal government involved in housing production, to virtually halt supply-side programs. The only surviving remnant was a sharply curtailed Section 202 housing program which dwindled to approximately 6–8,000 units per year.

A Shift Has Occurred Towards Demand-Side Programs

In addition to potential cost savings, demand-side programs have been considered to have the advantage of offering participants a wider choice of options such as staying in one's own dwelling unit instead of moving to a housing complex in a particular location. This advantage has been thought to be particularly attractive to older persons, the great majority of whom indicate a strong preference to age in place. The largest demand-side program is the Section 8 rent certificate program. In 1987 there were approximately 813,000 Section 8 Certificates and vouchers which subsidized rents for low- and moderate-income tenants who lived in existing housing approved by public housing authorities administering the program. The housing allowance experiment which provided more latitude in how housing subsidies could be spent and where participants could live than the Section 8 program found that elderly, in comparison to non-elderly, more often used the support to reduce their housing costs, rather than move. A full-fledged housing allowance program has not yet gained political support, in part hindered by its expected costs (approximately $30 billion, $5 billion of which would be for the elderly), recent concerns about its potential savings, and continued disagreements about the merits of demand-side vs. supply-side programs.

Linking Housing and Services: Moving Beyond Bricks and Mortar

For over 20 years advocates of policies to link federally assisted housing for the elderly with services struggled to place the issue on the federal agenda (Pynoos, 1992b). Even though evidence mounted that much of the federally assisted housing stock lacked services, funds were not allocated from HUD's budget nor targeted from agencies such as HHS to assist residents. The policy process itself served as a serious barrier to linking housing and services (Nachison, 1985). Various congressional committees and separate bureaucracies, zealous in maintaining their independence and authority, created and administered discrete housing, social services, health, and income support programs. Because linking housing with services ranked fairly low on the agendas of federal legislative committees or agencies, no overarching, coordinating policy developed to encourage it (Pynoos, 1990). Housing finance policy traditionally focused on building new units for healthy, active older persons, rather than on changing suitability over time (Pynoos, 1992a). Long-term care policy, with the exception of the 2176 Medicaid waiver program, almost exclusively focused on financing nursing-home care. Even the limited federal assistance allocated to in-home services was not been well coordinated with housing.

While the policies of two key components, housing and long-term care, developed independently, it became increasingly clear that housing was part of the long-term care continuum (Lawton, 1991). After almost a decade of lobbying by advocates who argued for a type of supportive housing that fit between housing for independent older persons and a nursing home, a HUD-funded Congregate Housing Services Program (CHSP) was created to provide service coordination and a variety of services to older tenants in public and Section 202 housing. The experiment involved 63 sites in which two meals a day and services such as homemaking were provided to approximately 3,000 frail older persons.

The launching of the CHSP demonstration proved to be controversial. HHS was reluctant to pay for the services out of its budget because it did not consider itself a housing agency. Proponents of the program argued that it was better off under the auspices of HUD anyway, because that would help preserve its housing orientation. They feared that if HHS controlled CHSP, it would adopt a medical model (e.g. target very frail older persons) in spite of the fact that it was based on social services. Even the evaluation proved contentious: HUD concluded that the demonstration indicated that CHSP did not demonstrate that it saved money that otherwise would have been spent on nursing home care and therefore was not cost effective. This viewpoint prompted a Congressional hearing about the CHSP in which HUD was accused of altering the evaluator conclusions to make the program appear unsuccessful when, in fact, the report indicated otherwise. Staff of the Hebrew Rehabilitation Center, the CHSP evaluator, testified that the evaluation was never intended to directly answer questions of cost-effectiveness. Nevertheless, as evidence of the program's potential, they pointed out that the CHSP served a number of older persons who had previously lived in nursing homes and that the agencies carrying out the program had effectively administered it. At the insistence of Congress, the CHSP program was continued but because of budget constraints and the continued lack of enthusiasm of the administration, it was confined to the same number of participants at the original sites. However, based on its first demonstration, the second CHSP phase involved stricter targeting to clients with more severe activity limitations, and elimination of the original two-meal-per-day requirement and tailoring of services.

In the absence of appropriate federal policies, many housing sponsors and service providers created innovative approaches to serving frail older tenants of government assisted housing. For example, a number of states, localities, and housing sponsors, using their own funds, created programs that provided case managers or service coordinators in subsidized housing. Several training programs were created under the auspices of national organizations such as the American Association of

Homes for the Aged to improve the skills of managers in assessing the problems of tenants and connecting them to services. In 1988, with assistance from the Robert Wood Johnson Foundation's "Supportive Services in Senior Housing Program," ten state housing finance agencies (HFAS) developed a market-driven, consumer-oriented model of service coordination and service delivery. The demonstration found that HFAS and housing sponsors were willing and able to commit funds to hire service coordinators and that likewise many tenants, who were generally above the income of those in the CHSP program, were willing to pay for services (Lanspery, 1990).

In the early 1990s what Kingdon (1984) refers to as an "open policy window" offered advocates of linking housing and services an unprecedented opportunity. During the 1980s Democrats, long the supporters of higher housing budgets and supply-side programs, were stymied by a Republican-controlled Senate and administration. In 1988, however, the Democrats gained control of both the House and the Senate. By that time concerns about homelessness, housing affordability, and the potential loss of several hundred thousand low- and moderate-income federally assisted units because of expiring contracts had raised the priority of housing on the federal agenda.

Over the next several years, under the leadership of Senator Alan Cranston (D-CA), the ground was laid for the passage of a major new housing bill, the first one in over ten years. Given the federal deficit and the prevailing shift towards demand-side programs, the resulting Cranston-Gonzales National Affordable Housing Act (NAHA) of 1990 had an underlying premise that federal funds should be used to leverage support from states, localities, and other sources, including residents themselves.

Even though housing for the elderly was not considered among the highest priorities of those advocating for a new bill, elderly advocates took advantage of the situation to lobby for several new policy initiatives in the area of supportive housing. Their effort in this area was aided by advocates for younger disabled persons and the homeless, who also sought to create housing that was linked to services.

NAHA was considered a landmark bill by advocates for the elderly because it contained several major provisions aimed at creating supportive housing. First, it revised the Section 202 program to allow federal funds to be used by private non-profit organizations and consumer cooperatives for building supportive housing targeted at frail elderly. Up to 15 percent of the funds could be designated for services. Second, service coordinators were considered an allowable cost in Section 202 housing with the proviso that such projects serve principally frail older persons. Third, the act authorized up to $51 million over a two-year period for a revised CHSP to cover both services and retrofitting of individual units and public and common spaces to meet the special needs of frail older and younger disabled, persons. Fourth, a demonstration ("HOPE for Elderly Independence") involving 1,500 frail older participants was created to test the effectiveness of a combination of housing vouchers and services on their independence. HOPE was particularly favored by the administration because of its demand-side approach and cost-sharing provisions (40 percent federal, 50 percent state and local, 10 percent participant). Fifth, the act supported the concept of older persons using the equity in their homes to provide them with additional income through federal government insurance for up to 25,000 home equity conversion mortgages.

Future Direction

In the next several decades housing policy for the elderly is likely to focus on meeting the needs of a very large group of frail older persons who will need supportive residential settings with services and who otherwise would be candidates for nursing home care. The projected increase for the population most likely to require assistance—those over age 85—will number approximately 8 million persons by the year 2030. Developments in this area will be driven by three forces: the high costs of nursing home care, the realization that many frail older persons can be cared for more humanely in residential settings, and the demand for alternatives to institutionalization by older persons and their families. A number of policy options are under consideration including expanding supportive housing, developing new forms of assisted living, and untying services from housing. The prospects for such initiatives, however, must be evaluated in the context of constrained federal housing budgets and increasing competition from other groups for resources.

Expanding Supportive Housing

NAHA signalled several new directions in federal policy to serve the needs of frail persons in existing federally assisted housing. However, the authorizations accompanying NAHA did not contain enough funds to meet even the modest objectives that the act set out to achieve. For example, authorizations were insufficient to provide service coordinators in all Section 202 and public housing projects. Only those projects which had a majority of tenants considered frail could qualify for service coordinators. Decisions concerning which of eligible projects would actually receive funds were made by lottery. While HUD indicated that service coordinators were an allowable cost in projects for which special federal allocations were unavailable, they had to compete with other needs such as maintenance and security. Moreover, the bill did not cover other federally assisted housing programs and required the vast majority of funding for services to come from non-HUD sources such as other federal agencies, state and local government, and participants themselves. The next step, supported by the 1992 housing bill, would be to insure that service coordination and services are available to all residents who need them in public and Section 202 housing and then to extend these programs to other federally assisted housing programs such as Section 8 new construction.

Even if adequate funds were provided for retro-fitting, service coordination and services, concerns exist that the concentration of frail older persons would be too great in particular developments, causing them to lose their heterogeneity and residential qualities. Moreover, housing a greater number of frail older persons is also likely to raise serious regulatory issues. For example, federally assisted housing complexes do not generally meet the building code standards for non-ambulatory residents (e.g. persons who walk with a pronged cane, walker, or who need assistance) or those with mental disabilities who might have difficulty with exiting building in an emergency. Some of these problems might be mitigated by creating a special wing of a building with widened corridors, sprinklers, and easy evacuation. It may be that ultimately, however, very frail persons will be better off and more efficiently served in new forms of housing such as assisted living that are planned to meet their needs.

Developing Assisted Living

Assisted living is a residential setting in which professionally managed and administered services are provided in order to keep frail persons physically and psychologically active (Regnier, in press). It falls on a traditional housing continuum between congregate or supportive housing and skilled nursing care. Typically, residents have their own individual apartment units made up of a sleeping and living area, kitchenette, and bathroom. Shared spaces include a dining room, recreation and social areas. Services include meals, housekeeping, and medication monitoring, which in some complexes can be purchased *a la carte.*

Assisted living combines elements of housing and long-term care. In the late 1980s and early 1990s, several hundred assisted living complexes were built by the private sector for individuals who could afford the costs which ranged between $1,500 and $2,500 per month. The financing of assisted living for low- and moderate-income persons has faced serious roadblocks because of the difficulty of combining funds from a variety of housing and service programs. Ideally, assisted living would be able to draw on such programs as HUD low-interest mortgage insurance, Section 8 certificates, SSI, Title XX, and Medicaid. Each of these programs is likely to have a different view of its role and responsibility in regard to assisted living. For example, Medicaid funds for community-based care are available primarily through waiver programs targeted to persons who would otherwise be in nursing homes. While assisted living may target those at the border of nursing homes, such programs have had difficulty proving that savings will result. In addition, how to regulate such settings is yet to be resolved because it bridges housing and nursing care.

Untying Housing and Services

NAHA reforms to create more supportive housing and developments in the area of assisted living represent a housing approach to better link housing and services. Limited funding for coordination and services under NAHA, however, suggests the difficulty in obtaining adequate support from housing budgets to meet the needs of tenants of federally assisted housing. Moreover, many older persons with similar or even more severe problems live in other parts of the housing stock without the benefit of relatively safe environments, supportive services, and housing subsidies. Even if federally assisted housing now occupied by the elderly were turned into supportive housing, it would still be inadequate to meet the needs of the growing number of frail older persons because of the limited number of units and unavailability in many geographic areas.

A more progressive policy would untie or unbundle the combination of housing and services. It would provide a range of physically supportive environments and portable services so that frail older persons would have residential options from which to choose. These options could include multi-unit apartments, assisted living complexes, small group homes, shared housing, and staying in one's own home or apartment. Such a policy, which has evolved recently in Scandinavia (Gottschalk, 1992) and is under consideration in England (Clapham and Monroe, 1990), would provide frail older persons with greater choice in selecting residential settings based on their preferences in relation to such factors as privacy or sociability. There would be little difference in the level of service that is provided within or without nursing homes. For reasons of efficiency, specialized facilities could be restricted to those with high levels of disability who would benefit by companionship, close support of resident staff, and proximity to communal facilities.

The HOPE for Elderly Independence housing voucher and services demonstration program is promising in that it does not tie benefits to a particular building or complex. Such a program has the potential to allow individuals greater freedom of choice, especially relative to staying in their own residences, and could be used by homeowners as well as renters. It also has the administrative advantage of concentrating housing and service funds in one agency, thereby potentially avoiding coordination problems. Voucher programs, however, are unproven and contain a number of possible problems. For example, elderly persons who reside in physically inadequate housing units may not qualify unless they move or can upgrade their units. For upgrading to occur, the voucher amount must be high enough to provide an incentive for alterations or funds must be available from other sources, such as home repair/modifications programs, which are currently in short supply (Pynoos, 1992a). In addition, unless a case manager or service coordinator is available to help arrange for services, many older people with multiple needs many have difficulty using the program. Creating a policy that provides an adequate range of suitable housing options and supportive services would move the United States closer to Northern European countries, where the trend has been to halt the construction of nursing homes, convert them into a form of sheltered housing, create new types of supportive housing, and untie care from housing (Gottschalk, 1992).

Increasing Competition from Other Needy Groups for Housing Resources

Meeting the needs of the growing number of frail older persons for supportive housing and services is taking place in the context of limited federal funds and increasing competition from other groups for housing resources, as illustrated by competition for public housing among the elderly and disabled younger persons. As noted above, the inclusion of supportive housing options in NAHA owed much to the efforts of groups representing younger disabled and older frail persons. Even though they tended to deal separately with issues and proposed differed approaches, each helped the other in that they advocated for a similar cause—using HUD's funds to provide for supportive environments and services. However, during the early 1990s the common ground that united them began to shake. While NAHA provided some additional resources for specialized housing and services, it was nowhere near the amount needed. Consequently, competition intensified among younger and older groups for existing scarce housing resources.

The competition among the elderly and younger disabled over federally assisted housing had its roots in the late 1960s when the United States began a process of deinstitutionalizing persons from mental health and chronic care settings where many had lived for considerable periods of time. The underlying philosophy of deinstitutionalization was that persons with mental problems could function better in the community and lead more normal lives through the use of newly developed drugs, social services, and living arrangements that included half-way houses, small group homes, apartments, and individual homes. During this period a number of laws were passed such as Section 504 of the Rehabilitation Act of 1973, which prohibited discrimination against handicapped persons, and the Fair Housing Act of 1988, which expanded Title VIII of the Civil Rights Act of 1968 to preclude discriminatory housing practices based on handicap and familial status.

While the goals of the reformers were noble, the programs intended to accompany deinstitutionalization were not forthcoming. Particularly in the area of housing, very few alternatives were created to meet the needs of persons with mental disabilities. In order to begin addressing such housing needs, the Section 202 program was divided into two parts: one for the elderly and disabled, and the second to support small group homes for those with mental disabilities. However, the Section 202 program at that point had been reduced to only about 12,000 units. Furthermore, neighborhoods often objected to housing persons with mental disabilities and strictly enforced zoning codes to avoid new types of housing. With few available alternatives, persons with mental disabilities and their advocates began to turn with increased frequency to Section 202 housing and public housing. Both programs had in legislative language over time created provisions for the disabled and the handicapped, although as noted above Section 202 had a separate program for younger persons and the elderly program had a cap of 10 percent of units for disabled residents. Public housing has had no such restrictions or limits.

The largest impact was felt in public housing where an increasing number of younger disabled persons applied to and became tenants. This movement was accelerated by federal priority provisions that gave a preference to applicants who were displaced by public action, spent more than 50 percent of their income for housing, or lived in very dilapidated housing (including homelessness). In 1991 it was estimated that approximately 30,000 of the approximately 300,000 units of public housing for the elderly and disabled were occupied by younger persons.

The movement of younger persons with mental disabilities into housing that was occupied primarily by older persons led to a great deal of controversy. On the one hand, advocates for the disabled argued that their clients were in need of and had a right to such housing. On the other hand, organizations such as AARP and AAHA pointed out the merits of age-specific housing and made the case that the mixing of these populations did not work well and that, as a result, older persons in need of housing were more likely to leave such complexes, remain more secluded in their existing units, or not apply in the first place. During 1992 advocates for the elderly introduced legislation to allow the preservation of federally assisted housing specifically for the elderly while those supporting younger disabled persons fought to prevent their exclusion from such programs.

Housing disabled younger persons in projects that had previously been primarily for the elderly illustrates several problems. First, it occurred at the same time that programs were emerging to provide assistance to help older frail persons age in place in federally assisted housing. If that option is precluded by the entrance of younger persons, other programs will have to be created to support the growing number of older persons who are frail, have low incomes and lack family supports that would enable them to live independently. Second, the successful mixing of younger mentally disabled persons with elderly would likely necessitate additional staff and services. In the budget climate of the early 1990s such resources are likely to only come from other already funded programs, thereby raising additional conflicts. Third, it represents a challenge to the view that older persons hold a sacrosanct position in terms of their need for and access to federal housing assistance. Further evidence of this erosion is found in arguments to retarget funds from elderly housing programs to those serving other population groups whom some analysts consider more needy. For example, Khadduri and Nelson (1992), noting the relatively high percentage of elderly in federally assisted housing programs (e.g. 35 percent of eligible elderly renters compared with 28 percent of eligible younger families received rental assistance), argued that, on the basis of worst case needs, assistance should be targeted more heavily to families and less to elderly. In support of their argument the authors note the persistence of poverty among single-parent families and the relatively small size and high asset level of the age cohort that will turn 62 in the next five years. Analysts on the other side of the issue point out that poverty is more persistent among the elderly than other age groups, and the cohort of elderly renters who are over 75 years of age—a group with fewer assets than younger renters—will grow dramatically during the period between 1990 and 2000.

Conclusions

Over the last 40 years there have been dramatic shifts in the nature of housing problems of the elderly and the response of the federal government in meeting them. As housing conditions have improved, there has been an increasing emphasis on addressing problems of affordability, suitability, and service linkages. The solution to these problems calls for a reconceptualization of housing beyond bricks and mortar and will require the close coordination of different branches of government in order to expand supportive housing options, develop assisted living, and untie housing and services. The federal budget deficit, competition among groups for housing resources, and increasing concerns about the costs of entitlement programs will make this task all the more difficult, resulting in requirements for greater participant co-payments and targeting to the "very" needy (e.g. those who are very poor and frail). Overall solutions to these problems will necessitate major reforms in both long-term care and housing policy.

REFERENCES

Brice, G.C. & Gorey, K.M. 1991. Facilitating federally subsidized housing managerial role expansion: Beyond "bricks and mortar" to life space intervention with vulnerable older tenants. *Journal of Applied Gerontology, 4*, 486–498.

Clapham, D. & Monroe, M. 1990. Ambiguities and contradictions in the provision of sheltered housing for older people. *Journal of Social Policy, 19*, 27–45.

Congressional Budget Office. 1988. *Changes in the Living Arrangements of the Elderly: 1960–2030*. Washington: U.S. Government Printing Office.

Dolbeare, C. 1986. "How the Income Tax System Subsidizes Housing for the Affluent." In R. Bratt, C. Hartman, & A. Meyerson, eds., *Critical Perspectives on Housing*. Philadelphia, PA: Temple University Press.

Gottschalk, G. 1992. *Housing for frail older persons in Denmark*. Presented at a conference on Housing Policy for Frail Persons: International Perspectives and Prospects. Andrus Gerontology Center, Los Angeles, CA.

Hare, P. & Ostler, J. 1987. *Creating an Accessory Apartment*. New York: McGraw Hill.

Heumann, L. 1988. Assisting the frail elderly living in subsidized housing for the independent elderly. *The Gerontologist, 28*, 625–631.

Holshouser, W. & Waltman, F. 1988. *Aging in Place: The Demographics and Service Needs of the Elderly in Urban Public Housing*. Boston, MA: Citizens Housing and Planning Association.

Horne, J. & Baldwin, L. 1988. *Home-Sharing and Other Lifestyle Options.* Glenview, IL.: Scott, Foresman.

Kasper, J. 1988. *Aging Alone: Profiles.* Baltimore, MD: The Commonwealth Fund Commission on Elderly People Living Alone.

Khadduri, J. & Nelson, K. 1992. To whom should limited housing resources be directed? *Housing Policy Debate, 3*, 54–55.

Kingdon, J.W. 1984. *Agendas, Alternatives, and Public Policies.* Boston: Little Brown.

Lanspery, S. 1990. *Techniques and models for integrating and upgrading services into senior housing*. Paper presented at American Society on Aging Special Program on Housing, April, 1990.

Lawton, M.P. 1991. New housing programs: book review. *The Gerontologist, 31*, 418–420.

Mikelsons, M. & Turner, M. 1991. *Housing Conditions of the Elderly in the 1980s: A Data Book*. Washington, DC: The Urban Institute.

Nachison, J.S. 1985. Congregate housing for the low and moderate income elderly—A needed federal state partnership. *Journal of Housing for the Elderly, 3*, 65–80.

Pynoos, J. 1990. "Public Policy and Aging in Place: Identifying the Problems and Possible Solutions." In Tilson, D., ed., *Aging in Place: Supporting the Frail Elderly in Residential Environments* (pp. 167–208), Glenview, IL: Scott, Foresman.

———. 1992a. Strategies for home modification and repair. *Generations, XVI*, 21–26.

———. 1992b. Linking housing and services for the elderly. *Journal of Aging and Social Policy, 4*, 157–177.

Regnier, V. (in press). *New Concepts in Assisted Living: Design Innovation from the United States and Northern Europe*. New York: Van Nostrand.

Soldo, B. & Longino, C. 1988. "Social and Physical Environments for the Vulnerable Aged." In Institute of Medicine, *America's Aging: the Social and Built Environment in an Older Society* (pp. 103–133), Washington: National Academy Press.

Stone, M. 1990. Shelter poverty and the elderly. *Journal of Aging and Social Policy, 2*, 84.

Struyk, R.; Page, D.; Newman, S.; et al. 1989. *Providing Supportive Services to the Frail Elderly in Federally Assisted Housing*. Washington: Urban Institute Press.

Welfeld, I. 1988. *Where We Live: A Social History of American Housing*. New York: Simon and Schuster.

CHAPTER 6

Health Care Policies

Rosemary McCaslin

Introduction

As we enter the 1990s the need for change in the way health care is delivered in the United States has become a major public issue. Among the questions being asked about the existing health care system is whether it is capable of meeting the needs of a growing elderly population. Whatever plan of general reorganization is ultimately chosen will have to address health care policies for the aged.

The population of the United States (and, indeed, the world) is rapidly aging. The lay public has recently become aware of this important fact of which professionals have been aware for some time. Within this century medicine has made striking advances in its ability to treat infectious disease, formerly a major cause of death in the early years of life. As a result more people are living through childhood to become adults and, subsequently, old people. Medicine has not yet made comparable breakthroughs in the treatment of diseases which take their toll in adulthood (e.g., cancer and cardiovascular disease) and thus has not yet succeeded in dramatically affecting the length of the potential lifespan. But we have created a large and increasing population of elderly people who will survive into the sixth, seventh, and eighth decades of life. As stated in chapter 1, the oldest of the old are those whose numbers are increasing fastest. This is an important issue for health care because age-related disabilities most often begin after age 75.

The aging of the population carries important implications for future needs in health and related services. As people age, a variety of physical, emotional, and social factors take their toll on health and vitality. For example, up to 85 percent of persons aged 65 and over have been found to have some chronic health problem, 13 percent of which are severe. Chronic illness rates are estimated to have increased from 30 percent in 1930 to 80 percent in 1970 and have replaced acute diseases as the major cause of death and disability in the U.S. (Rice and Feldman, 1983). Chronic illness often results in decreased physical mobility and other limitations in functional abilities, and these disabilities also increase with age. About 20 percent of the elderly suffer some limitations in activities of daily living with about four percent being severely disabled. Again, the oldest old suffer the most disability. Among persons aged 85 and over, 60 percent are limited in their activities and at least 30 percent are unable to carry out functions necessary for independent living (Busse, 1980; National Clearinghouse on Aging, 1981).

Current health care policies in the United States carry an enormous and increasing financial cost that is heavily impacted by population aging. The rise in health care costs has been especially striking over the twenty years since Medicare and Medicaid (the two largest health programs used by older persons) were enacted. In 1967 total U.S. expenditures for health amounted to $51 billion, 6.4 percent of the Gross National Product (GNP). Public expenditures per capita for the same year totalled $248. By comparison, in 1986 total U.S. health expenditure amounted to $454 billion or 10.8 percent of the GNP and public expenditure per capita had risen to $1,580.

The cost of health care for the elderly has also risen over time. In 1977 these costs were $43 billion or 2.3 percent of the GNP and public expenditures per capita for the elderly were $1,785. By 1984 the comparable figures were a total expenditure of $120 billion or 3.3 percent of the GNP with a per capita public expenditure of $4,202. These costs included $54 billion for hospital care, $25 billion for nursing home care, $25 billion for physicians' services, and $16 billion for other health care.

Most of this dramatic increase in health care costs can be attributed to inflation but it has also been affected by population growth and changes in the services being provided and utilized over time. Some of these changes in service have been a response to the needs of an aging population; others are a function of changing medical technologies. Regardless of the reasons for increased health care costs, they are reaching a level that is no longer affordable (HCFA, 1986; Waldo and Lazenby, 1986; Levit, et al., 1985).

The existing health care system is hard pressed to meet the needs of persons now old, and we know that the number of elderly persons requiring health care will increase dramatically by the year 2020 when the "baby boom" generation reaches late life. Thus, to plan effectively for the future, it is important to understand what health care services are currently available to the elderly and what are the strengths and weaknesses of those services.

Major U.S. Health Care Programs

Acute Care: Medicare

It is notable, given the prevalence of chronic health problems among the elderly, that the most prominent U.S. health care program specifically for the aged is primarily focused on the treatment of acute episodes of treatable illness. Popularly known as Medicare, Title XVIII of the Social Security Act was enacted in 1965. Medicare Part A is a hospital insurance program, financed through employer/employee payroll taxes and provided automatically to persons over age 65. Medicare Part B, covering outpatient services, is an optional program that requires the recipient to pay a monthly premium (presently about $2,000). The particulars of coverage under these programs are modified periodically by Congress.

Medicare Part A provides coverage for hospitalizations of up to 90 days duration. A deductible equal to approximately one day of care (currently about $550) must be paid by the patient, and co-insurance payments are required after 60 days of hospital care. Following an acute hospital stay, Part A will also pay for up to 100 days of rehabilitative care in a skilled nursing facility. However, the actual length of covered periods of skilled care are much shorter, based on weekly reviews of the patient's capacity for continued improvement. Nursing care must also be provided in Medicare-certified facilities. These are few because the nursing home must agree to provide service for the relatively low amount of payment available through Medicare as well as to being subject to a large number of Medicare regulations.

Part A also reimburses elderly and disabled persons confined to their homes for physician-prescribed skilled health services including nursing, physical therapy, home health aides, and medical equipment. Since 1980 previous hospitalization is not required to receive home services under Medicare but services must be prescribed for treatment or rehabilitation of acute conditions. Additionally, Part A will pay for limited hospice services for patients whose death is imminent.

Medicare Part B pays for physicians' services, related medical services (e.g., lab work), and medical supplies ordered by a physician (e.g., canes, walkers, bathroom appliances). Services not covered include medications, dental care, and prescription eyeglasses. Medicare payments for specific medical services are usually much lower than the amount typically charged by service providers. Unless the health care provider accepts Medicare consignment, agreeing to provide services for Medicare payment alone, the patient is responsible for that portion of his/her medical bills that exceeds the Medicare payment.

In the 1980s Medicare shifted its reimbursement policy from one based on fees for specific services to a prospective payment policy in which providers receive a fixed payment based on the patient's diagnosis. These payments are based on an official list of several hundred Diagnosis Related Groups and are commonly referred to as the DRG system. There has been considerable concern and some documentation that the DRG system would result in shorter hospital stays, patients being discharged with more serious conditions, and a responding increase in home health services to meet the needs of elderly discharged to home while still bedridden (Estes and Wood, 1986; Fischer and Eustis, 1988). It has also been observed that hospitals have increasingly created skilled nursing units within their own facilities so they can provide the longer inpatient stays needed by many elderly patients, drawing Medicare reimbursement both from a period of acute treatment and one geared to rehabilitation.

Medicare is clearly not intended to cover long term maintenance services or assistance with chronic conditions. Even so, health care providers are often able to adapt diagnoses and orders for treatment so that a small part of the need for long term care can be provided under Medicare as rehabilitative services. In recent years Medicare expenditures for home health care have grown at an annual rate above 20 percent (Benjamin, 1986). In 1985 they accounted for 4.7 percent ($2.257 billion) of the Part A budget and 0.2 percent ($33 million) of the Part B budget (HCFA, 1986). Yet the need for such services is far greater; it has been estimated that over 19 percent of non-institutionalized Medicare enrollers suffer from chronic limitations in activities of daily living (Gornick et al., 1985).

Institutional Long-Term Care

Medicaid

Frail and ill elderly have been cared for in a variety of institutional settings over the years. The particular institution to which the aged have been assigned at any given point in time has been determined to a large extent by the public funding policies of that era. Initially the elderly were not differentiated from other persons unable to care for themselves. When poorhouses were instituted in the 17th century, elderly too frail to work were among their residents. This form of care evolved into county-based public facilities, augmented by private boarding houses. Later, when state mental institutions were built in the early 19th century, funding for dependent populations was shifted to state budgets and there was a massive transfer of elderly patients from county nursing homes to state hospitals (Grob, 1986).

The first systematic national attention to long term care needs of the elderly came with the Kerr-Mills act of 1960. This voluntary program enabled states to designate funds for the building of public hospitals and, especially, nursing homes. The result was considerable expansion of the nursing home industry.

The most important public program addressing institutional long term care for the elderly today is Title XIX of the Social Security Act, Medicaid, enacted in 1965 along with Medicare. Medicaid is intended to make basic health services available to persons of limited financial means, including those who may be elderly. It is funded jointly by the Federal and State governments; a minimum set of services must be provided and each state may choose to place limits on or to extend its program's coverage. The basic range of services that must be provided includes inpatient hospitalization, outpatient care, laboratory and X-ray services, skilled nursing home care and home health care for adults, physicians' services, family planning, rural health services, and screening, diagnosis, and treatment for children and adolescents. Services that a state may choose to provide include medications, eyeglasses, unskilled nursing home care, inpatient psychiatric care for the elderly and children, physical therapy, and dental services. As with Medicare, payments under Medicaid tend to be low and not all health care providers are willing to treat patients covered by this system.

In spite of the broad mandate of Medicaid, the financing of nursing home care has become a very large part of this program. In 1984, 31.4 percent of the Medicaid budget was allocated to skilled and intermediate care facilities serving the elderly. Looked at another way, $32 billion was spent on nursing home care in 1984 and Medicaid covered 43 percent of this cost (HCFA, 1985).

Medicaid's prominence in the financing of institutional care for the elderly stems largely from the lack of alternatives. Skilled nursing home care is sufficiently expensive to be beyond the means of most elderly and their families. (In recent years these costs have been in the range of $20,000 to $25,000 per year in most locales.) Standard health insurance policies do not cover such care and it is only very recently that insurance companies have begun to experiment with policies written specifically for long term care coverage.

Medicaid is intended for the medically indigent, and elderly persons who require nursing home care find themselves in this category rather quickly. In the course of making private payment to nursing homes, elderly "spend down" their assets until they are sufficiently impoverished to be eligible for Medicaid. Numerous studies have indicated that about two-thirds of elderly persons become Medicaid eligible in 13 weeks, and 80 to 90 percent within two years. Making a bad situation worse, in most states the assets of the spouse of a nursing home patient are included in what must be spent, leaving the survivors impoverished and eligible for Medicaid should they need such care. At the same time there are elderly who may spend down all of their (and their spouse's) assets, yet remain ineligible for Medicaid coverage because their income exceeds the program's limits in their particular state (Quadagno, Meyer, & Turner, 1991). Clearly, Medicaid does not cover nursing home care for all elderly nor is it the ideal source of coverage for many.

Medicaid also provides limited home health services to the poor elderly. There is considerable variation among states, but in the majority Medicaid home health services are estimated to reach less than one percent of eligible individuals needing such care. In 1982 402,000 persons received home health care through Medicaid; the cost of these services was $429 million. By comparison, Medicaid covered care in a nursing home for 1.3 million persons in that same year at a cost of $13.3 billion. Growth rates for Medicaid home health services have varied over recent years from decreases of 6.2 percent to increases as high as 9.2 percent per annum. During the same period the cost of these programs has tended to double each year (Benjamin, 1986).

Veterans Administration

The United States Veterans Administration (VA) system operates the largest independent health care system in the world, including 172 hospitals, 117 nursing home care units, and 16 domiciliaries (sheltered living environments). Contracts with 3,400 community nursing homes further expand the VA system's long term care capacity. At present nearly half of the 30 million veterans in this country are over the age of 55. Further, the aging of the veteran population is expected to peak earlier than that of the general population. By the year 2000, 9 million persons, about two-thirds of males over the age of 65, will be veterans. The number of veterans older than 75 years will grow by 343 percent from 1980 to 2000 (Rathbone-McCuan, Harbert, & Fulton, 1991; Saltz, Rathbone-McCuan, & Moses, 1989; Veterans Administration, 1984).

This rapid increase in age and concomitant need for health care among veterans has begun to stress the considerable resources of the VA system. Recently it became necessary to institute a means test for treatment not specific to service-connected disorders. In 1986 the VA utilized 40,000 long-term care beds, yet served only 20 percent of veterans in need of nursing home care. By the year 2010 it is expected that between 110,000 and 140,000 beds will be needed (U.S. Senate, 1987). It is not yet entirely clear what mix of VA and non-VA resources will be able to meet these increasing needs.

The VA system also provides a range of home care and episodic services. These include 73 home care programs, 37 adult day health care services (22 through community contracts), 88 respite care programs, and 2 hospices. Additionally, a community residential care program provides payment to and supervision of non-family caregivers for 12 million elderly and disabled veterans living in over 3,000 private homes (Saltz, Rathbone-McCuan, & Moses, 1989).

One important element of the VA system's future planning is its 10 Geriatric Research, Education, and Clinical Centers and its 11 Interdisciplinary Team Training in Geriatrics programs. These are major efforts to train the health care providers who will be needed to care for elderly veterans and to foster research that can help shape future geriatric care programs. Professionals trained by these programs will not only improve VA services but provide leadership for the larger task of reorganizing the country's entire health care system.

Home Health Care

Home health care services have existed in the United States for the past century, in various forms and under a variety of auspices. As early as 1796 the Boston Dispensary provided such services to poor patients. Beginning in the 1880s programs began to proliferate under voluntary charitable auspices including Visiting Nurses Associations (VNA), charity organization societies, and settlement houses. In 1898 Los Angeles was the first county health department to sponsor home health services for the poor, and in 1909 Metropolitan Life became the first insurance company to offer these services to policyholders. Hospitals began to enter the home health care field in large numbers in the late 1940s as a means of reducing the cost of care. Most of these early programs were focused on maternal and child health and on infectious diseases; health education was emphasized in conjunction with treatment (Leiby, 1978; Mundinger, 1983; Rosen, 1958).

Many of these seminal programs have survived to the present, with varying foci over time, as VNAs, Family Service of America (FSA) agencies, and public health departments. Over time they have developed and refined service delivery models which usually include professional supervision and backup of paraprofessional service providers as a means to extend service and reduce cost.

The potential importance of these services in maintaining the health of both individuals and society has probably never been greater than it is today. The existing health care system, focused primarily on cure of acute illness, is both inappropriate and unnecessarily expensive for the long term care needs of the elderly. Yet existing home health care and related community-based services are too fragmented and underdeveloped to constitute an effective and efficient alternative system.

The current array of home health care services for the elderly has been shaped largely by public benefits programs. Most important among these in addition to Medicare, Medicaid, and the Veterans Administration are the Social Services Block Grant and the Older Americans Act. Local providers within state and federal programs frequently include VNA and FSA agencies as well as private home health care businesses, the descendants of private duty nursing. VNAs, for example, constituted 12 percent of home health agencies in the mid-80s (Salvatore, 1985).

Social Services Block Grant and the Older Americans Act

Many gap-filling, supportive services are made available to persons in need of home health care through the Social Services Block Grant, formerly Title XX of the Social Security Act. It provides grants-in-aid to states which can be used for various services in the home to low-income and elderly individuals. The incorporation of Title XX into the block grants reduced funds available for home care by spreading fewer dollars among more programs. Nevertheless, in 1985 all states included homemaker, chore, and home management services under this program; adult day care was included by about half the states. Home-delivered services account for approximately 11 percent of recipients (307,000 persons) and about 14 percent of expenditures ($555 million) (O'Shaughnessy, et al., 1985).

The Administration on Aging (AoA) administers funds from Title III of the Older americans Act through an extensive network of State Units on Aging (SUAs) and Area Agencies on Aging (AAAs). These services for the elderly usually include homemakers, home delivered meals, case management, assessment, adult day care, and respite care. In 1985 40 percent of Title III funds ($265 million) was allocated to supportive in-home services and an additional 10 percent ($68 million) to home-delivered meals programs (O'Shaughnessy, et al., 1985).

Private Agencies

In addition to publicly funded services, there has been significant growth in recent years in home health agencies in the private sector. The number of proprietary home health agencies increased by 1,360 percent from 1972 to 1982 while similar hospital-based services grew by 64 percent (Bergthold and Estes, 1986). These entrepreneurial and institutional initiatives have been viewed, in part, as responses to liberalization of Medicare regulations (Roberts and Heinrich, 1985) as well as to a growing awareness of the elderly population as a potential market for private health care services. It is possible that the emergence of long term care insurance will spur further growth in this sector. Private market growth, however, has been partially offset by closures of some voluntary agencies and reduction of services by others that could not financially tolerate changes in Medicare reimbursement policies (Stewart, 1979).

Home health care services from all sources reach about one percent of the U.S. population (Berk and Bernstein, 1985). Yet they remain unavailable for many persons in need. While their cost in both public and private monies is considerable and growing, it remains much lower than that of comparable care provided in an institutional setting. Better utilization of home health care, therefore, is likely to be a cost-effective strategy for addressing unmet needs among persons with chronic disabilities.

Family Caregiving

Public and private services that are available to assist disabled elderly are heavily supplemented by informal caregiving by family members. In fact 80–85 percent of all home care for these patients is provided by family (Manton and Liu, 1984). Family assistance involves 2.2 million spouses, adult children, and other relatives caring for 1.3 million older persons (Stone and Cafferata, 1985). Research conducted on the effects of caregiving on the caregiver has shown that families often pay a high price in reduced employment, stress, and ill health (e.g., Brody, 1985; Poulshock and Deimling, 1984; Cantor, 1983). In spite of their burden, families have not been found to reduce caregiving activities when formal home health services are provided (e.g., Hooyman, Gonyea, and Montgomery, 1985).

It is likely that families will always provide much of the care needed by their aged members and that elderly persons will always prefer that some types of care come from family members rather than from formal agencies. These realities should be taken into account in any reorganization of the health care system. A population with a relatively large proportion of older persons will also, necessarily, contain a large number of middle-aged caregivers. The latter will need services that mitigate the stress of caregiving. These might include respite care, support groups, and preventive health programs such as exercise and stress reduction education. The needs of family caregivers are an important reminder that effective health care policies for the elderly must be part of a larger health care system for persons of all ages.

Future Policy Directions

International Perspectives: National Health Insurance

The United States is virtually the only post-industrial nation that does not have a national health insurance system. Under such programs, health care is usually guaranteed to all persons as a right of citizenship. The costs of health care are covered through taxes rather than individual payment for service, and decisions about the availability of particular services and their reimbursement rates are made by a central authority.

National health insurance has been a subject of sometimes heated debate in the United States for many years. At various points in time, bills have been introduced in Congress and the Senate to enact both limited and wide-reaching versions of nationalized health care. In recent years similar bills have been put forward in some state legislatures. Until very recently, however, all such proposals have been defeated, largely due to lobbying efforts by the American Medical Association (AMA), which has considered national health insurance to be anathema.

However, public opinion now seems to be turning in favor of national health insurance and even the AMA has come to support the need for such change. The astronomical rise in health care costs not only has strained the health care system itself but also has become burdensome to the business community. Many employers have reduced their workers' health insurance coverage or created more part-time positions for which they do not have to provide these benefits. As a result an increasing number of Americans have no health insurance coverage. These uninsured workers and their families further stress public health care programs; they often cannot afford routine medical services and seek care only when their health problems become serious.

Because of the widely felt impact of these problems, there is now considerable pressure for reform of American health care. However, no consensus has yet emerged as to the direction such reform should take. Current proposals range from those calling for complete federalization of health care to those for management systems to better coordinate existing private insurance companies. Throughout these debates, there has been considerable examination of the national health programs of other countries to determine what has been proven effective.

The system most often proposed as a possible model for the United States is the Canadian health care system. In that model, major decisions about the type and quantity of services to be provided and their costs are made centrally. Actual service delivery is widely dispersed and makes use of both public facilities and private practitioners. The Canadian approach is viewed as well-managed and cost-conscious yet as retaining a good deal of autonomy for practitioners and choice for consumers.

The ultimate shape of a reorganized United States health care system will also be influenced by several recent experiments in services for the elderly. Among the most important of these are Health Maintenance Organizations, long term care insurance, rationing plans, and catastrophic health care proposals.

Health Maintenance Organizations

Health Maintenance Organizations (HMOs) have existed in this country for half a century but have gained increased acceptance over the past twenty years. In an HMO a set, monthly pre-payment is used to cover the costs of whatever services are actually needed by a member. Financial success, therefore, depends on reducing the amount and expense of care that is required. In other words it is in the HMO's best interest to keep its members as healthy as possible. As a result preventive care is encouraged and more expensive medical interventions are used only when necessary. HMOs have been shown repeatedly, for example, to have lower rates of elective and controversial surgeries (e.g., hysterectomies) than do other types of health care systems.

In recent years new HMOs have been developed along with variations such as Planned Provider Organizations (PPDs). The latter consist of contractual relations among a group of private practitioners to pool their finances on an HMO model. HMOs have also begun to enroll more elderly members and a national demonstration project has been evaluating the feasibility of an expanded model for the elderly, the Social Health Maintenance Organization (SHMO).

SHMOs attempt to expand prepaid health care coverage to include community and nursing home care in coordination with a complete acute care medical system. The demonstration projects are attempting to make this broader model affordable by enrolling a wide cross-section of elderly in terms of their health and service needs. They have utilized both Medicare and Medicaid as sources of premiums along with private payment. In the first two-and-a-half years of this experiment, over 14,000 Medicare beneficiaries were enrolled at four sites. The results of these demonstration projects are still being evaluated (Leutz et al., 1988).

Long Term Care Insurance

Private health insurance policies that augment Medicare coverage have become increasing common. In 1977, for example, two-thirds of Medicare enrollers also had a "medigap" policy (Cafferata, 1985). On the other hand, a study by the American Association of Retired Persons found that more than 3 million elderly cannot afford such private insurance, yet do not qualify for Medicaid (Older Americans Report, 1990). The coverage of these types of insurance policies usually parallels Medicare guidelines and thus addresses skilled nursing care only for short-term, rehabilitative purposes.

To date private insurance has been little involved in the financing of long term care for the elderly. In 1984, for example, private insurance reimbursed only 0.8 percent of a total cost of $32 billion for nursing home care (HCFA, 1985). During the 1980s the private insurance industry began to experiment with long term care policies. By the middle of the decade, some 70 companies had sold such policies to at least 300,000 persons (Schaeffer, Blum, and Richmond, 1986). However, long term care insurance remains expensive, relatively narrow in coverage, and not well-understood by the public (Wiener, Ehrenworth, and Spence, 1987). Given the potential expense of long term care, a large insurance pool would be required to increase the viability of such policies. It has been suggested that tax incentives be used to encourage employers and other groups to include long term care insurance among their benefits. This approach should result in a broader age range of insured and thus a more adequate risk pool and lower cost per policy (National Chamber Foundation, 1986).

Rationing and Catastrophic Health Policy

Various proposals have been put forward to address issues at the extremes of the health care continuum. At one point federal legislation was passed that would have protected elderly individuals against the enormous expenses of "catastrophic" illnesses, i.e. those requiring treatment whose cost and duration far exceeds the usual coverage of either private insurance or public programs. This act was subsequently repealed, however, because it had been financed solely from assessments on Medicare recipients. Use of such a small risk pool created a higher cost than most older Americans were willing to assume. Similar coverage spread across the entire population would be less costly and is likely to be an element of broader national insurance programs.

A few states have tried an opposite approach to containing extreme medical costs, i.e. rationing their provision. Most attempts to create rationing systems have utilized blue ribbon panels to rank the social importance of services according to a number of variables including cost, age of recipient, and resulting improvement in functioning or longevity. Not surprisingly, these programs have been highly controversial and it is not yet clear whether they are likely to become widespread or whether this approach will be accepted as part of national health care decision-making.

Issues in Health Care for the Elderly

The acute care models on which most health services and benefit programs are based tend to encourage institution-based care. Services needed to prevent further disability, to maintain optimal functioning, and to rehabilitate or improve functioning over a long period of time are seldom covered by public programs and are beyond the resources of low and middle income families. That many such services can be provided by paraprofessionals also disqualifies them from coverage in some programs. More intensive and costly services are encouraged, especially those which must occur in a hospital setting even though they may not be most appropriate for the medical situation. At the same time, types of care that might ultimately reduce total care needs are discouraged.

Limitations and restrictions in existing home health services have left critical gaps in coverage, especially for low to middle income elderly and their families who cannot afford to purchase care in the private market, yet are not eligible for public programs. Were affordable home health services available to these frail elderly, nursing home placement (ultimately at public expense) could often be delayed if not avoided. Restrictions on the amount of care allowed under programs such as Medicare have a similar result in channelling patients who could be cared for at home into expensive long term institutional care facilities.

Too little is known about the burden placed on family members by gaps in appropriate and accessible home care. When private purchase of costly services is encouraged, the financial effects must be felt by many family members beyond the identified elderly patient. If needed services are not available and family members provide care, loss of wages and the stress of caregiving can affect the entire family. And if disabled elderly are not helped to achieve and maintain their maximum level of functioning and family members must be diverted to caregiving roles, the productive potential of both patient and caregiver are lost to the community.

Services that are available are surprisingly under-utilized, especially by the elderly. Fears that increased service accessibility will encourage excessive use have been shown to be unfounded. In the case of home health care, a study of utilization within Canada's universally available program reports that only about 10 percent of the elderly use these services each year (Moen, 1978). Many elderly appear to feel that their situation must be described as extremely desperate to justify requesting assistance (McCaslin and Calvert, 1975). Resulting delays in retaining appropriate help are likely to exacerbate the health problem and may render it less amenable to home-delivered interventions.

Older people demonstrate a pronounced reluctance to make use of any type of formal service, preferring family assistance in most situations (e.g., McCaslin, 1988). Attitudes about help-taking and cultural stigmas associated with "welfare" programs may be partially to blame. The resulting lack of accurate public knowledge about available services is seriously compounded by the real difficulty of utilizing a fragmented system of care.

Health and mental health services that are available are offered under such a wide variety of auspices and eligibility standards that the average consumer cannot be expected to know how to access them. Medical professionals are not much better informed about the range of services their patients may need. Available services are often rendered inaccessible by factors such as geographic distance, lack of transportation assistance, waiting lists, and language barriers. Once available services are accessed, they often present the neophyte clients with unfamiliar rules and expectations which may or may not be congruent with their own culture and experience.

Effective models must be developed that can coordinate the multiple public programs that now provide and enable geriatric services both among themselves and in conjunction with private services and markets. And these fragmented services must also be better coordinated with an even wider range of health-related and supportive services that are necessary to maintain the health and well-being of disabled and medically-dependent individuals.

Within varying state and local systems there is a further need to develop more effective models for coordinating the activities and inputs of the multiple professionals whose skills are necessary in long term care: physician assistants; psychologists; physical, speech, respiratory, and occupational therapists; nutritionists; and others. In geriatrics multidisciplinary team practice is coming to be seen as essential for effective treatment and care. Such practice is demanding, complex, and has received very little empirical investigation (i.e. McCaslin, O'Day and Endter, 1987). Models of team practice that do exist are geared to acute care requirements; these models need to be adapted to the realities of home-delivered care and extended to allow for preventive interventions and self-help strategies. Geriatric team practice also needs to involve family members more effectively and consistently in the decision-making process.

Additionally, team practitioners need to develop more effective methods of reaching persons who would benefit from their services at a time when the individual and family will be most amenable to accepting assistance. Existing frameworks for anticipating the institutions with which people are likely to have contact at points of situational change and decision-making (Meyer, 1976) could be incorporated into multidisciplinary approaches. Team practice as well as case management practice can also improve methods of monitoring changes in patient status and care needs over time. Here, too, changes in the resources, availability, and needs of family caregivers must be taken into account. For all of these pragmatic and humane reasons, increased attention to effective and efficient models of home health care organization and delivery is imperative.

Concluding Comments

It is quite likely that there will be some major reorganization of the United States health care system within the next decade. Whatever form that reorganization takes must accommodate the needs of a growing elderly population. Conversely, the health care needs of older persons would be better served by a more rationally designed general health care system.

Health care policies must be developed that simultaneously consider quality of care, cost of care, and ethical means of distributing services. The current health care system is neither effective nor efficient in meeting the service needs of elderly persons and it fails entirely to address questions of which services have priority for which populations.

The tasks that lie ahead are complex and challenging and will likely require very different ways of thinking than those that have shaped current health care policies. Difficult as this work will be, it is also a most exciting time for professionals concerned about health care for the elderly. If the right decisions are made, not only can major improvements be made in health care policy but also in the health and well-being of all persons.

REFERENCES

Benjamin, A.E. 1986. State variations in home health expenditures and utilization under Medicare and Medicaid. *Home Health Care Services Quarterly, 7(1)*, 5–28.

Bergthold, L.A. & Estes, C. L. 1986. *The impact of Medicare policy on home health care*. Paper presented at the Annual Scientific Meetings of the Gerontological Society of America, Chicago, Illinois.

Berk, M.L & Bernstein, A. 1985. Use of home health services: Some findings from the National Medical Care Expenditure Survey. *Home Health Care Services Quarterly, 6*, 13–23.

Brody, E.M. 1985. Parent care as a normative family stress. *The Gerontologist, 25*, 19–29.

Busse, E.W. 1980. "Old Age." In S.I. Greenspan & G.H. Pollack, eds., *The Course of Life: Psychoanalytic Contributions toward Understanding Personality Development*, Vol. III: Adulthood and the aging process. Bethesda, MD: National Institutes of Mental Health.

Cafferata, G.L. 1985. Private health insurance of the Medicare population and the Baucus legislation." *Medical Care, 23*, 1086–1096.

Cantor, M.H. 1983. Strain among caregivers: A study of experience in the United States. *The Gerontologist, 23*, 597–604.

Estes, C. & Wood, J. 1986. The non-profit sector and community based care for the elderly in the U.S.: A disappearing resource. *Social Science and Medicine*, *23*, 1261–1266.

Fischer, L.R. & Eustis, N.N. 1988. DRGs and family care for the elderly: A case study. *The Gerontologist*, *28*, 383–389.

Gornick, M. et al. 1985. Twenty years of Medicare and Medicaid: Covered populations use of benefits, and program expenditures. *Health Care Financing Review/1985 Annual Supplement* (HCFA Pub. No. 03217). Washington, DC: Health Care Financing Administration.

Grob, G.N. 1986. "Explaining Old Age History: The Need for Empiricism." In D. Van Tassel & P.N. Stearns, eds., *Old Age in a Bureaucratic Society*, New York: Greenwood.

Health Care Financing Administration (HCFA). 1985. *Health Care Financing Review: 20 Years of Medicare and Medicaid*. Washington, DC: U.S. Government Printing Office.

Health Care Financing Administration (HCFA). 1986. *HCFA Statistics* (HCFA Pub. No. 03229). Washington, DC: U.S. Government Printing Office.

Hooyman, N.; Gonyea, J.; & Montgomery, R. 1985. The impact of in-home services termination on family caregivers. *The Gerontologist*, *25*, 141–145.

Leiby, J. 1978. *A History of Social Welfare and Social Work in the United States*. New York: Columbia University Press.

Leutz, W.; Abrahams, R.; Greenlick, M.; Kane, R.; & Prottas, J. 1988. Targeting expanded care to the aged: Early SHMO experience. *The Gerontologist*, *28*, 4–17.

Levit, K.R. et al. 1985. National health expenditures, 1984. *Health Care Financing Review*, *7*, 1–35.

Manton, K.G. & Liu, L. 1984. *The future growth of the long-term care population: Projections based on the 1977 National Nursing Home Survey and the 1982 Long-Term Care Survey*. Paper presented at the 3rd National Leadership Conference on Long-Term Care Financing. Washington, DC.

McCaslin, R. 1988. Reframing research on service use among the elderly: An analysis of recent findings. *The Gerontologist*, *28*, 592–599.

McCaslin, R. & Calvert, W.R. 1975. Social indicators in black and white: Some ethnic considerations in delivery of services to the elderly. *Journal of Gerontology*, *30*, 60–66.

McCaslin, R.; O'Day, M.; & Endter, S. eds. 1987. *Social Work Education for Multidisciplinary Practice*. Berkeley, CA: University of California School of Social Welfare.

Meyer, C.H. 1976. *Social Work Practice: The Changing Landscape* (2nd ed.). New York: Free Press.

Moen, E. 1978. The reluctance of the elderly to accept help. *Social Relations, 25*, 293–303.

Mundinger, M.O. 1983. *Home Care Controversy: Too Little, Too Late, Too Costly*. Rockville, MD: Aspen Systems.

National Chamber Foundation. 1986. "Private sector task force on catastrophic and long-term health care alternatives." In *Private sector policy options for addressing catastrophic and long-term health needs.* Washington: Author.

National Clearinghouse on Aging. 1981. *Statistical Notes,* No. 6. Washington: Author.

Older Americans Report. 1990 (January, 26). Washington, DC: American Association of Retired Persons.

O'Shaughnessy, C.; Price, R.; & Griffith, J. 1985. *Financing and delivery of long-term care services for the elderly.* Washington, DC: Congressional Research Service, The Library of Congress.

Poulshock, S.W. & Deimling, G.T. 1984. Families caring for elders in residence: Issues in the measurement of burden. *Journal of Gerontology, 39*, 230–239.

Quadagno, J.; Meyer, M.H.; & Turner, J.B. 1991. Falling into the Medicaid gap: The hidden long-term care dilemma. *The Gerontologist, 31*, 521–526.

Rathbone-McCuan, E.; Harbert, T.L.; & Fulton, J.R. 1991. Evaluation as an imperative for social services preservation: A challenge to the department of veterans affairs. *Journal of Social Work Education, 27*, 114–124.

Rice, D.P. & Feldman, J.J. 1983. Living longer in the United States: Demographic changes and health needs of the elderly. *Milbank Memorial Fund Quarterly/Health and Society, 61*, 362–395.

Roberts, D.E. & Heinrich, J. 1985. Public health nursing comes of age. *American Journal of Public Health, 75*, 1162–1172.

Rosen, G. 1958. *A History of Public Health.* New York: MD Publications.

Saltz, C.C.; Rathbone-McCuan, E.; & Moses, D. 1989. *Gerontological social work training opportunities in the Veterans Administration System.*

Paper presented at the Annual Program Meeting of the Council on Social Work Education, San Francisco, California.

Salvatore, T. 1985. Organizational adaptation in the VNA: Paradigm change in the voluntary sector. *Home Health Care Services Quarterly*, 6, 19–31.

Schaeffer, C.; Blum, A.: & Richmond, S. 1986. "Insurance for Long-term Care." *Changing Times*, September, 113–117.

Stewart, J.E. 1979. *Home Health Care*. St. Louis, MO: C.V. Mosby.

Stone, R. & Cafferata, G.L. 1985. *Caregivers of the frail elderly: A national profile*. Unpublished paper prepared for the National Center for Health Services Research and Health Care Technology Assessment.

United States Senate Special Committee on Aging. 1987. *Developments in Aging: The Long-Term Care Challenge*. Vol. 3. Washington, DC: U.S. Government Printing Office.

Veterans Administration (VA). 1984. *Survey of social work service research in the Veterans Administration*. Unpublished manuscript, Veterans Administration Research and Program Evaluation Committee. Washington, DC: Author.

Waldo, D.R. & Lazenby, H.C. 1986. Demographic characteristics and health care use and expenditures by the aged in the United States: 1977–1984. *Health Care Financing Review*, 6, 1–29.

Wiener, J.M.; Ehrenworth, D.A.; & Spence, D.A. 1987. Private long-term care insurance: Cost, coverage, and restrictions. *The Gerontologist*, 27 (4), 487–493.

PART III

Service Programs for the Elderly

CHAPTER 7

Social Service Programs for Older Adults and Their Families

Service Use and Barriers

David E. Biegel
Kathleen J. Farkas
Nancy Wadsworth

A number of new social service programs for the elderly have developed over the past three decades, stimulated to a large degree by the passage of the Older Americans Act in 1965 which put in place a variety of federally funded services designed to cover a broad spectrum of needs of the elderly. Existing social services are varied and include senior centers, nutrition programs, transportation programs, telephone reassurance and friendly visiting, adult day care, adult protective services, self-help groups, and services for caregivers.

Service use is extensive; a recent study by the National Center for Health Statistics reported that 5.7 million persons aged 65 years and older, or 21 percent of the elderly, used one or more of a selected group of community-based services within the past 12 months (NCHS, 1986). However, considerable evidence also indicates that there are a variety of barriers that prevent utilization of social service programs by the elderly. Studies of service-utilization patterns have found that many older people eligible for service programs do not use them (U.S. General Accounting Office, 1977; Krout, 1984). Service delivery barriers are especially significant for minority elderly (Kulys, 1990;

Holmes, 1982; Guttman and Cuellar, 1982) and for those elderly, such as the blind and visually disabled or elderly with mental health problems, whose service needs span both the aging network as well as other, more specialized service delivery systems (Biegel, Shore, and Silverman, 1989).

Inquiries into service utilization require an understanding of three interlocking factors: (1) the characteristics of the service delivery system which provides funding and administrative structure; (2) the characteristics of the service providers and the setting in which the service is provided; and (3) the characteristics of the persons eligible for the services. These factors can either be facilitators which encourage service use or barriers which may discourage and/or prevent service use.

There have been a number of studies which have tried to explain or predict service utilization by the elderly and examined the role of predisposing, enabling, and need factors in predicting the use of medical services. The use of this model has been extended to examine social service use and was adapted by Noelker and Bass (1989) to include the influence of informal support systems on service use. Though helpful in explaining the role and significance of particular variables in predicting service use, service use prediction models have generally not been able to explain significant amounts of the variance in service use.

Another perspective on service use, the barrier perspective, shifts the question from "What factors explain service use?" to "Why do people not use services?" Barriers can be conceptualized in many different ways. One approach is to separate barriers into three conceptual levels: system level barriers, agency level barriers, and individual level barriers (Biegel and Farkas, 1989). Systems level barriers include political, economic, and social forces which shape the development of policy. Examples of these barriers include: accessibility of services—service availability, cost, location and availability of transportation; hours of service; auspices of service; provision of information about services to potential referral agents and users of services; and fragmentation of services as reflected by lack of linkages with other service systems and providers, both formal and informal (Austin, 1991; Wallace, 1990; Hughes and Guihan, 1990; Petchers and Milligan, 1988; Noelker and Bass, 1989).

Agency level barriers are those that directly affect service delivery, such as skills, attitudes and behavior of staff, and cultural sensitivity (Biegel, Petchers, Snyder, and Beisgen, 1989; Biegel, Shore, and Silverman, 1989). Individual level barriers refer to personal and family attitudes and behaviors toward the services offered, such as lack of knowledge of services in general, not knowing where to go for help with specific problems/issues, negative attitudes toward and unwillingness to accept help, and role of family and other informal network members in discouraging and/or preventing service use. Other barriers relate to the health status characteristics of the elderly and may include health problems, such as chronic illness, or physical mobility problems and activity restrictions. (Biegel and Farkas, 1989; Petchers and Milligan, 1988).

This paper describes selected community-based social services available to older adults in terms of: (1) purpose or goals of the service; (2) the target population and/or the eligibility requirements; and (3) the location of the service. Where available, research findings concerning the extent of participation in particular services and data concerning the effectiveness of particular services are also discussed. In addition individual services are discussed in terms of the barriers to utilization which may exist at one of three levels: the system level, the agency or staff level, and/or at the level of the individual or family as discussed above.

Senior Centers

Overview of Senior Centers

A Senior Center is defined as "a community focal point on aging where older persons as individuals or groups come together for services and activities which enhance their dignity, support their independence, and encourage their involvement in and with the community" (National Council on the Aging, 1978, as cited in Gelfand and Gelfand, 1982, p. 181). Since their inception Senior Centers have provided a place for older people to gather and engage in a variety of activities and services. Senior Centers vary widely by size, structure, and range of services.

Funding for Senior Centers is rarely from a single source. Most often funding is sought for various service components through different funding streams, usually through some combination of federal, state, and local and sometimes non-governmental sources of revenue. Most receive a substantial percentage of their funding from local sources (Gelfand, 1988). Federal sources for funding of Senior Centers include Title lll of the Older Americans Act, which funds multipurpose Senior Center construction, operation, and nutrition services, along with some specialized programs. Block Grants from the Department of Housing and Community Development can be used for developing, improving, and coordinating Senior Center activities and facilities. General Revenue Sharing Funds can be allocated, and ACTION Volunteer programs, as well as federally-funded employment programs, may offer additional personnel resources. Higher Education Act funds can assist in training Center staff. State and local funds may be allocated through Social Services Block Grants; State Units on Aging administer Older Americans Act funding and add the required 10 percent match. In addition, in some states legislatures appropriate funds for Senior Centers. Other states and cities may finance Centers through bond issues or levies. Additional sources of funding may be garnered from civic or religious organizations, foundations, United Way, contributions from the Center's elderly participants, creative utilization of in-kind contributions of space and volunteers, and by the use of fundraisers.

Participation in Senior Centers

Senior Centers have become one of the most visible and popular services to older people. Krout (1988) estimated that there are approximately 10,000 to 12,000 Senior Centers in this country serving between 5 and 8 million people aged 60 and over. The National Center for Health Statistics (1986) reports that in 1984 15 percent of the population aged 65 and over in the U.S., or 4 million persons, had attended a Senior Center in the previous year. Krout, Cutler and Coward (1990) state that these percentages reflect 4 to 12 times greater usage than reported for any other community-based service for older people.

Eligibility criteria for publicly funded Senior Centers are age-based. One must be at least 60 years old to participate in a Center, but specific programs within the Center may use other criteria in addition to chronological age. The nutrition programs include spouses of eligible participants regardless of the spouse's age. Some sites, due to funding limitations, have set priorities for service eligibility on the basis of need in addition to, or in lieu of, age. There exists some support for an age-integrated service delivery strategy in that the members of Senior Centers expressed a higher preference for interaction with people of all ages than did non-members in a general population survey (Daum, 1982).

A recent study examined the extent to which frail elderly have been integrated into multi-service Senior Centers. This survey of 300 centers in New York state found that Center directors believed that a membership of more than 10 percent impaired elders would tax their staff's current training levels and the programming abilities (Cox and Monk, 1990). Programs for the frail require larger and more specialized staff than is available at most senior Centers (Krout et al., 1990). There has also been some concern expressed that inclusion of too high a percentage of frail elders may change the nature and perception of senior centers and discourage participation by the well elderly.

Participation rates at Senior Centers range from 8 percent to 21 percent of the local elderly population (Krout, 1988). Issues concerning participation in Senior Center services and activities can be studied from a variety of perspectives. A number of studies compare characteristics of elderly who participate in Senior Center activities with non-participants. Ralston (1984), looking at a sample of black elderly who were attenders or non-attenders, found the groups were similar to the extent that non-attenders were considered potential Center participants.

Few studies have examined the set of characteristics which might predict Center participation (Krout et al., 1990). Ferraro and Cobb's results from a ten-month study of 48 white Center participants found that frequent attendance was more likely among those elderly people who used the Center primarily as a social agency, but that long-time attendance was found among those who regarded the Center as a voluntary organization (Ferraro and Cobb, 1987). In a secondary analysis of the 1984 Supplement on Aging to the National Health Interview Survey, Krout et al. (1990) examined predictors of participation in Senior Centers. The array of predictor variables included lower income, higher levels of social interaction, increasing age up to 85, living alone, fewer ADL and IADL difficulties, higher education up to post-high school, being female, and living in central city or rural nonfarm places (Krout et al., 1990).

Activities of Senior Centers

Senior Centers have great latitude in the type, amount, and frequency of services and activities which they provide. Centers may provide services directly under the Older Americans Act, or they may coordinate with other local service providers and may use local funds and resources to develop their service and activity packages. Traditionally Senior Centers have provided a combination of recreation/educational activities, services and information, and referral to other service programs (Cohen, 1972; Lease and Wagner, 1975). Examples of recreation /educational activities include arts and crafts, various classes, hobby groups, physical activities, excursions, and forums. Service programs would include those activities which are directed toward alleviating or preventing various health and social problems. Examples of services provided at Centers are meals, legal and income counseling, and screening clinics for common health problems of elderly people. Services provided by the Centers but delivered in the community are friendly visiting, homemaker assistance, handyman and chore services, and other outreach programs. Information and referral to a variety of services may be seen as a separate category of activities or may be included under the general rubric of service activity.

The number and variety of services and activities available at Senior Centers have grown over the past ten years. Krout's 1985 study of activities and services of 755 Senior Centers shows that services such as recreation, health/nutrition, and information are most likely to be offered; the in-home services, personal counseling, and income supplements are least likely services to be found at Senior Centers. The service package available at Senior Centers varies with location. Krout's study (1985) found that the mean number of services provided in Centers was 17.6 and the mean number of activities was 11.1. Centers located in smaller, less urban communities provided fewer services than Centers in larger areas (Krout, 1987).

Systems Level Barriers

Senior Centers rely upon complex and diverse funding streams. Federal, state and local funds as well as private funding sources are used to fund the various activities and services. Each of these funding streams may have different reporting mechanisms and/or different eligibility requirements. Considerable administrative skill is needed to manage the reporting requirements to support broad-spectrum service and activity programs. Funders tend to target special services with little or no funding for operation, while needs increase due to a growing elderly population; in a tight economy, allocations may remain the same or be reduced. As with all social service programs in a tight economy, competition among service providers for dwindling resources has increased. The national funding trend to shifting away from programs for "well-elderly" in favor of services for the frail and impaired can be seen to have an impact upon the traditional packages of activities and services available in Senior Centers. Jirovec, Erich, and Sanders (1989) found that obstacles to Center participation included accessibility problems related to lack of transportation and lack of financial resources.

Agency Level Barriers

Many of the agency level barriers directly follow from the systems level. Administrative and bureaucratic red tape go hand in hand with the complex funding picture for Senior Centers. Strategic issues regarding fundraising, coordination, and collaboration of a range of services for different target groups presents a challenge for administrators who must try to reach such a broad target population and broad range of services. Staffing is often a problem; recruiting and retaining qualified staff is difficult for agencies in which most positions are at an entry-level with few opportunities for promotion. Senior Centers often rely on volunteer help who require considerable management support and direction. Other difficulties experienced by Senior Center staff can include dealing with government mandates, lack of adequate staffing levels, and the uncertainty of ongoing funding (Salamon and Trubin, 1983).

Personal and Family Barriers

While eligibility is age-based, programming at Senior Centers can never meet all of the heterogeneous and changing needs of the elderly population. The growth and survival of Senior Centers in some communities may be due to the fact that they are not perceived as providing services to the poor, the very ill, or minorities. (Krout et al., 1990). In fact the shift toward funding more services for the vulnerable aged and minorities could be a barrier for some participants who prefer not to be associated with those who are less able or different. Yearwood and Dressel (1983), in a study of a single Southern rural center, found that general cooperation between white and black participants was interspersed with sporadic racial antagonism. Salamon and Trubin (1983) touched upon some of these issues in a study of difficulties in Senior Center life. Problems these authors documented included the fact that many Center participants did not want to be associated with older, frailer members; difficulty of new members entering into an established system; and perceived differences between members. Accessibility can be a barrier for some elderly, especially in rural areas where distances are great. Centers usually serve a specific geographical area; some potential participants may not have a center available to them. In addition, poor health can restrict participation in Senior Centers by elderly individuals. This is an especially significant barrier for those Senior Centers that do not provide transportation services or who do not offer programming to elders with health or activity restrictions.

Nutrition Programs

Overview of Nutrition Programs

A national study of food consumption conducted by the Department of Agriculture in 1965 stated that 95 million Americans did not consume an adequate diet; 6 to 8 million were older adults. These data laid the groundwork for federal funding of nutrition services which have become the most widely used and best known program of the Older Americans Act (Huttman, 1985). In 1973 an amendment to the Older Americans Act provided for one (or more) hot meals served in a congregate setting for adults 60 or more years of age and their spouses of any age. Since their inception nutrition programs have been popular and well-received and have been the cornerstone of many Senior Center programs. Nutritional programs are funded and monitored through the Area Agencies on Aging, and represent the largest single component in AoA expenditures. According to the National Association of Nutrition and Aging Services Programs, the federal appropriation for Title IIIc Nutrition Services (Congregate Meals programs) in 1992 was approximately 365 million dollars. Appropriations for home-delivered meals were 84 million dollars (Personal communication, Connie Benton-Wolfe, May 7, 1992).

Participation in Nutrition Programs

Nutrition programs can be discussed in terms of congregate meals and home delivered meals. Congregate meal programs are open to people age 60 and older and their spouses, regardless of age. Home delivered meals are provided to those elders aged 60 or older who qualify as home-bound according to accepted medical criteria. Most participants of the home delivered meals are aged 75 or older and are low-income. It is estimated that the current need is much greater than the number being served, and waiting lists for this program can be long (Huttman, 1985). Statistics from the National Center for Health Statistics show that 2.1 million people (5 percent of people aged

65 and older living in the community) reported using congregate meals programs in 1984. In this same year 2 percent of persons 65 and older living in the community (497,000) reported they used home delivered meals services (National Center for Health Statistics, 1986).

Activities of Nutrition Programs

The goals of the congregate meal program are to: improve health through a low-cost, nutritious meal which is served in a congregate setting; increase the incentive to maintain social well-being; improve the elder's capability to prepare nutritious meals at home by offering nutrition education, shopping assistance, and transportation to markets. Nutrition programs are required to offer counseling and referral to other service-providers and to have outreach services to the isolated elderly. The program is intended to reflect cultural pluralism, but Huttman (1985) has criticized the program by pointing out that congregate meal programs are less available in rural areas and that there are too few sites in ethnic and low-income areas. Congregate meal sites are open 5 or more days per week and offer hot meals that meet 1/3 of the U.S. Department of Agriculture's RDA requirement . Federal funds pay 90 percent of the cost and require a 10 percent local match. Sites are prohibited from charging for meals; at the same time, they are required to inform participants of the opportunity to donate from 25 cents to one dollar per meal. Nutrition programs are encouraged to use volunteers to enhance the opportunity for social contact. In some sites volunteers are the mainstay of the service (Gelfand, 1988). Nutrition programs also include home-delivered meals. Home delivery programs are usually staffed by volunteer teams consisting of a driver and a visitor.

Systems Barriers

While costs have risen, appropriations, after controlling for inflation, have not. The 10 percent local match can be problematic in some areas for program development as well as for maintaining current levels of operations. Nationally there is declining participation in congregate meal programs. Nutrition programs may be unable to address individual tastes of elderly participants, due to the need to standardize menus so as to keep costs down. In addition, dietary regulations do not allow the elderly to take food home.

Agency Barriers

Sites can serve only a limited number of elderly and long waiting lists have developed at some sites. This is especially true for the home-delivered meals programs in the face of the increasing numbers of impaired elderly in the community. One solution used in the congregate meals program is to rotate clients on an every-other-day basis. Enforcement of strict health codes can create barriers for on-site preparation of meals, especially for organizations which do not have sophisticated staff or facilities for food preparation (Gelfand, 1988). However, this barrier can be addressed by instituting a catering system. Nutrition programs are often staffed by volunteers who require staff attention in terms of recruitment, supervision, and retention. The older aged volunteers who deliver meals often have their own health problems, while younger volunteers are largely unavailable because of employment.

Personal and Family Barriers

Sites operate only five days per week. People who depend upon these meals do not have access to these services during holidays or weekends. The elderly may have complaints about the quality of food and the taste. Participants must be physically or mentally able to get to the site or be completely homebound to qualify for home-delivered meals. Lack of cultural sensitivity and flexibility regarding ethnic foods present particular barriers for ethnic elderly.

Transportation Services

Overview of Transportation Services

Transportation programs are vitally important as an adjunct to community-based aging services. Transportation provides access to health and social services; increases mobility of seniors for social, psychological and physical benefits; and assures access for physically impaired and isolated elderly (Harbert and Ginsberg, 1979). Many older adults have difficulty accessing services and activities due to the lack of appropriate public transportation or may no longer be able to drive or to afford the expense and upkeep of a personal automobile. Recent studies show that about one-third of the elderly do not drive a car. Older women and minorities are less likely to drive than are white men. Half of elderly white women, half of all black elderly, and almost three-fourths of Mexican-American elderly do not drive (Huttman, 1985). For some, age-related perceptual and physical changes may make driving difficult or unsafe.

Transportation can be provided to elderly people using several strategies: (1) by providing reduced fares on existing mass transit systems; (2) by providing specialized transportation systems; or (3) by enlisting volunteer escorts to provide transportation or to accompany the elderly on mass or specialized transportation. These different models of services vary in their flexibility with respect to destination, routes, scheduling, and other services available.

The 1975 Urban Mass Transportation Act (UMTA) provided transportation to handicapped people through the provisions of funds for the purchase of handicapped-access busses and vans for Title lll services. The act also covered operational expenses such as gas, repairs, and insurance, but was rescinded in 1981. Funding for transportation services is currently available through The Older Americans Act, Title lll, which provides transportation to and from nutrition programs. Medicaid requires that each state plan include transportation for medical appointments for eligible recipients. Escort service is another support program which is used by older clients. This program provides an escort who helps the older person to get around, who may also serve as an interpreter or help with communication for speech or hearing impaired persons (Harbert and Ginsberg, 1979).

Participation in Transportation Programs

In 1984 1.2 million elderly (5 percent of the population aged 65 and older living in the community) used some type of transportation service (NCHS, 1986). Eligibility varies for the different types of transportation programs, but most use an age criterion. UMTA-funded programs require an individual to be handicapped and/or 60 years of age or older. For transportation under the Medicaid program, an individual must be Medicaid eligible, and then transportation is provided to and from medical appointments only. For reduced-fare programs, proof of age and travel during non-peak hours is required. Some programs have looked at both age and need criteria and developed transportation services for elderly and handicapped people (Noel and Chadda, 1987).

Systems Barriers

Mass transit services are planned, developed, and funded based upon the needs of an entire region. While the elderly are part of the picture, the services designed and offered may not exactly match the needs of the elderly. The planning bodies for transit systems and for social services are distinct, so that the needs of the elderly are compared to needs of the general population and of other special interest groups in planning large scale services such as mass transit.

Many specialized services may not be coordinated over wide areas. For example, a person living a block out of the city limits may not be able to ride the city's specialized bus system. A transportation system which is geared to meeting the needs of elderly people is bound to be attractive to most groups of people, providing such specialized services can increase the demand for them and quickly decrease the costs. Eligibility criteria and the application process for specialized transportation services often are rigorous and thus serve to limit the number of participants.

Agency Barriers

Transportation services, by definition, require the use of a motor vehicle as well as the staff to operate and maintain it and to schedule and coordinate the services. Scheduling is a particular problem with portal-to-portal services since service routes are developed in response to the needs of individuals. For services which have fixed routes, the scheduling problems are transferred to the individual who must time his or her appointments with the bus schedule. Programs which use volunteer drivers and escorts would appear to have the least problems since the elderly person and the volunteer arrange their own schedules. Volunteer programs, however, can experience problems with recruitment.

As with many social services, transportation is generally less available in rural areas than in cities and suburbs (Huttman, 1985). Regardless of setting, programs vary greatly in extensiveness, frequency, and responsiveness of services. Sponsors of specialized transportation programs can include public, county, and regional paratransit systems, and private nonprofit systems including volunteer organizations. Funds may be allocated to specific agencies in order to coordinate services throughout a region so that individual agencies may have to give up some of their transportation dollars and control of their own specialized programs to be part of a larger system.

Basic staff needs for transportation programs include drivers as well as people who schedule and coordinate the services. Drivers working with the elderly may need additional training to understand sensory, memory, and motor impairments, and incontinence which can accompany the aging process. A driver whose priority is to keep the time schedule rather than to wait an extra five minutes so an elder can keep a doctor's appointment, for example, will need additional training in the purpose of the service.

For those organizations which must purchase a vehicle, the start-up costs, including the purchase price, insurance and liability coverage, and driver training are high. Ongoing costs of such transportation programs include the maintenance and repair of the vehicles, licenses, registration, and insurance.

Personal and Family Barriers

While mass transit is available to all and reduced fares available to many, it may not be possible for the elderly to use the service easily. The nature of most mass transit systems facilitates access for all areas of a region and a network of routes provide access to other parts of a town or city. For the elderly, however, the amount of walking required and the number of transfers necessary may make the mass transit system too difficult to navigate. Elderly people who live in neighborhoods where there are high levels of crime are vulnerable during waits at the bus stop or subway station. Even when crime is not an issue, the waits at the station can be exhausting and inconvenient.

The stigma associated with using transportation programs is low, since all people need and use transportation. However, to the extent that programs are means-tested, there may be stigma in using these services. Some elderly do not know about specialized services and/or do not know how to request the service. Still others may be reluctant to ask for help because they don't want to be too much of a burden.

Physical disability and sensory impairment can prevent some elderly from using even the most specialized portal-to-portal transportation. Most transportation programs require that the person be able to walk to the curb and to get on the bus without assistance. For frail elderly, an escort may be necessary to help the person get ready for the bus and to accompany him or her on the trip.

Telephone Reassurance and Friendly Visiting Programs

Overview of Telephone Reassurance and Friendly Visiting Programs

Telephone reassurance and friendly visiting programs are designed to provide regular contact, either in person or by telephone, to persons who are isolated and in need of social contact. The goals of these programs are: to provide regular contact with isolated elderly; to provide reassurance; and to provide a link to other formal services as required. Programs can be sponsored by any type of agency or community organization that is interested in developing such services.

Activities of Telephone Reassurance and Friendly Visiting Programs

The activities of telephone reassurance and friendly visiting programs are simple. Telephone reassurance programs assign a caller who "checks in" with the elder every day, at a prearranged time, provides some social contact, and arranges for needed chores. If there is no answer, the caller has the number of a designated relative, friend, or neighbor who can investigate. In an emergency situation, appropriate professional help is dispatched. Friendly visiting programs offer companionship and socialization and may provide information and a link to other services. Visits may occur weekly or monthly. Volunteer visitors may read to participants or write letters for them and do other small tasks. Monk (1988) discusses the use of various communication approaches to increase social contact among isolated elderly and presents cable and two-way television, computer games, and lifeline emergency systems as possible adjuncts to telephone reassurance and friendly visiting efforts.

Telephone reassurance and visiting programs are often staffed by volunteers, many of whom are elderly themselves and participate in programs such as Retired Senior Volunteer Program (RSVP), Senior Companions, or Senior AIDES. They are funded by private, nonprofit organizations, through Social Service Community Block Grants, or through Title lll of the Older Americans Act. These programs are relatively inexpensive and administratively uncomplicated.

System Barriers

Telephone reassurance and friendly visiting are not services which can stand alone but should be part of a larger constellation of social and health services offered to older people. Telephone reassurance and friendly visiting programs usually operate under the aegis of a larger program, such as a Senior Center, or they may be operated by a volunteer organization in cooperation with a hospital or social service agency. Funding for programs like these are often scant and programs may share staff and other administrative resources. In the shadow of larger organizations, programs like telephone reassurance may not receive the administrative attention or funding they need to manage the services, the record keeping, and the staff efficiently.

Agency Barriers

Staffing appears to be the primary agency barrier to telephone reassurance and friendly visiting programs. Most of these programs rely on volunteers who need special training, monitoring, and professional back-up in difficult cases. Staff must know how to screen for and train volunteers and maintain their interest and enthusiasm for the work since reliability of volunteers is essential to program success. Accuracy of record-keeping of both client information and resource information for clients is crucial.

Personal and Family Barriers

Reaching isolated people is difficult by definition. One central barrier is the lack of awareness of available programs by those elderly with minimal social contact and few social resources. The client's sense of privacy or personality may hinder attempts to connect him or her with a volunteer caller or visitor. From the volunteer's perspective isolated people often have problems which impede communication, such as mental illness, speech and hearing impairments, or physical disabilities. Daily encounters with some people who need contact may not always be pleasant or productive. Volunteers must develop non-judgmental attitudes and learn to be persistent without being overbearing in order to fulfill the task. Like all programs which attempt to foster relationships between people whose backgrounds are different, telephone reassurance programs must incorporate training on cultural differences and norms. Language can be a very steep barrier for people whose first language is not English unless the program has made special efforts to recruit bilingual and bicultural staff.

Adult Day Care

Overview of Adult Day Care

Adult day care offers structured, comprehensive health, social, and related support services in a protective setting during any part of the day (but less than 24-hour care) for impaired elderly and their caregivers. Programs are designed to meet the needs of functionally impaired adults through individual plans of care. Program goals, structure, and viability are controversial issues; nevertheless, the number of day care programs has grown over the last twenty years (U.S. Senate Committee on Labor and Human Resources, 1988). Approximately 1,400 day care programs are listed in the most recent edition of the National Day Care Directory, twice the number listed in the early 80s.

Early studies found evidence for two categories of adult day care, the health oriented model and social services oriented model. These models varied in participants, staffing, services, costs, and auspices (Weissert, 1976, 1977). A more recent study (Weissert, et al., 1989) has expanded the categorization of adult day care into three models which will be described more fully below.

The debate on the effectiveness of adult day care as an alternative to institutional care, and whether or not it prevents institutionalization, continues in the literature (Weissert, et al., 1989; Rathbone-McCuan, 1990). Day care programs can be seen as a relatively inexpensive part of the continuum of community-based services for frail and impaired elders. Analysis of cost data has shown that 6 hours of adult day care typically costs about $30 plus an hour of transportation costs; this is considerably lower than the $40 per hour charge for a home health nurse, and also lower than the $25 cost of a four-hour homemaker visit (Weissert, et al., 1989).

Participation in Adult Day Care

In one of the most comprehensive studies of adult day care to date, Weissert, et al. (1989) examined a representative sample of 60 adult day care centers and described three models of care, each of which serves a separate subpopulation and which were identifiable by revenue type, auspices, and staffing. Two of the models were identified by auspices and the third by the special population served. Auspice Model One centers are affiliated with nursing homes or rehabilitation centers and typically serve an older, white, more physically disabled rather than mentally impaired population. These programs generally are supported by philanthropic and self-pay sources. Auspice Model Two centers are those affiliated with general hospitals or social service agencies or housing agencies. The population served by Auspice Model Two typically are people of color who are unmarried, female, and not dependent in activities of daily living. Over 40 percent of the people served in Model Two centers suffered from a mental disorder and 16 percent had been admitted to an inpatient facility at some time in their lives for mental health problems, compared with 8 percent of those in Model One and 9.6 percent in Model Three. Medicaid payments were the primary source of revenue for Model Two centers. Auspice Model Three centers, termed Special Purpose centers, served a homogenous group, such as blind elderly or veterans.

Twenty-seven percent of the programs studies were classified as Auspice Model One, 62.2 percent were Auspice Model Two, and 11.2 percent were labeled Auspice Model Three, or Special Purpose. Daily census patterns in the facilities studied ranged from 5.6 to 42.2; the average number of participants per day was 20 (Weissert, et al., 1989). Model Two Centers were found to have the most frequent attendance patterns with an average of 3.7 days per week per participant compared to 3.1 days per week in Model One and 2.5 days per week in Special Purpose centers. Other authors have identified adult day care programs which serve special populations such as developmentally disabled elderly (Zimpel, 1990), Alzheimer's disease patients (Conrad and Guttman, 1991), isolated elderly (Williams, 1984), and Jewish survivors of concentration camps (Fried and Waxman, 1988).

Activities of Adult Day Care Programs

Case management, health assessment, nutrition education, therapeutic diets, transportation, and counseling are among the most frequently provided services; other activities can include nursing services, personal care services, and various therapeutic activities. Case mix and auspices have been shown to be associated with type and variety of services offered (Weissert, et al., 1989). As one might predict, Model One centers provided more therapeutic and health services, while Model Two center programs were focused upon social and supportive services. Kirwin (1986) suggests a compromise strategy of integrating adult day care programming with Senior Center programming to increase service options and decrease costs.

Families of impaired elderly people are often included in adult day care programming and are seen to be important in the operation of these programs. Hedenstrom and Ostwald (1988) studied programs in Minnesota and found that families are frequently involved in social activities, counseling sessions, and support groups. Programs which arrange services around the needs of families and other caregivers, which provide services such as transportation, and offer services during extended hours are thought to be more viable than those which do not (Adams, 1988).

While elderly people are the direct recipients of services provided by adult day care programs, families also are thought to receive some benefits from service. Strain, Chappell, and Blandford (1987) found that life satisfaction improved for both the informal caregivers and the adult day care participants while the elder attended the program. However, Johnson and Maguire (1989) did not find that day care participation was related to reduction in caregiver stress.

System Barriers

With no national program that provides funding for all models of day care, programs often provide care based upon the type of funding available rather than upon the type of services needed. Even though federal sources have been estimated to provide 50 percent of revenue supporting adult day care programs (Weissert, et al., 1989), there are no federal guidelines for day care programs. The result is that programs develop unevenly depending upon the funding regulations of a particular source, which typically is Medicaid. It should be noted, however, that standards for adult day care have been developed by the National Council on Aging and some states have licensing standards as well.

Agency Barriers

Planners of adult day care programs must not only understand the types of physical and mental impairments prevalent among the various subpopulations of elderly who use these programs, but also be able to recognize the implications of these needs for program staffing and service needs. Programs must be designed to meet the needs of the group targeted as well as the needs of their caregivers. Butrin (1985) discusses the fact that the expression of a desire for a program does not guarantee high service utilization rates. Many agencies which might have access to the client group may not have the expertise to develop and manage adult day care programs.

Many of the agency level barriers discussed in the section on Senior Centers could also apply to a discussion of adult day care. Additional issues for adult day care centers would be the increased staff training and the increased staff-to-client ratio necessary to care for impaired people. The reporting requirements of the funding sources, especially Medicaid, are often lengthy and complicated, taking additional administrative and staff time from service provision. Adult day care centers are as much a place as they are a service, and the need for a safe, comfortable environment, which must be secure so that clients cannot wander, can be expensive. Liability and other insurance costs present additional barriers.

Personal and Family Barriers

The personal and family barriers to using adult day care services initially involve the decision to seek such a service. Families are often reluctant to give up the caregiving role to a stranger or may feel a sense of failure in asking for help. The elderly clients may be fearful of leaving a familiar environment, or reluctant to adapt to new people and new routines, or concerned that adult day care is the first step to nursing home placement. After the person is enrolled in the service, the barriers become those of cost, convenience, and transportation. It should be noted, however, that unlike institutionalization, adult day care usage represents repetitive choices by families. That is, families must decide *each day* to bring their elder to the day care center, addressing such issues as the elder's desire to go that day, the weather, etc. Even though adult day care has been shown to be one of the best bargains in long term care services, the out-of-pocket costs can be prohibitive for many families. Family caregivers who work hours different from the day care program hours find additional barriers in trying to arrange for interim care. However, if these barriers can be overcome, the elderly and their families can benefit from adult day care. Regardless of the adult day care model used, the Weissert study found that participants and caregivers both are very satisfied with the care received in these programs (Weissert, et al. 1989, p. 649).

Self-Help Groups

Overview of Self-Help Groups

Self-help groups for all ages have grown tremendously during the past ten years (Kurtz, 1990). Three concepts are involved in self-help efforts: mutual aid, social transaction, and advocacy on behalf of a particular interest group. By utilizing self-help experiences, many people become aware of services and may be more inclined to seek them out and use them. Self-help groups may not only increase demand for services but also can call attention to the strengths, weaknesses, and gaps in the formal service structure (Powell, 1987). Self-help experiences can be especially valuable for older adults because they provide the opportunity for socialization, intellectual stimulation, and mutual support. Self-help groups also can create opportunities to develop leadership skills and encourage empowerment and personal growth (Powell, 1987). Self-help available outside of formal groups has been associated with measures of health, self-esteem, and overall adjustment in a sample of elderly people living in retirement hotels and apartments (Stein, Linn, and Stein, 1982). The concept of self-help and mutual support can be found in a variety of social support efforts with the elderly and is not limited to formal groups designated as self-help groups.

Participation in Self-Help Groups

Estimates of participation of elderly people in self-help efforts are not available because of the nature of the service and the fact that there are so many different types of organizations which might be defined as offering self-help. Elderly people may participate in any of the various age integrated self-help groups, but there are also groups which are focused particularly for elderly participants. Examples of these age-specific groups include: Alzheimer's disease caregiver support groups, Gray Panthers, and the Older Women's League. Various program models of self-help groups for the elderly exist, including programs which train elderly volunteers to develop helping relationships with neighbors (Morrow-Howell and Ozawa, 1987); self-help communities in day centers for physically frail handicapped elderly (Friedlander, 1982); and widow-to-widow groups to address needs of older women (Adlersberg and Thorne, 1990).

Activities of Self-Help Groups

The activities of self-help groups are tailored to the particular task or focus of each group. Zimmer (1988) has suggested that the effectiveness of any self-help group for older people can be understood in the context of late-life learning. She proposes that there are three types of learning which are tied to group stages: (1) education and skills training; (2) mutual aid/peer support; and (3) social action and advocacy. The format for group meetings varies by the type of organization. Activities can involve sharing of personal experiences, group discussions of particular topics, and/or presentations by outside speakers. Some self-help efforts are staffed by professional leaders while others are composed only of group members who assume the responsibility for organizing and running the meetings and activities.

System Barriers

Systems level barriers apply to self-help groups which have a national or regional organizational structure as well as to local grass-roots organizations. A central characteristic of some self-help efforts is to restrict the amount of professional leadership or the amount of formal linkages with other service providers in the community. Since many self-help groups are singularly focused upon a particular problem or disease, the lack of formal relationships with professionals and/or service organizations may impede advocacy efforts or limit funding opportunities.

Agency Barriers

With the exceptions of the peer/professionally led groups of the Alzheimer's Association, self-help groups do not routinely operate out of an agency base. The level of administrative expertise, the type and amount of resources, and the type of staffing available may vary widely among groups and between different chapters of the same group. For self-help groups which are not affiliated with national offices, the success of fund-raising, publicity, and continuity may fall solely upon the energy and commitment of a few core members. Since self-help groups are not funded by any particular source of revenue, fund-raising is a crucial issue and may create barriers to expansion or survival for groups unable to develop successful funding strategies.

Personal and Family Barriers

For a service to be effective, the participants need to see the value of the activity or effort. Elderly people or their families who do not see self-disclosure or group activity as a positive step toward a goal will not view self-help as useful. Similar feelings about the usefulness of self-disclosure and group support may exist among different ethnic/racial groups. For people sensitive to issues of stigma and labeling, becoming associated with some types of self-help groups may present too much fear and anxiety. The effort to travel to meetings may be too great, especially if transportation is not available. One of the draws of self-help, however, is the cost and the availability of services. Attendance at self-help groups is free and some groups, Alcoholics Anonymous, for example, have meetings at all times of day and night and at many locations.

Adult Protective Services

Overview of Adult Protective Services

Adult protective services programs offer legal protection and special services to older adults who are at risk for physical harm, financial exploitation, physical abuse, emotional abuse, or unnecessary institutionalization. Professional protective service workers assess the situation of elders to determine the extent of their physical and mental abilities as well as the effectiveness of their support system. A plan is constructed to prevent or reduce risk from harm, using the least restrictive alternatives available. The protective service worker's role is to coordinate health, mental health, and social or legal services on the client's behalf. Protective services programs also advocate for the rights of the elderly in institutions as well as in the community. Since the early 1980s most adult protective services programs seek to prevent elder abuse, neglect, and exploitation through some combination of case-management and legal interventions (Bookin and Dunkle, 1985; Zborowsky, 1985).

Participation in Adult Protective Services Programs

A potential protective services client lacks the capacity to act effectively in his or her own behalf and may not have relatives or others willing or able to assume appropriate support. In a ten-year review of adult protective service cases in South Carolina, Cash and Valentine (1987) reported that the typical client was an elderly woman with low income. Recent studies have shown that reported cases of elder abuse and neglect fall short of the estimates of incidence (Dolon and Blakely, 1989). Fredriksen (1989) analyzed the caseload of an adult protective services program. He found a low rate of substantiation of abuse and, therefore, a low rate of service because of the difficulty in securing evidence and the lack of client cooperation. A study of physicians in Alabama found that a majority of physicians recognized their responsibility to report elder abuse, but 75 percent were unsure of how they should report it and to whom (Daniels, Baumhover, and Clark-Daniels, 1989).

Activities of Adult Protective Service Programs

Programs which deal with protective services involve medical, social, and legal services. Assessment is a large part of the service since the outcome of the assessment is instrumental in determining whether or not a person will be involved in steps to appoint a guardian or other legally responsible person. Social service agencies are not the only source of adult protective service programming; there are examples of efforts in the legal and medical communities to improve services to impaired individuals (Schwartz, 1982; Daniels, et al., 1989).

System Barriers

The overlap of social, medical, and legal systems in protective services can create problems of interagency and interdisciplinary coordination. These systems are often unaccustomed to interagency collaboration and have differing perceptions of their roles in relation to protective services. Each system, for example, has its own guidelines and approaches to providing service. Funding is inadequate to meet the need because these clients are "invisible"; the extent of the need is not clearly documented. Danger of paternalism and inappropriate action on the part of actors within various systems can also present barriers to service development.

Agency Barriers

Protective services staff must be expert in assessing risk situations and knowledgeable about the community's legal and social norms for guardianship. Workers must have access to a range of legal, health, mental health, and social services not only to complete a thorough assessment but also to develop care plans. Since the decision about whether or not a person is able to manage successfully in the community is often subjective, staff attitudes about personal freedom and safety are as important as their substantive knowledge of the aging process. Some agencies may shy away from protective services work because of the legal interventions potentially required. Daniels, et al. (1989) found that physicians cited the prospect of lengthy court appearances and the likelihood of angering the abuser as factors that created barriers to reporting elder abuse. Adult protective services work is full of ethical dilemmas and involves taking some risks in pursuing least restrictive alternatives. Because of the interdisciplinary nature and intensity of the work, battles over turf are common. Agencies which cannot productively manage interagency conflict in order to develop collaborative arrangements will have difficulty in providing services effectively.

Personal and Family Barriers

Fear and shame are among the central barriers to seeking adult protective services (Dolon and Blakely, 1989). Clients may fear people in their families will seek retribution if others are called into the situation. For families as well as the elders themselves, seeking guardianship or being forced to accept guardianship is stigmatizing. The fact that protective service workers often are seen as authority figures who can remove someone from his or her home can create an antagonism between professionals, neighbors, families, and clients. An additional barrier to service is that many of the people in need do not have the ability to recognize their plight and to ask for help.

Services for Family Caregivers

Overview of Services for Family Caregivers

The majority of disabled older persons live in the community and are cared for by families. As many researchers have shown, it is a myth that the elderly are abandoned by their families. Rather, family members provide extensive support and represent the elderly's most significant resource. In 1977, the U.S. General Accounting Office estimated that 70–80 percent of supportive care to older persons is provided by family members (U.S. General Accounting Office, 1977). More recent research has substantiated the significant levels of care being provided by families, friends, and neighbors. It is estimated that approximately 75 percent of non-institutionalized disabled elderly persons in the community rely solely on care from the informal support system. The more frail the elderly family member, the greater likelihood that children will assume more responsibility for care. The family is also the source of care most preferred by the elderly. There is growing awareness that family caregiving, though having positive aspects for the caregiver, is often stressful as well. This knowledge has led to the development of a number of service and policy initiatives designed to reduce caregiver burden and provide supportive assistance to enable families to continue their caregiving roles.

Activities of Caregiver Services

Caregiver interventions can be classified into three types: support group interventions, educational interventions, and clinical or direct service interventions (Biegel, Sales, and Schulz, 1991). Support group interventions are designed to provide caregivers with emotional support, informational support, and enhancement of coping skills with emphasis on the sharing of feelings, experiences, and coping strategies among group members. Sometimes these groups are led by professionals, sometimes they are peer led. Groups also vary to the extent to which they are time-limited or ongoing.

Educational interventions emphasize the provision by professionals of information and/or skills, usually in a group format, to better enable caregivers to meet their needs. Interventions vary in the degree to which they focus upon cognitive and skill development areas and can be classified into three principal types: cognitive information only, cognitive information plus self-enhancement and/or behavioral management skills, and self-enhancement and/or behavioral management skills only.

Clinical interventions, a direct treatment oriented service, is the most prevalent type of caregiver intervention found in the literature. This group of interventions varies much more than do either support group or educational interventions and can be broadly categorized into six different types: counseling/therapy, respite, behavioral/cognitive stimulation, hospice, day hospital, and general psycho-social interventions.

Examination of the effects of the above interventions on caregiver distress indicate that, overall, caregivers report very high levels of satisfaction with the interventions in which they have participated. However, interventions were less effective in reducing levels of caregiver distress, with reductions in levels of caregiver burden, and reductions in such enduring outcomes as caregiver depression reported in less than half of the interventions. Unfortunately the existing literature provides very little focus on the process of the interventions themselves. Thus even in the case of successful interventions we don't understand how an intervention actually affects caregiver distress, and, in the case of multifaceted interventions, whether particular parts of the intervention are more effective than others (Biegel, Sales, and Schulz, 1991).

System Barriers

The lack of financial resources for caregiver services is a significant barrier. Caregiver interventions are often seen as an adjunct to existing services, such as adult day care, rather than as a service by itself since the caregiver is a secondary client in the aging system. The result is that agencies often don't have sufficient resources and/or expertise to focus attention on caregiver needs.

Agency Barriers

Agencies often find that while caregiver services are greatly needed, they are often poorly attended. The ongoing nature of some caregiver support groups can serve as a barrier to participation by caregivers who are fearful of becoming "dependent" upon a group. For these caregivers a time-limited support group might be a more attractive option. An additional barrier is that the needs and interests of spouse and adult child caregivers are often quite different from each other. Yet group activities such as support groups and educational programs often combine spouse and adult child caregivers in the same group and fail to recognize their different needs. For example, while spouse caregivers may not want to talk about nursing home options, adult child caregivers want to hear about all the options potentially open to them.

Personal and Family Barriers

For caregivers who already feel burdened providing care to their elderly spouse or parent, participating in an educational program or support group might seem like an additional obligation. In addition, the lack of anyone to stay with their elder while the caregiver participates in a program or activity may represent an additional barrier, or lack of transportation may be a problem inhibiting caregiver participation. There have been some innovative attempts by agencies to address these issues through use of computer networks which provide information to individual caregivers as well as enable linkages among caregivers, or through programs that offer telephone ties between caregivers and also telephone tapes of educational information for caregivers.

Conclusion

Over the past thirty years an extensive system of social services has evolved in response to the needs of an increasingly older population. Despite the growth in the number and variety of services available to older persons, barriers which limit service access and utilization still exist at the systems level, the agency level, and at the individual level. This chapter has discussed these barriers in relation to a comprehensive, yet not exhaustive, list of commonly used services: senior center services, nutrition programs, transportation services, telephone reassurance and friendly visiting programs, adult day care, self-help groups, adult protective services, and services for family caregivers.

Many demographic, economic, and social issues will influence the development of social services over the next decades. The elderly will continue to grow in numbers as the baby boom cohort ages. Taeuber (1990) has projected that 20 percent of the U.S. population will be age 65 and over by the year 2030. Demographers estimate that the numbers will increase, but the nature of the needs and the demand for services are less clear. Future aged cohorts are expected to be better educated and healthier. Given the population increases, will the current age criteria for service be feasible? Two possible scenarios are that the defined age for entry into later life and for eligibility for service programs may be pushed upwards from 65 or that the criteria for program eligibility will become a measure of functional rather than chronological age. Program focus for some areas may shift from primarily treatment and remediation to programs of prevention and health maintenance given the characteristics and demands of the aging population.

Staff training needs can be expected to reflect these demographic and policy shifts. For example, professionals in the field of gerontology may very well be expected to understand and use a variety of health promotion techniques in addition to, or in prevention of, therapeutic measures. Future cohorts of older people are likely to increase the demand for exercise and nutritional efforts to maintain health and prevent disability. Changes in policy-makers' view of age criteria may also increase the need for specialists in disability across the lifespan rather than specialists focused upon the concerns of a particular age group. While the lifespan approach traditionally has been popular in training programs for gerontologists, the possibility of a decreased emphasis on chronological age may make this perspective even more useful for practitioners and program planners in the future.

Many of the services discussed in this chapter are supported by public funds. Services directed toward elderly people will compete with other services and other population groups for decreasing federal, state, and local resources. In fact, appropriations for the Administration on Aging, when adjusted for inflation, have been declining over the past decade (Binstock, 1991). The mechanisms for administration, funding, and evaluation of these efforts will need to keep pace not only with the changing needs of the client group but also with an increasingly competitive funding arena. Advocacy efforts on behalf of elderly people, as well, will need to reflect the increased levels of education, health, and political awareness of future cohorts as well as the needs of the poor, the frail, and the isolated elderly.

Certainly the debates regarding the issues of age versus need as discussed by Neugarten and Neugarten (1986) will be salient for policy makers and planners throughout the 1990s. Given these changes some of today's barriers may be lessened. Some of the personal and family barriers which influence service use by today's elderly may not be relevant to future cohorts of elderly and their families. For example, the life experiences of future cohorts of elderly may yield a very different perception of later life and retirement and the goods and services to which they feel entitled. Many will have benefited from federally sponsored programs, such as educational loans or mortgage assistance, during their adult lives and will not experience barriers of stigma in using services. On the other hand, systems and agency barriers may increase for some services or groups depending upon policy and political decisions regarding age-based services. Collaborative relationships among agencies and funding bodies may become more complex and restrictive, especially if the eligibility criteria are tightened or services are in short supply. Thus in the future a barriers perspective can remain a useful tool to learn more about service gaps and strengths to meet the needs of the elderly.

REFERENCES

Adams, R.G. 1988. Attitudes of decision makers toward adult day care. *Journal of Applied Gerontology*, *7*, 37–48.

Adlersberg, M. & Thorne, S. 1990. Emerging from the chrysalis: Older widows in transition. *Journal of Gerontological Nursing, 16,* 4–8.

Austin, C.D. 1991. Aging well: What are the odds? *Generations, 15,* 73–75.

Biegel, D.E. & Farkas, K.J. 1989. *Mental health and the elderly: Service delivery issues.* Cleveland, OH: Western Reserve Geriatric Education Center Interdisciplinary Monograph Series.

Biegel, D.E.; Sales, E.; & Schulz, R. 1991. *Family Caregiving and Chronic Illness: Alzheimer's Disease, Cancer, Heart Disease, Mental Illness, and Stroke.* Newbury Park, CA: Sage.

Biegel, D.E.; Shore, B.K.; & Silverman, M. 1989. Overcoming barriers to serving the aging/mental health client: A state initiative. *Journal of Gerontological Social Work, 13,* 147–165.

Binstock, R. 1991. From the great society to the aging society: Twenty-five years of the Older Americans Act. *Generations, XV,* 11–18.

Bookin, D. & Dunkle, R.E. 1985. Elder abuse: Issues for the practitioner. *Social Casework, 66,* 3–12.

Butrin, J. 1985. Day care: A new idea? Not really. *Journal of Gerontological Nursing, 11,* 19–22.

Cash, T. & Valentine, D. 1987. A decade of adult protective services: Case characteristics. *Journal of Gerontological Social Work, 10,* 47–60.

Cohen, M.L. 1972. *Senior Centers: A Focal Point for the Delivery of Services to Older People.* Washington, DC: National Council on Aging.

Conrad, K.J. & Guttman, R. 1991. Characteristics of Alzheimer's versus non-Alzheimer's adult day care centers. *Research on Aging, 13,* 96–116.

Cox, C. & Monk, A. 1990. Integrating the frail and well elderly: The experience of senior centers. *Journal of Gerontological Social Work, 15,* 131–147.

Daniels, R.S.; Baumhover, L.A.; & Clark-Daniels, C.L. 1989. Physicians' mandatory reporting of elder abuse. *Gerontologist, 29,* 321–327.

Daum, M. 1982. Preference for age-homogeneous versus age-heterogeneous social interaction. *Journal of Gerontological Social Work, 4,* 41–55.

Dolon, R. & Blakely, B. 1989. Elder abuse and neglect: A study of adult protective service workers in the United States. *Journal of Elder Abuse and Neglect, 1,* 31–37.

Ferraro, K.F. & Cobb, C. 1987. Participation in multipurpose senior centers. *Journal of Applied Gerontology, 6,* 429–447.

Fredriksen, K.I. 1989. Adult protective services: A caseload analysis. *Journal of Interpersonal Violence, 4,* 245–250.

Fried, H. & Waxman, H.M. 1988. Stockholm's Cafe 84: A unique day program for Jewish survivors of concentration camps. *Gerontologist, 28,* 253–255.

Friedlander, H. 1982. Differential use of groups in mainstreaming the handicapped elderly. *Social Work with Groups, 5,* 33–42.

Gelfand, D.E. 1988. *The Aging Network: Programs and Services.* New York: Springer Publishing Co.

Gelfand, D.E. & Gelfand, J.R. 1982. "Senior Centers and Support Networks." In D. Biegel & A. Naparstek, eds., *Community Support Systems and Mental Health: Practice, Policy and Research* (pp. 175–189), New York: Springer.

Guttman, D. & Cuellar, J.B. 1982. Barriers to equitable service. *Generations, 6,* 31–33.

Harbert, A.S. & Ginsberg, L.H. 1979. *Human Services for Older Adults: Concepts and Skills.* Belmont, CA: Wadsworth.

Hedenstrom, J. & Ostwald, S.K. 1988. Adult day care programs: Maintaining a therapeutic triad. *Home Health Care Services Quarterly, 9,* 85–102.

Holmes, M.B. 1982. *Services to minority elderly: Area agency, service provider, and minority elderly perspectives: Summary report.* Bronx, NY: Community Research Applications.

Hughes, S.L. & Guihan, M. 1990. Community-based long-term care: The experience of the living at home programs. *Journal of Gerontological Social Work, 15,* 103–129.

Huttman, E.D. 1985. *Social Services for the Elderly.* New York: The Free Press.

Jirovec, R.L.; Erich, J.A.; & Sanders, L.J. 1989. Patterns of senior center participation among low income urban elderly. *Journal of Gerontological Social Work, 13,* 115–132.

Johnson, M. & Maguire, M. 1989. Give me a break: Benefits of a caregiver support service. *Journal of Gerontological Nursing, 15,* 22–26.

Kirwin, P.M. 1986. Adult day care: An integrated model.[Special Issue: Social work and Alzheimer's disease: Practice issues with victims and their families.] *Journal of Gerontological Social Work, 9,* 59–71.

Krout, J.A. 1984. Notes on policy and practice: Utilization of services by the elderly. *Social Services Review, 52,* 281–290.

———. 1985. Senior center activities and services: findings from a national study. *Research on Aging, 7,* 455–471.

———. 1987. Rural-urban differences in senior center activities and services. *The Gerontologist, 27,* 92–97.

———. 1988. The frequency, duration, and stability of senior center attendance. *Journal of Gerontological Social Work, 13,* 3–19.

Krout, J.A.; Cutler, S.J.; & Coward, R.T. 1990. Correlates of senior center participation: A national analysis. *The Gerontologist, 30,* 72–79.

Kulys, R. 1990. "The Ethnic Factor in the Delivery of Social Services." In A. Monk, ed., *The Handbook of Gerontological Services.* New York: Columbia University Press.

Kurtz, L.F. 1990. The self-help movement: Review of the past decade of research. *Social Work with Groups, 13,* 101–115.

Lease, J. & Wagner. 1975. *Senior centers: A report of senior group programs in America.* Washington, DC: National Council on Aging.

Monk, A. 1988. Aging, loneliness, and communications. *American Behavioral Scientist, 31,* 532–563.

Morrow-Howell, N. & Ozawa, M.N. 1987. Helping network: Seniors to seniors. *Gerontologist, 27,* 17–20.

National Center for Health Statistics (NCHS). 1986. Aging in the eighties, age 65 years and over—Use of community services; preliminary data from the Supplement on Aging to the National Health Interview Survey: United States, January-June, 1984. *Advanced Data from Vital and Health Statistics, 124* (DHHS Publication no. (PHS) 86-1250, September 30). Hyattsville, MD: U.S. Public Health Service.

Neugarten, B.L. & Neugarten, D.A. 1986. Age in the aging society. *Daedalus, 115,* 31–49.

Noel, E.C. & Chadda, H.S. 1987. Consolidating elderly and handicapped transportation services. *Transportation Quarterly, 41,* 229–246.

Noelker, L.S. & Bass, D.M. 1989. Home care for the elderly persons: Linkages between formal and informal caregivers. *Journal of Gerontology, 44,* S63.

Petchers, M.K. & Milligan, S.E. 1988. Access to health care in a black urban elderly population. *The Gerontologist, 28,* 213–217.

Powell, T.J. 1987. *Self-Help Organizations and Professional Practice.* Silver Spring, MD: National Association of Social Workers.

Ralston, P.A. & Griggs, M.B. 1985. Factors affecting utilization of senior centers: Race, sex and socioeconomic differences. *Journal of Gerontological Social Work, 9*, 99–111.

Ralston, P.A. 1984. Senior center utilization by black elderly adults: Social attitudinal and knowledge correlates. *Journal of Gerontology, 39*, 224–229.

Rathbone-McCuan, E. 1990. Respite and Adult Day Services. In A. Monk, ed., *The Handbook of Gerontological Services*. New York: Columbia University Press.

Salamon, M.J. & Trubin, P. 1983. Difficulties in senior center life: Group behaviors. *Clinical Gerontologist, 2*, 23–37.

Schwartz, S.A. 1982. Guardianship. *Physical and Occupational Therapy in Geriatrics, 2*, 63–66.

Stein, S.; Linn, M.S.; & Stein, E.M. 1982. The relationship of self-help networks to physical and psychosocial functioning. *Journal of the American Geriatric Society, 30*, 764–768.

Strain, L.A.; Chappell, N.L.; & Blandford, A.A. 1987. Changes in life satisfaction among participants of adult day care and their informal caregivers. *Journal of Gerontological Social Work, 11*, 115–129.

Taeuber, C. 1990. "Diversity: The Dramatic Reality." In S.A. Bass, E.A. Kutza, & F.M. Torres-Gill, eds., *Diversity in Aging: Challenges Facing Planners and Policy-Makers in the 1990s*. Glenview, IL: Scott, Foresman.

U.S. Senate Committee on Labor and Human Resources. 1988. *A bill to amend the public health service and to establish a lifecare long-term care program and for other purpose*. 100th Congress, Session 2, S2681. Washington, DC: U.S. Government Printing Office.

United States General Accounting Office. 1977. *The well-being of older people in Cleveland, Ohio: Report to the Congress*. Washington, DC: U.S. Government Printing Office.

Wallace, S.P. 1990. No-care zone; availability, accessibility, and acceptability in community-based long-term care. *The Gerontologist, 30*, 254–261.

Weissert, W.G. 1976. Two models of geriatric day care: Findings from a comparative study. *The Gerontologist, 16*, 420–427.

———. 1977. Adult day care programs in the United States: Current research project and a survey of 10 centers. *Public Health Reports, 92*, 49–56.

Weissert, W.G.; Elston, J.M. et al. 1989. Models of adult day care: Findings from a National survey. *Gerontologist, 29,* 640–649.

Williams, C. 1984. Reaching isolated older people: l. An alternative model of day services. *Journal of Gerontological Social Work, 8,* 35–49.

Yearwood, A.W. & Dressel, P.L. 1983. Interracial dynamics in a southern rural senior center. *Gerontologist, 23,* 512–517.

Zborowsky, E.K. 1985. Developments in protective services: A challenge for social workers. Special Issue: Gerontological social work practice in the community. *Journal of Gerontological Social Work, 8,* 71–83.

Zimmer, A.H. 1988. Self-help groups and late-life learning. Special Issue: Late-life learning. *Generations, 12,* 19–21.

Zimpel, B. 1990. Sharing activities: The Oneida County A.R.C. Cornhill Senior Center Integration Project. Special Issue: Activities with developmentally disabled elderly and older adults. Activities. *Adaptation and Aging, 15*(1/2), 131–139.

Note

Georgia Anetzberger and Arlene Snyder are thanked for their helpful comments in reviewing an earlier draft of this chapter.

CHAPTER 8

Income Security

Martha Baum

During the 1980s a sharp reversal in the outlays for social welfare has taken place in the United States. It is not surprising that the supposedly sacrosanct "safety net" programs suffered the most. These are "exceptionalist" programs specifically intended for disadvantaged target groups. Program vulnerability is high because, in the United States at least, where there is a larger share of such programs compared to other welfare states, programs for poor people operate in an atmosphere of hostility (Kahn, 1979). In such an atmosphere, benefits are inadequate at best and may be reduced further and even disappear in a budgetary crisis (Schorr, 1986). Programs for the aged in this category include Supplementary Security Income (SSI) and Medicaid.

The elderly have fared better in the changed political climate than other population age groups, especially the youngest adults and the children. Old people have fared relatively well in great measure because of Social Security, which proved astonishingly resistant to very serious attempts to undermine and even abolish the social insurance program. Some now would even argue that the elderly are doing too well and should give up some of their largesse. The Ford Foundation Report, The Common Good (1989), for example, notes that the aggregate poverty rate for the aged is now lower than for the under-65 population. The Report repeatedly endorses a proposal to tax elderly retirees and survivors for any income received over the amount that has been paid into Social Security. The Common Good is generally sympathetic to hardship among all age groups, yet seems not to take into account that it is not that the elderly are doing so much better in the aggregate but that other age groups have been deprived of income by harsh budget cuts over the last decade. This is especially true for programs such as Aid to Families with Dependent Children (AFDC) for which The Common Good proposes to increase outlays, in part through additionally taxing the elderly.

The repeated refrain among those who write about social welfare policy and programs around the world is that the aging population is a burgeoning problem. There are so many old people, and they are getting older and older and more and more costly to care for. But is the United States really justified in thinking that its government, directly or indirectly, does too much for the aged? There is an inference that persons who are not working, although perhaps they should be supported at some level, should not be enjoying any of the luxuries of life as some elderly clearly are. By contrast, very few voices are raised in protest over the very steep redistribution of income from the poor to the rich among the non-elderly (Shapiro and Greenstein, 1988, p. 15). Those under 65 who are well-to-do have received tax advantages of an astonishing magnitude (Winnick, 1988), yet there has been little commentary (Schorr, 1986).

In reality people in the group defined as old have quite disparate fates. Very few are anything like wealthy, and many are desperately poor in spite of repeated past efforts to improve the lot of the elderly. Statistics from the 1986 census (U.S. Bureau of the Census, 1988a) show that in families with heads 65 and over 15.1 percent (one in every seven) had incomes of less than $10,000, while at the other extreme about one-fifth (22.0 percent) had incomes of $35,000 and over. Families, who are usually married couples, are very much more likely to be above the poverty level than "unrelated individuals." Among the latter 13.4 percent had incomes of less than $5,000. These incomes were below and often well below the poverty level by the official definition in 1986, which was $6,630 for an older couple household and $5,255 for an older individual living alone. Another fifth (21.8 percent) of elderly "unrelated individuals" just straddled the poverty line with income levels of between $5,000 and $6,999. Although these figures show many elderly still in want, the situation for the proportions in poverty has been recently reversed slightly in favor of the over-65 population.

In 1969, for example, the poverty rate for persons over 65 (23.3 percent) was twice as large as for all persons in the United States (12.1 percent), but by 1980 the poverty rate for persons over 65 (15.7 percent) had drawn much closer to the poverty rate for all persons (13.0 percent) (Karger and Stoesz, 1990, p. 94). By 1986 the rate for all persons (13.6 percent) had increased slightly again, and the elderly were at an advantage (12.4 percent). Smeeding (1990, p. 369) shows, however, that if one leaves out the children, adults 18 to 64 are actually less likely to be below the poverty line than those 65 and over.

Within that poverty rate for the elderly were concealed terrible discrepancies: only 11.0 percent of the white elderly but 31.1 percent of the black elderly and 37.7 percent of the Hispanic elderly were in poverty (Karger and Stoesz, 1990, p. 94). Those living alone, the oldest, and those without any income beyond what was provided by Social Security were the most likely to be poor. In fact single, widowed, and divorced women are the most deprived of all older people and black women suffer the most of all (Abramovitz, 1988; Atchley, 1980; Cianciolo, 1990). There remain, in spite of improvements over the years, huge numbers of elderly persons who are in need of adequate nutrition, housing, and health care and who lack any of the small amenities of life. Yet they belong to the group, older Americans, who survived the 1980s relatively well in terms of income supports.

The star of the admittedly flawed drama was Social Security, especially Title II, Old Age and Survivors Insurance (OASI). Although the Reagan administration with popular support and majority control in the Senate, was disposed toward dismantling as many welfare programs as possible, a hard wall of resistance defended Social Security (Achenbaum, 1986). Not only the elderly, a growing political constituency, but most of the younger generation wished to continue the program in spite of increased deductions from their paychecks (Harris and Associates, 1981). Younger adults saw the program not only in terms of their own futures but also as a conduit of welcome income support for aging relatives (Kingson, Hirshorn, and Cornman, 1986). Social

Security got chipped away at, especially in the Amendments of 1983 (Svahn and Ross, 1983), but its essence was preserved.

After decades of growth and expansion, however, there is little doubt that the welfare state is in decline in the United States for the foreseeable future, and that the elderly will necessarily be adversely affected. In the next section, the emergence, growth, and diversity of income security programs in the United States until toward the end of the 1970s will be described briefly.

Brief History of Income Security Programs in the United States

"There is no reason why everybody in the United States shouldn't be covered. I see no reason why every child from the day he is born shouldn't be a member of the social security system. When he begins to grow up, he should know he will have old age benefits direct from the insurance system to which he will belong all his life. If he is out of work, he gets a benefit. If he is sick or crippled, he gets a benefit" (Perkins, 1946). This was the way Franklin D. Roosevelt was heard to describe his plans for Social Security over and over again to his closest collaborators in 1933. The legislation that was passed in 1935 did not meet these universal cradle-to-the-grave standards. Over the next several decades, however, the Social Security system has become by far the strongest pillar for financial support for old people. Over 90 percent of those 65 and over have qualified for benefits since the 1970s (Kennedy, Thomas, and Schmulowicz, 1975).

The United States was unusually reluctant and tardy in its entry into the welfare field. As Bremner (1956) described the situation, from the value perspective of "rugged individualism" the very notion of a system of relief seemed blasphemous. Most western industrialized countries moved into old age pension systems between 1880 and 1922. From the 1930s to the 1950s these initial programs were elaborated into comprehensive systems of income support and social insurance that encompassed entire national populations (Flora and Heidenheimer, 1981). In the United States almost nothing federal of any scope was implemented before the "Big Bang" of the Social Security Act of 1935 (Furniss and Tilton, 1977). By that time, the nation was beset by bankruptcies, bank failures, and staggering unemployment (Schlesinger, 1977). Data from that period emphasize that older people were the most affected by these disastrous conditions (Douglas, 1939). Economic insecurity was the focus of a number of new efforts (Achenbaum, 1978), but none of the measures taken brought relief to more than a small proportion of the population. Federal intervention received massive popular support, although there was considerable opposition from both political and private sector sources when Roosevelt attempted to enact Social Security legislation (Altmeyer, 1966; Leuchtenberg, 1963; Witte, 1962).

With curtailments and compromises the Act of 1935 was passed. Core welfare state policies such as old age pensions and social insurance did belatedly emerge in the United States, although national health insurance never did make it through the legislative process (Weir, Orloff, and Skopol, 1988). For decades after the New Deal era there was a commitment to minimize the impact of a market economy on the financial fortunes of its citizens, but movement towards adequate coverage has been incremental with various social benefits often remaining fiscally and symbolically separated (Weir, et al., 1988). Nevertheless, steady growth occurred through the early 1970s. As will be discussed shortly, one reason for growth, but also for lack of governmental control over some income programs, was the encouragement in the United States for private sector involvement in the welfare state (Stevens, 1988).

Social Insurance

The Social Security legislation which was passed in 1935 actually contained two separate parts or Titles. Title I encompassed social assistance, a set of means-tested income benefit programs for the indigent, including Old Age Assistance. Title II, which is what most people mean when they refer to Social Security, encompassed the key social insurance programs. The insurance programs also include unemployment compensation and benefits to the permanently disabled, but Social Security is best known for financial support to the elderly. Social insurance is a system whereby people are compelled through payroll taxes to insure themselves against the possibility of their own indigence resulting from the loss of a job, the death of the family breadwinner, or physical disability (Karger and Stoesz, 1990).

There was considerable political struggle as to whether the new Social Security insurance programs should be financed out of general revenues or out of the employees' pockets (Karger and Stoesz, 1990). In the end a compromise was reached and joint employee-employer contributions were agreed upon (Rich and Baum, 1984). The intention of Title II of the Social Security Act was to maintain income within some limits by replacing lost earnings. It is universal coverage: the individual must make a contribution, but then he or she and any survivors are entitled to benefits. Social Security was designed to have and continues to have redistributive properties via the adequacy principle which allocates 90 percent of past earnings to beneficiaries in the lowest income brackets. At the same time it offers additional compensation through the equity principle by allowing higher earners to receive additional benefits in sharply decreasing proportions from a second and third bracket representing middle and high incomes (Rich and Baum, 1984). The payroll tax is regressive in the sense that it is only levied up to a certain amount of salary or wages, and thus the highest earners are not fully taxed (Rich and Baum, 1984).

The system got off to a modest start with a payroll tax of one percent—to be matched by the employer—on the first $3,000 of income. Other features such as disability and hospital insurance were added over time, and the tax generally increased until by 1984 the rate was seven percent for both employee and employer, covering incomes up to $37,000 (Rich and Baum, 1984). And payments continue to increase, although Congress is beginning to be disturbed by the evidence that Social Security taxes are biting more and more heavily into the paychecks of lower-income people while "reforms" in income tax rates have favored the well-to-do (*New York Times*, March 25, 1990). Taking all things together, income after taxes and transfers was more unequal in the United States in 1985 than it had been in 1966 (Pechman, 1985). By 1988 the United States was paying out 26 percent of Gross National Product (GNP) for all social insurance programs and the largest proportion of monies by far was going to elderly retirees and survivors. By contrast, the public assistance programs cost only 10 percent of GNP (U.S. Bureau of the Census, 1988b). In 1984 the average OASDHI (Old Age, Survivors, Disabled and Hospital Insurance) beneficiary received $460.47 a month while the average Supplementary Security Income (SSI) recipient received only $221.87 a month (Rosen, Fanshel, and Leitz, 1987).

The economic well-being of the elderly generally has improved as Social Security underwent modifications through the 1950s, 1960s, and 1970s (Clark, 1990). In the early phase only about 50 to 60 percent of older persons were covered by social insurance, but by 1985 91 percent of households aged 65 years of age and over were receiving some benefits from this source (Schorr, 1986).

In the 1970s real benefits were increased with the introduction of Cost of Living Adjustments (COLAs) to increase benefits to match rises in prices or rises in wages. But this double standard for triggering increases was deemed too costly and it was "decoupled" in 1977 (Robertson, 1978). The relevant Amendment to the Act was modified to address inflation only and with specific stipulations. There continued to be increases in payroll contributions and tax rates to match the new benefits (Cianciolo, 1990). Nevertheless, the program was viewed as an enormous success (Karger and Stoesz, 1990). Without Social Security, according to Harrington (1987), the poverty rate for the elderly would have soared compared with that of the total population, rather than declining steadily since 1969.

But there were portents of troubled times to come. In the late 1970s President Carter faced a deteriorating economy and was trying hard to balance supporting social programs with fiscal conservatism (Hargrove, 1988). Expanding entitlement did not fit easily with a resurgent free market capitalist ideology (Myles, 1984).

Supplemental Security Income

Supplementary Security Income is the successor to public assistance programs for the needy aged, blind, and disabled. Old Age Assistance had been one of the key features of the original Social Security Act (Title I). When states chose to comply with federal requirements, the federal government paid one-half of the assistance payment in accordance with a matching formula (Schottland, 1968). Although eventually all states participated, the monthly supplements the states added to the universal federal grant varied widely. In 1973, for example, when the program was about to be terminated, six states had average payments below $60 monthly while nine states had payments above $100 (Kennedy, Thomas, and Schmulowitz, 1975). These public assistance programs are the ones labelled "safety net," but in reality there were 51 safety nets, counting all the 50 states and the District of Columbia, each of which had its own eligibility criteria and payment standards (Schorr, 1986).

In 1972 legislation was passed in an effort to remedy the plight of the poorest of the poor. President Richard Nixon proposed a Family Assistance Plan to place an income floor under all the people of the United States (Karger and Stoesz, 1990). This proposal was rejected but a compromise plan, Supplemental Security Income (SSI), was accepted, which replaced Old Age Assistance altogether. Under Title VI of the Act the aged, the blind, and the totally and permanently disabled were to be provided with a "federally guaranteed" income administered by the Social Security Administration (Ball, 1973). It was a "first and only" program in the United States to guarantee support to the "worthy poor," but it remained a public assistance and not an insurance program (Burke and Burke, 1974). In passing the legislation Congress made SSI recipients ineligible for Food Stamps. This was a program on which many impoverished older persons had come to depend, and 45 of the 50 states enacted their own legislation by 1975 granting automatic eligibility to Food Stamps for SSI recipients (U.S. House Select Committee on Aging, 1975). There is a very small income and assets disregard for recipients, and in 1987 the maximum benefit was 74.8 percent and 88.9

percent of the poverty level for elderly individuals and couples respectively (Karger and Stoesz, 1990).

The cash assistance from SSI is meager, and some 27 states offer a supplement to the payment as expected by the federal government. However, these payment supplements in the large majority of cases do not bring the total payment above the poverty line (Rich and Baum, 1984). State contributions tended to be small, and many of the 51 "safety nets" reneged altogether (Rich and Baum, 1984). At least under the Social Security Administration the SSI purchasing power remains fairly constant since the poverty threshold is adjusted yearly by using the Consumer Price Index (CPI) (Derthick, 1979; U.S. Bureau of the Census, 1984). It has been argued, however, that the poverty index is an inadequate measure of what it takes to support a household. The index is calculated based on the estimate of food costs for the household times three, on the assumption that food should cost about one-third of household maintenance needs. Not only is the cost of food based on the Thrifty Food Plan, which is an emergency diet and inadequate for regular use, but other household maintenance costs have risen more rapidly than food over recent years (Munnell, 1982).

An estimated 45 percent of eligible old people do not enroll in SSI (Menafee, Edwards, and Schieber, 1981). It is not clear whether failure to enroll is primarily due to the humiliating means testing procedures for income and assets or simply to lack of knowledge of program availability (Schorr, 1986). Whatever the reason, not participating makes the elderly poor person have great difficulty obtaining Medicaid (The Common Good, 1989). Other elderly may lose Medicaid because not all states automatically grant eligibility to SSI recipients (Rich and Baum, 1984). Medicaid can be highly beneficial since it covers long-term care, an issue American politicians have as yet failed to address.

Twenty-one states have a General Assistance program that serves a similar clientele. Aged, blind or disabled, and dependent individuals and families who fall through the safety net may receive help from this source (Karger and Stoesz, 1990). These state- and 10 community-administered programs usually offer assistance only to a very restricted clientele, and the grants tend to be very small.

There were many elderly who were left out of the improved well-being for older people in the 1960s and 1970s, and some of the in-kind programs that augmented their resources were curtailed in the last decade (Clark, 1990). Beyond elderly below the poverty line, there are also a large group of "tweeters," whose incomes are just above the poverty line and so deprive them of SSI related in-kind services (Smeeding, 1986). Many needy elderly did not get a sufficient Social Security check and had to be supplemented by SSI. Others had only SSI to turn to. Better off old people had additional sources of income.

Private Pension Plans

Social benefits to retirees have grown in part due to the encouragement of the United States government for the private sector to become involved in the welfare state (Stevens, 1988). Private-sector benefits, originally known as "welfare capitalism," have a long history in this country (Brandes, 1976). Building schools, housing, even whole towns for workers and their families were ventures in an early paternalistic phase. Soon, however, efforts of private companies became more modest and centered on financial support during crises and on pension plans (Brody, 1980). A very wide variety of organizations both public and private are now involved in the unpenetrable tangle sometimes referred to as the "welfare mess" (Morris, 1986; Stoesz, 1989).

Although it was developed in the latter part of the nineteenth century, the concept of the pension plan had the most rapid growth after the 1950s (Rich and Baum, 1984). Pension plans were inaugurated in response to labor demands when the government refused to act, and millions of workers became involved, but the private pension often proved to be a delusion because of fraud, mismanagement, and restrictive rules for distributing benefits. As a Department of Labor official declared in testimony before Congress, if you remain in good health and stay with the same company until you are 65 years old and if the company is still in business, and if your department has not been abolished, and if you haven't been laid off for too long a period, and if there is enough money in the fund, and if the fund has been prudently managed, you will get a pension (U.S. Department of Labor, 1971).

After several ineffective attempts at corrective legislation, the Employee Retirement Income Security Act (ERISA) was enacted in 1974 (Cummings, 1974). The Act did not require employers to have pension plans, an omission that has been highly criticized because of consequent inequities in income among retirees (Crystal, 1982). It did, however, establish certain protection addressing the two major deficiencies discovered in private pension plans: bad management and the denial of benefits due to an interrupted work schedule or insufficient years in a company (U.S. Department of Labor, 1975). Issues of fairness and universal access still attracted unfavorable attention, and efforts were made but without success to create a Minimum Universal Pension System (MUPS) (President's Commission on Pension Policy, 1981).

ERISA did address other issues around pensions. Before the entry of the federal government, business, and also state and local governments, played an important role in pensions (Berkowitz and McQuaid, 1980). A few selected federal employee groups were covered by pension plans even before Social Security, and there were a plethora of state and local community retirement pension plans (Tilove, 1976). These latter were likely to be highly unstable because of political overpromising and the precarious financing underlying lower level public pension plans (Achenbaum, 1986). ERISA provided more stability by linking many of the programs with Social Security (Rich and Baum, 1984). Efforts are still ongoing, however, to create a uniform integrated system out of a public pension assortment still fraught with inequities (Crandall, 1980).

Private pensions were encouraged by the federal government through incentives which tax exempted employee and employer benefits. Those who contributed to private pension plans were "sheltered" from taxation until drawing income in retirement. After a slow start in the 1950s, by 1980 pension plan benefits were being distributed to one-fifth of older Americans and almost half of the labor force was enrolled (Grad, 1983). Since the late 1970s private pension coverage has declined moderately (The Common Good, 1989). The decline or levelling off is occurring even though ERISA produced two models to increase pension coverage.

The Keogh Act was legislated in 1962 to assist the self-employed who were not covered by private pensions. Such workers could yearly contribute a portion of their incomes to a fund that was tax free and accrued tax free interest. The contributions increased over time until, by 1988, 20 percent of earned self-employment income to a maximum of $30,000 of net income (i.e. minus business expenses) could be contributed (Bernstein, 1990). In 1984 Congress decided that persons with self-employment should be given "pension parity" with corporations. As a result, those eligible for Defined Benefit Keogh Plans, such as physicians in private practice, can sometimes shelter nearly all of their net earnings (Bernstein, 1990).

Provision was also made through ERISA for the individual who is not covered by any employer pension plan through Individual Retirement Accounts (IRAs). An eligible worker can deposit up to 15 percent of income, not to exceed $2,000, into a tax sheltered plan (Rich and Baum, 1984). The overt intent of IRAs was to help the worker who was least likely to be included in private pension plans. But initial provisions of the 1981 Economic Recovery and Tax Act also were aimed at undermining Social Security (Karger and Stoesz, 1990). By allowing annual contributions to IRAs to be deducted from Social Security payroll taxes, workers would be encouraged to use those taxes for IRA investments (Ferrara, 1984). This plan was blocked, but for several years constraints were relaxed so that those who already had private pension plans could also participate in tax-sheltered IRAs. By 1983 20 percent of the population had IRAs. Thirty-five billion dollars were transferred to IRA accounts in 1983 and again in 1984. Tax-sheltered IRAs are still available but tax-sheltering is again only available to a limited segment of the population.

There are an incredibly large number of private pension plans and the diversity at face value seems great (Ippolito, 1990; Quinn and Burkhauser, 1990). Most worker participants, however, about 80 percent, are enrolled in Defined Benefit Programs where pension benefits are federally guaranteed up to a stipulated maximum should plans be terminated (Clark and

McDermed, 1988). Only certain segments of the population participate. Union workers, full-time wage and salaried workers, and those earning higher incomes are far more likely to benefit. Because the results are so inequitable, there is cause for concern over the revenues in taxes foregone by sheltering private pensions (Karger and Stoesz, 1990, p. 130). In 1985 alone lost taxes from all private pension plans taken together amounted to $66 billion. Overall, those who will receive least income from private pensions are the ones who will get least from public sources as well. Even for those included, there is a degree of uncertainty about eventual outcomes that governmental regulations have only partially remedied (Clark and McDermed, 1988). And private pensions do not speak to compensation for inflation; the COLAs in the public sector are not matched in the private sector.

Many questions have been raised about private pension plans in their present forms given available data (Munnell, 1982; Rankin, 1984). Private pension advocates have claimed that pensions encourage investment while Social Security taxes work against investment, but a recent investigation into this hypothesis found no supporting evidence (Merton and Bernstein, 1987). Nor apparently can Social Security alone be blamed for the early exodus of older persons from the labor force, since a recent survey (The Employee Benefit Research Institute, 1986) found most private employers have instituted pension provisions that embody strong incentives to older workers to retire early. Both the public sector and the private sector are evidently working together to reduce significantly the size of the 65-and-over work force. The Reverse Annuity Mortgage (RAM) has not drawn a large response from the elderly for whom it was designed (The Common Good, 1989). Moon (1977) explains that the value of home equity is adjusted downward to allow the older occupants to remain in their home during the remaining lifetime. The reduced amount of the granted mortgage is treated as a rental fee. The bargain sounds tempting, but few older people derive any useful income from their homes (Struyk and Soldo, 1980). The market appears potentially large but about 40 percent of older Americans are renting or living in the homes of others, and another more than 10 percent still owe money to the bank (Kendig, 1990). Many more homes owned by the elderly are of insufficient value for equity (The Common Good, 1989), and institutional barriers such as contingency clauses have made others hesitant to engage in RAMs (Hancock, 1987; Wheeler, 1986). Finally, some older people refuse to encumber their estates for surviving relatives through remortgaging.

Overall, then, the mix of public and private income security options has increased over recent decades, and so has the relative well-being of the aged in the United States. The 1980s have brought threats to Social Security and more and more dependence on the private sector, which serves segments of society which have more resources. Existing inequities have as a result deepened over the 1980 decade, as will be considered in the next segment.

Income Security in the 1980s and Beyond

After a difficult start, retirement came to be seen as a "good thing" by all ages in the United States population (Rose and Mogey, 1972; Harris, 1978). Retirement no longer was perceived as a "roleless role" (Burgess, 1960) but more as an earned privilege and an opportunity (Miller, 1965). Major studies carried out in the late 1960s and early 1970s showed large majorities of retired people expressing satisfaction with the experience (Cottrell and Atchley, 1969; Heidbreder, 1972; Streib and Schneider, 1971). Much of the acceptance of the retirement status could be laid to trust in a "social contract" for income protection in old age as symbolized by the Social Security Act in the United States (Baum and Baum, 1980).

Data from the early 1980s (Munnell, 1982) show Social Security provides the largest share (40 percent) of over-65 household income. Using 1984 data, Ycas and Grad (1987) show similar patterns of resource distribution and break the overall pattern down into income groups. Again about two-fifths (38 percent) of all income for aged households comes from Social Security; only one percent is from public assistance (SSI). Assets such as property, savings, and stock and bond holdings account for 28 percent of income for all aged households; earnings contribute 16 percent of income. Private pensions, though presumably very widespread, contribute only six percent. Looking at opposite income extremes within aged households, the breakdown by income source shifts. Aged households with incomes of less than $5,000 depend on Social Security for 77 percent of their income and public assistance for 14 percent. Only one percent stems from private pensions. Even at the opposite or higher income end, aged households with incomes of $20,000 or more depend on Social Security for one-fifth or 20 percent of their incomes. Special government pensions make a relatively large contribution, close to 10 percent, to these better off households, but assets (39 percent) followed by earnings (23 percent) are the largest contributors. It is worth noting that the proportion coming from private pensions for these better off aged households is not different from that of all such households—only 6 percent.

The dependence of the poorest households on Social Security for what is obviously a very meager income but just about all they have is enormous. In the late 1970s and early 1980s, the very existence of this insurance plan for old age was threatened. Economic deterioration accompanied by high inflation and other factors made Social Security financing inadequate (U.S. Senate Special Committee on Aging, 1981). A Harris poll (December, 1981) uncovered a crisis of confidence among the people of the United States. Three national groups, the Advisory Council on Social Security, the National Committee on Social Security Reform, and the President's Commission on Pension Policy developed recommendations for "saving Social Security" (Rich and Baum, 1984, p. 68).

At the same time attacks on the system were mounting, and the weaknesses of the economy were blamed on the excesses of the welfare state. Public uncertainty and the ambivalence of many Americans toward centralized government provided presidential candidate and later President Reagan with an opportunity for an integrated ideological attack (Glazer, 1984). The Reagan administration was bolstered by a Republican majority in the Senate and by contributions from conservative "think tanks," such as the American Enterprise Institute and Heritage House (Karger and Stoesz, 1990). The responses of more liberal analysts during this period were vacillating (Schultze, 1977) or defensive (Howe, 1982; Piven and Cloward, 1971). By the mid to late 1980s well-known academicians such as Murray (1984) and Sandell (1988) proclaimed the New Deal to be dead and its agenda obsolete. But the conservative "agenda" did not completely overcome the welfare state and its popularity.

In spite of all the controversy, Social Security was "saved" (Svahn and Ross, 1983). In April, 1983 President Reagan signed into law the new Social Security Amendments passed in that year, praising the bipartisan compromise that culminated in the Amendments. As Svahn and Ross (1983) note, the compromise tried to reconcile the widespread support for Social Security with the undeniable evidence that OASDI expenditures had exceeded revenues since 1975. The major changes in the Act included the following (Svahn and Ross, 1983, pp. 22–23).

1. Delay the annual cost of living benefits (COLAs) from June to January of each year. (SSI recipients were exempted from this wage/price "stabilizer" provision and SSI couples were granted a very small increase in benefits).
2. Make up to half the benefits received by higher income beneficiaries subject to income taxes.
3. Gradually raise the retirement age for benefits early in the next century: from 2015 on one must be 66 to receive full benefits (and Medicare).
4. Called for earlier implementation of scheduled payroll tax increases.

These changes have affected all Social Security beneficiaries and future beneficiaries to some extent, and accelerated payroll taxes implemented several times during the 1980s placed an unexpectedly heavy burden on those still in the labor force. A festering problem is that the surplus revenues being created by these sacrifices were to be placed in a special fund to guarantee pensions for an anticipated boom in retirees and their dependents. At the present time the federal government is treating the surplus as general revenue, however, and it could well be diverted into current consumption (The Common Good, 1989). Although temporarily saved, Social Security remains in jeopardy (Munnell, 1982).

A brief note on health care is introduced at this point because there is such an impact on income security for the elderly. In spite of large expenditures on Medicare ($100 billion per year) and Medicaid ($50 billion per year) (Gibson and Waldo, 1981), the elderly are highly vulnerable to financial deprivation through ill health (The Common Good, 1989). Medicare is running out of funds even as the mandated hospital insurance has become almost useless for many eligible elderly because of increases in pre-payments and co-payments (Moon and Smeeding, 1989). Long-term care has become a harsh necessity for steadily increasing numbers of handicapped old persons, but nursing home costs are enormous and Medicare covers only the most modest fraction of such costs (The Common Good, 1989). Medicaid does include nursing care for the eligible poor, but those who are not poor must "spend down" and become destitute before they are eligible. Mentally ill older people tend to be warehoused untreated in state hospitals (Biegel and Farkas, 1989), a policy that affects proportionately more minority elderly than non-minority (Markides and Mindel, 1987).

Relief at the continuation of Social Security has led to some underestimation of the impact on those over 65 in the 1980s. Clark (1990) points out that there has been an erosion in income security resources for older people in a number of ways. The social tide has turned from increasing real benefits in Social Security to reducing the generosity of future benefits. SSI, food stamps, Medicaid, and other in-kind benefits were curtailed in the 1980s. The elderly poor in fact have not fared well since 1982 when the impact of the 1981 legislation began to be felt (Morris, 1987). As Burt and Pittman (1985) suggest, the extent of this adverse impact is difficult to estimate. For those receiving only SSI, cuts in in-kind services may amount to 10 percent or more of their average federal paychecks (Burt and Pittman, 1985). "Block" grants to the states under the Omnibus Budget and Reconciliation Act transferred more responsibilities to the states along with cuts in appropriations. While all states did not suffer equally, it has been estimated that the cuts created losses of around 4.0 percent of income in all households with $10,000 or less (Moon and Sawhill, 1984).

Budget cuts were very severe for voluntary social welfare agencies under the Reagan administration. Between 1982 and 1985 these non-profit agencies, which make extensive use of voluntary personnel and provide services for all age groups, lost $9 billion or 35 percent of federal aid (Schorr, 1986). These monies were not recouped: appeals to private corporations to furnish more assistance were not heeded, and private individuals have less discretionary income due to family income declines in the late 1970s through 1985 (Economic Policy Institute, 1986).

The federal government has been whittling away at Social Security with COLA delays and taxes on benefits. The "savings" from taxing the pensions of the relatively well-off elderly are not applied to helping those with inadequate income in old age who, as always, are the big losers (Weir, et al., 1988). Many have worked most of their adult lives but never received wages sufficient to rise above poverty (Levitan and Shapiro, 1987). In 1987 13.6 percent of the elderly were in extreme poverty; 8.6 percent of men 65 and over and 15.2 percent of women. Income deficiencies for both groups increase with age. For men 85 years of age and over the proportion in extreme poverty rises to 13.3 percent; for women 85 and over to 19.7 percent. The highest incidence of poverty occurred among the oldest widows relying entirely on Social Security benefits (U.S. Senate Special Committee on Aging, 1988). Inequities in the treatment of women originating from the onset of Social Security have persisted in spite of attempts at remediation (Schulz, 1988). Sidel (1986) shows that one in five older women live in poverty, and that about 90 percent of such women are single, that is, either never married, widowed, or divorced. These women had histories of low paying jobs, little savings, no private pensions, and little from Social Security (Estes, Gerard, and Clark, 1984). Whether husbands were deceased or divorced, little was left to their former wives. Among these virtually destitute old women, minorities were over-represented; while 13.1 percent of white were represented, 21.1 percent were Hispanic, 35.5 percent were black, and 30.3 percent were other minorities, i.e., Native American Indians and Asian/Pacific Islanders (Sidel, 1986).

Markides and Mindel (1987) demonstrate the relative poverty of all minority aged, although men are not as deprived as women relatively speaking. They cogently argue that ethnic minorities are disadvantaged by a "social insurance" that is intended to be only a supplement to savings and other pension programs. Because minority members in the United States are likely to be ineligible for private pension programs and subject to long periods of unemployment or underemployment which reduce public benefits, they are doubly disadvantaged all their lives and on into old age (Markides and Mindel, 1987).

Income security in the United States in old age is currently an issue of concern. The mainstay Social Security is under continuous attack, and the "safety net" is visibly full of holes. Other post-industrial countries are often doing better by social welfare.

Comparing Social Welfare States

The strong responsibilities of the Western European and other nation states to promote the public welfare are not fundamentally challenged (Weir, et al., 1988). In the United States, however, the legitimacy of the welfare role of the federal government is a matter of debate. We do comparatively less for our citizens but let them go without any very serious attempt at salvage (Myles, 1984). Although other nations also face economic problems and have aging populations at least as advanced, the long-standing commitment to public pensions as the only way to ensure adequate and socially acceptable levels of income distribution to older members endures (Schulz and Myles, 1990). The United States, by contrast, seems to have accepted the notion of an "inexorable limit of welfare capitalism" as other nations have not (Flora and Heidenheimer, 1981). This country seems to be backing off far more rapidly given rising costs of social provision and increased attention to "individual enhancement" (Morris, 1987). The United States will pass over the responsibility to the private sector for the delivery of services, even though the "market approach" to health care has been a dismal failure (Morris, 1987).

Although threatened by assertions about economic breakdown and dismayed by the worst recession since the 1930s (Wilensky, 1976; O'Connor, 1973), most welfare states do not appear to be seriously endangered (Heidenheimer, Heclo, and Teich-Adams, 1983). They exhibited patterns of rapid growth after World War II and into the mid-seventies, at which point growth slowed sharply (Friedman, 1987). The commitment to insure some stability in citizen well-being to shelter against the turbulence of global economics, however, remains intact (Sherer, 1987). The general situation in Western Europe, Canada, and to a lesser extent the United Kingdom can best be described as undergoing adjustment and retrenchment.

The United Kingdom probably comes closest to the United States in recent efforts to reduce welfare expenditures and involve the private sector (Critchfield, 1990), although Judge (1987) maintains that the change represents a shift to a "mixed economy" of welfare rather than a divesting of responsibility by the government. Like the United States and the United Kingdom, Canada also chose a conservative government in the 1980s, but that country has retained its social welfare provision with modest retrenchment and some reevaluation of the programs in reaching the poor (Torczyner, 1987). In Italy public social expenditures have actually continued to rise well into the 1980s, but recently growth has begun to slow as it did earlier in other countries (Ascoli, 1987). West Germany and Sweden have remained comprehensive welfare states. West Germany became the first nation to adopt pension programs and, with minor adjustments, that country remains a comparatively equitable and adequate welfare system (Federico, 1984, p. 64). Sweden underwent a temporary political upheaval in the early to mid-1980s about social provision, which eventually led to some service consolidation, but the welfare state has become an irreversible fact of life in twentieth-century Sweden (Olson, 1987).

The United States has spent heavily on service provision but done less well in caring for the poor. In a highly informative summary of the adjusted disposable income levels for the elderly in eight different countries, Smeeding (1990) demonstrates that the United States is in the solid middle range for national mean income for all persons 65 and over, with only the Netherlands doing much better and the United Kingdom, Australia, and West Germany scoring lower. Canada, Sweden, and Norway are in the same range of means as the United States. If, however, the percent of elderly below the poverty line is the subject of consideration, the United States has a far larger proportion of poor old people than any other country except the United Kingdom (Smeeding, 1990). Excluding Israel, which is a special case in this context, the United States has in fact a far larger proportion of people in poverty after reaching age 65 than Australia, Canada, West Germany, and Switzerland. In Sweden, the Netherlands, and Norway the proportion of elderly below the poverty line is infinitesimal. A partial explanation of this apparent contradiction between mean adjusted disposable incomes and proportions below the poverty line lies in the fact that the mean obscures larger variabilities within age groups in the United States. In this country there are relatively small percentages of middle-class elderly but relatively large proportions of well-off elderly, a distribution which distorts the mean upward. The United States has more inequality in income distribution among its elderly population than other countries (Smeeding, 1990).

The United States, once moving upward steadily if gradually, has been withdrawing very heavily from its welfare state commitment. Compared with other countries the federal state has attempted far more radically to shed responsibilities for citizen welfare. Other countries face uncertain economic futures, fears about unemployment, and huge numbers of persons 65 and over. Except for the United Kingdom, however, they are engaged in rather modest adjustments which make the extent of decentralization and privatization in the United States appear extreme. These factors will necessarily intrude on the social work profession and social work roles.

The Roles of Social Workers

The United States has not succeeded in establishing a sense of national community (Schorr, 1986). This country inched for several decades toward the acceptance of ultimate federal responsibility for citizen well-being, but then retreated. Social provision increasingly has been shifted toward individual states and communities whether or not these public entities are willing and/or able to take on the task. Public entities are advised to seek partnerships with private for-profit organizations to accomplish service goals. Inevitably, the traditional settings providing care have lost ground to other arrangements. The impact on the roles of social workers—and on the profession itself—are likely to be profound.

Karger and Stoesz (1990), using a structural approach, lucidly discuss the shift from an emphasis on government and voluntary agencies as the primary sectors of social provision to a new scene where the corporate sector and private practice are taking over much of the territory. Social work, as a profession, grew from a spirit of altruism and concern for others, and practitioners were prepared to address social problems other groups spurned. Although uncomfortable with the bureaucratic inability to respond effectively to human needs in the particular, social workers nevertheless often played influential roles in federal and state bureaucracies. In the voluntary sector, in agencies operating for "cost" not profit, social workers could be more creative and respond to the grass roots. Under Reagan voluntary agencies were financially starved, and government bureaucratic intervention decreased.

The corporate sector, unfamiliar ground to social workers, by contrast, increasingly exploits growing service markets in long-term care, health maintenance, and corrections. What is perhaps most troubling to social welfare professionals in this development is that the profit motive inhibits the provision of goods and services to uninsured persons of limited means. Social workers are unused to the priorities of corporate management, but social workers are nevertheless beginning to participate as clinical practitioners in Employee Assistance Programs, and industrial social work programs are growing.

As opportunities in the traditional bases of service provision have declined, the interest of social workers in private practice has increased. If economic opportunities for professionals in private practice to serve the disadvantaged are preserved either directly or indirectly, then the traditional social work mission will be continued. But many in the profession fear that as social work becomes commercialized, there will be a turning away from public welfare and grassroots service.

As welfare policy becomes fragmented over the public and private sectors and Federal authority diminishes, it will doubtless become more difficult for social workers to address the issues that lead to program change as they have in the past. Lowy (1985) saw direct service social workers as providing data to shape policy and planning from a front-line advocacy perspective. Social workers engaged in indirect service such as administration and planning would use the knowledge accumulated to move outward both within and without the social work profession to present a coherent brief for supporting people in need. Being situated in human service corporations or in private practice as these sectors grow and traditional settings shrink will inevitably produce more conflict within the profession and make bridges to other interested parties more difficult.

Yet as Federico (1984) very persuasively demonstrates, the need for humane and adequate welfare programs persists. There are new technological advances supposedly designed to improve human lives, but social change of this nature has produced other problems in this country, such as boredom, apathy, drug dependence, and, most fundamentally, the specter of unemployment and underemployment coupled with a greater likelihood that disadvantaged social members will be pushed farther out of the mainstream. The unique ability of the social worker to speak to social problems attacking society persists even during, perhaps especially during, social change. It follows that social workers should continue to fulfill the functions just mentioned. In addition, social workers should also work with members of this society to help them to understand changes, to participate in processes that affect change, and to become linked to the resources needed. Federico cites four areas currently of special relevance for social welfare that are particularly pertinent for the present and future fate of the aged population in the United States.

1. Poverty and the under-class phenomenon have grown in response to Reagan attacks on programs for the poor, who are increasingly isolated from the mainstream. There are also "new poor" groups who are homeless and rootless as a consequence of the early 1980s recession, from which many once steady workers have never re-

covered. This economically and socially afflicted cohort has already had its impact on older people and will continue to do so more visibly as larger proportions move into old age.

2. Both immigration patterns and population growth need attention. Immigrants from Asia are currently victims of persecution, and, unlike earlier waves, are poor, uneducated, unskilled, and non-English speaking. This is true of Cubans and Haitians as well. Population growth is highest among Hispanics who are over-reaching blacks on birth rates. Recent immigrants and growing numbers of ethnic minorities, over-represented among the elderly poor even now, threaten to increase in the future.
3. Changing life styles have led to a very diverse constellation such as single parents, divorced parents, two-earner families, step-parent families, individuals living alone, all of which contribute to a family base from which it is more difficult to give assistance to the growing number of old people who are highly dependent on families financially as well as in other life spheres.
4. Changing regional relations include the clustering of immigrants and old people in selected areas of the country, and the movement of younger persons out of depressed industrial and sunbelt areas seeking better work opportunities. Some elderly benefit by the ability to move to more desirable climates, but increasingly elderly persons will find themselves subsisting in inhospitable regional areas or left behind as their children move away to seek greener pastures.

Problems and Prospects

Many elderly in the United States have an apparently solid base of income security. Buffered by Social Security and with other financial means at their disposal, people over 65 can enjoy some well earned leisure after retirement from a long work life and the empty nest. For all the income security programs intended for the elderly, however, a large proportion of older people are in poverty or near-poverty. The well-being may be transitory. There is no integration among the various programs, and most programs—even Social Security—favor those who were better off over their earlier lifetimes and thus able to shore up financial resources. Social Security continues to slip, always causing income injury via delaying COLAs to all elderly but especially injuring those who already have the least. The data on younger cohorts suggest that the apparent affluence of the elderly is a passing stage in American life as more of our people will reach old age with fewer income supports, although the numbers will increase for the next several decades. Especially frightening for many old people—and their children as well—is the prospect of illness and incapacitation. Unlike other countries, the United States offers no universal health coverage or insurance.

The problems detailed by Federico make it imperative for the elderly and those who give them informal support that the Federal government grasp firm control in at least two areas of life. While some observers of the scene call for targeting to reduce expenditures for social welfare in a multi-cultural society such as our own, in the United States only the universal program of social insurance, Social Security, has worked. It has been frequently suggested, however, that this standby is badly in need of reform. One frequent idea has been to improve on the idea of a guaranteed income for everyone in the United States by ensuring an above-the-poverty-line, regularly adjusted for inflation payment. The monies would come from general revenues and thus apply universally but allow everyone to contribute according to ability to pay. The other area is of course universal basic health care, perhaps modeled after the Canadian system. Both of these initiatives would go far to solve some of the most urgent issues in aging which are mounting steadily. Social workers could advocate for these initiatives across all settings in which they work and with all others engaged in social welfare activities from whatever perspective or position. The corporate sector would very probably draw sighs of relief for the most part, for they are finding fringe benefit activities increasingly burdensome. Social workers in the traditional realms and in private practice would surely benefit in their efforts to help all in need.

These prospects could well come to pass since poverty and associated problems are burgeoning in this society, and they would quite effectively serve the most basic needs of all persons but especially the most disadvantaged elderly whose ranks are certain to swell in future years. It also would prevent the potentially disruptive specter—already beginning to emerge—of people moving from state to state seeking the best bargains in economic and health benefits. These might not be the elderly themselves, but it could be younger relatives the elders would much miss. Aged minorities and recent very needy immigrants would also have a solid enough support floor, so that they need not compete with one another for resources or become pariahs in the areas where they live. One of the reasons for federal intervention in the first place in this country was the inequities among the states in serving the people. The states are hurting fiscally and being challenged over unequal treatment by their residents. Now is the time to go really federal for the basic needs. If tax breaks were reduced for the private sector, the "new" Social Security would be affordable, for universal programs are inexpensive administratively. The government could support research in health care at a socially acceptable level but leave much of the expensive technologically advanced innovative treatments to the private sector. These prospects seem feasible, for the social fabric is deteriorating, as the mass media continually report. All problems, of course, will by no means be solved. But social workers would be buttressed in their work at state and local levels to pursue their mission with individuals, families, support groups, and communities.

REFERENCES

Abramovitz, M. 1988. *Regulating the Lives of Women: Social Welfare Policy from Colonial Times to the Present.* Boston: Southend Press.

Achenbaum, A.W. 1978. *Old Age in the New Land: The American Experiences Since 1790.* Baltimore, MD: The Johns Hopkins University Press.

———. 1986. *Social Security: Visions and Revisions.* Cambridge, MA: Cambridge University Press.

Altmeyer, A. 1966. *The Formative Years of Social Security.* Madison, WI: University of Wisconsin Press.

Atchley, R.C. 1980. *The Social Forces in Later Life.* Belmont, CA: Wadsworth.

Ball, R. 1973. Social Security Amendments of 1972: Summary and Legislative History. *Social Security Bulletin, 3,* 25.

Baum, M. & Baum, R.C. 1980. *Growing Old: A Societal Perspective.* Englewood Cliffs, NJ: Prentice-Hall.

Berkowitz, E. & McQuaid, K. 1980. *Creating the Welfare State: The Political Economy of Welfare Reform.* New York: Praeger.

Bernstein, A. 1990. *Tax Guide for College Teachers.* Washington, DC: Academic Information Service.

Biegel, D.E. & Farkas, K.J. 1989. *Mental health and the elderly: Service delivery issues.* Western Reserve Geriatric Education Center. Interdisciplinary Monograph Series. Cleveland, OH: Case Western Reserve University.

Brandes, S. 1976. *American Welfare Capitalism, 1880–1940.* Chicago: University of Chicago Press.

Bremner, R. 1956. *From the Depths: The Discovery of Poverty in the United States.* New York: New York University Press.

Brody, D. 1980. The rise and decline of welfare capitalism. In D. Brody (Ed.) *Workers in Industrial America.* New York: Oxford University Press.

Burgess, E.W. 1960. *Aging in Western Societies.* Chicago: University of Chicago Press.

Burke, V. & Burke, V. 1974. *Nixon's Good Deed: Welfare Reform.* New York: Columbia University Press.

Burt, M.R. & Pittman, K.J. 1985. *Testing the Social Safety Net.* Washington, DC: The Urban Institute.

Cianciolo, P. 1990. *Social security: The experience of women.* Unpublished dissertation. Pittsburgh, PA: University of Pittsburgh.

Clark, R.L. 1990. "Income Maintenance Policies in the United States." In R.H. Binstock & L. George (Eds.) *Handbook of Aging and the Social Sciences.* Third edition. (pp. 383–397), San Diego: Academic Press.

Clark, R. & McDermed, A. 1988. Pension wealth and job changes: The effects of vesting, portability, and lump-sum distributions. *Gerontologist, 28,* 524–32.

The common good. 1989. *Social Welfare and the American Future.* New York: Ford Foundation Report.

Cottrell, F. & Atchley, R.C. 1969. *Women in Retirement: A Preliminary Report.* Oxford, OH: Scripps Foundation for Research in Population Problems.

Crandall, R.C. 1980. *Gerontology: A Behavioral Approach.* Reading, MA: Addison-Wesley.

Critchfield, R. 1990. "Thatcher's Battle of Britain." *World Monitor 3,* 34–46.

Crystal, S. 1982. *America's Old Age Crisis: Public Policy and the Two Worlds of Aging.* New York: Basic Books.

Cummings, F. 1974. Reforming private pensions. *The Annals, 415,* 80–94.

Derthick, M. 1979. *Policy-Making for Social Security.* Washington, DC: The Brookings Institute.

Douglas, P.H. 1939. *Social Security in the United States.* New York: McGraw-Hill.

Economic Policy Institute 1986. *Family Incomes in Trouble.* Washington, DC: Economic Policy Institute.

Employee Benefit Research Institute. 1986. Features of employer health plans. *Issue Brief, 60,* 11.

Estes, C.L.; Gerard, L.; & Clark, A. 1984. Women and the economics of aging. *International Journal of Health Services, 14,* 55–68.

Federico, R.C. 1984. *Social Welfare Institution.* Fourth edition. Lexington, MA: D.C. Heath.

Ferrara, P. 1984. *Rebuilding Social Security.* Washington, DC: Heritage Foundation.

Flora, P. & Heidenheimer, A. 1981. *The Development of Welfare State Programs in Europe and America.* New Brunswick, NJ: Transaction Books.

Friedman, R.R. 1987. "Welfare states: A Summary of Trends." In R.R. Friedman, N. Gilbert & M. Sherer (Eds.), *Modern Welfare States* (pp. 282–289). Brighton, U.K.: Wheatsheaf Books.

Furniss, N. & Tilton, T. 1977. *The Case for the Welfare State.* Bloomington, IN: Indiana University Press.

Gibson R.M. & Waldo, D. 1981. National health expenditures, 1980. *Health Care Financing Review, 3:* 1–54.

Glazer, N. 1984. "The Social Policy of the Reagan Administration." In D.L. Baldwin (Ed.), *The social contract revisited* (pp. 221–244). Washington, DC: The Urban Institute.

Grad, S. 1982. *Income of the Population 55 and Over.* Washington, DC: Social Security Administration.

Grad, S. 1983. *Income of the Population 55 and Over.* Washington, DC: Department of Health and Human Services, Office of Research and Statistics.

Hancock, J.A. (Ed.) 1987. *Housing the Elderly.* New Brunswick, NJ: Center for Urban Policy Research.

Hargrove, E.C. 1988. *Jimmy Carter as President: Leadership and the Politics of the Public Good.* Baton Rouge, LA: Louisiana State University Press.

Harrington, M. with Greenstein, R. and Norton, E.H. 1987. *Who Are the Poor?* Washington, DC: Justice For All.

Harris, C.S. 1978. *Fact book on aging: A profile of America's older population.* Washington, DC: National Council on Aging.

Harris, L. and Associates, Inc. 1981. *Aging in the eighties: America in transition.* Washington, DC: National Council on Aging.

Heidbreder, E. 1972. Factors in retirement adjustment: White collar/blue collar experiences. *Industrial Gerontology 12,* 69–79.

Heidenheimer, A.J., Heclo, J. & Teich-Adams, C. 1983. *Comparative Public Policy: The Politics of Social Choice in Europe and America.* London: MacMillan.

Howe, I. 1982. *Beyond the Welfare State.* New York: Schocken Books.

Ippolito, R.A. 1990. *Pensions, Economics and Public Policy.* Homewood, IL: Dow Jones-Irwin.

Judge, K. 1987. "The British Welfare State in Transition." In R.R. Friedman, N. Gilbert & M. Sherer (Eds.), *Modern Welfare States* (pp. 1–43). Brighton, U.K.: Wheatsheaf Books.

Kahn, A.J. 1979. *Social Policy and Social Services.* Second edition. New York: Random House.

Karger, H.J. & Stoesz, D. 1990. *American Social Welfare Policy.* White Plains, NY: Longman.

Kendig, H.L. 1990. "Comparative Perspectives on Housing, Aging and Social Structure." In R.H. Binstock & L.K. George (Eds.),

Handbook on Aging and the Social Sciences. Third edition (pp. 288–307). San Diego: Academic Press.

Kennedy, L.D., Thomas, D. & Schmulowicz, J. 1975. Conversions to supplemental security income from assistance: A program records study. *Social Security Bulletin,* 38, 6, 30.

Kingson, E.R., Hirshorn, B.A. & Cornman, J.M. 1986. *Ties that Bind: The Interdependence of Generations.* Washington, DC: Seven Locks.

Leuchentenberg, W. 1963. *Franklin Roosevelt and the New Deal.* New York: Harper & Row.

Levitan, S.A. & Shapiro, S. 1987. *Working but Poor: America's Contradictions.* Baltimore: The Johns Hopkins University Press.

Lowy, L. 1985. *Social Work with the Aging.* Second edition. White Plains, NY: Longman.

Markides, K.S. & Mindell, C.H. 1987. *Aging and Ethnicity.* Newbury Park, CA: Sage.

Menafee, J.A., Edwards, B. & Schieber, S. 1981. Analysis on Nonparticipation in the SSI program. *Social Security Bulletin, 44,* 3–21.

Merton, C. & Bernstein, J.B. 1987. *Social Security: The System That Works.* New York: Basic Books.

Miller, S.J. 1965. "The Social Dilemma of the Aging Leisure Participant." In A.M. Rose & W.A. Peterson (Eds.), *Older People and Their Social World* (pp. 72–92). Philadelphia: F.A. Davis.

Moon, M. 1977. *The Measurement of Economic Welfare: Its Application to the Aged Poor.* New York: Academic Press.

Moon, M. and Sawhill, I.V. 1984. "Family Incomes: Gainers and Losers." In J.L. Palmer and I.V. Sawhill (Eds.), *The Reagan Record* (pp. 317–346). Cambridge, MA: Ballinger.

Moon, M. & Smeeding, T. 1989. "Can the Elderly Really Afford Long-Term Care?" In S. Sullivan & M. Lewin (Eds.), *The Care of Tomorrow's Elderly: Encouraging Initiatives and Reshaping Public Programs.* Washington, DC: University Press.

Morris, R. 1986. *Rethinking Social Welfare.* White Plains, NY: Longman.

———. 1987. "Re-thinking Welfare in the United States: The Welfare state in Transition." In R.R. Friedman, N. Gilbert and M. Sherer (Eds.), *Modern Welfare States* (pp. 83–108). Brighton, U.K.: Wheatsheaf Books.

Munnell, A.H. 1982. *The Economics of Private Pensions.* Washington, DC: The Brookings Institute.

Murray, C. 1984. *Losing Ground.* New York: Basic Books.

Myles, J. 1984. *Old Age in the Welfare State; The Political Economy of Public Pensions.* Boston: Little Brown.

New York Times (1990). The Week in Review, Sunday, March 25.

O'Connor, J. *(1973) The Fiscal Crisis of the State.* New York: St. Martins Press.

Olson, S. 1987. "Towards a Transformation of the Swedish Welfare State?" In R.R Friedman, N. Gilbert & M. Sherer (Eds.), *Modern Welfare States* (pp. 44–83). Brighton, U.K.: Wheatsheaf Press.

Pechman, J.A. 1985. *Who Paid the Taxes 1966–1985?* Washington, DC: Brookings Institute.

Perkins, F. 1946. *The Roosevelt I Knew.* New York: Viking Press.

Piven, F. & Cloward, R.A. 1971. *Regulating the Poor: The Functions of Public Welfare.* New York: Vintage Books.

President's Commission on Pension Policy. 1981. *Coming of Age: Toward a National Retirement Income Policy.* Washington, DC: National Planning Association.

Quinn, J.F. & Burkhauser, R.V. 1990. "Work and retirement." In R.H. Binstock & L.K. George (Eds.), *Handbook of Aging and the Social Sciences.* Third edition (pp. 308–327). San Diego: Academic Press.

Rankin, D. 1984. "Employee Benefit Plans under Fire." *New York Times,* December 16.

Rich, B.M. & Baum, M. 1984. *The Aging: A Guide to Public Policy.* Pittsburgh: Pittsburgh University Press.

Robertson, H. 1978. Financial status of social security program after the social security amendments of 1977. *Social Security Bulletin, 41,* 21–30.

Rose, C.L. & Mogey, J.M. 1972. Aging and preference for later retirement. *Aging and Human Development, 3,* 45–62.

Rosen, S.A., Fanshel, D. & Leitz, M.E. (Eds.). 1987. *Face of the Nation 1987.* Silver Spring, MD: National Association of Social Workers.

Sandel, M. 1988. "Democrats and Community." *The New Republic,* January 21.

Schlesinger, A. 1977. *The New Deal in Action.* Folcroft, PA: Folcroft Library Editions.

Schorr, A.L. 1986. *Common Decency.* New Haven, CT: Yale University Press.

Schottland, C.I. 1968. *The Social Security Program in the United States.* New York: Appleton-Century-Crofts.

Schultze, C. 1977. *The public use of private interest.* Washington, DC: Brookings Institute.

Schulz, J.H. 1988. *The Economics of Mandatory Retirement.* Fourth edition. Dover, MA: Auburn House.

Schulz, J.H. & Myles, J. 1990. "Old Age Pensions: A Comparative Perspective." In R.H. Binstock & L. George (Eds.), *Handbook of Aging and the Social Sciences.* Third edition (pp. 398–414). San Diego: Academic Press.

Shapiro, I. & Greenstein, R. 1988. *Holes in the Safety Nets.* Washington, DC: Center on Budget and Policy Priorities.

Sherer, M. 1987. "Welfare States: An Overview of Problems and Perspectives." In R.R. Friedman, N. Gilbert & M. Sherer (Eds.), *Modern Welfare States* (pp. 290–298). Brighton, U.K.: Wheatsheaf Books.

Sidel, R. 1986. *Women and Children Last.* New York: Viking Penguin.

Smeeding, T.M. 1986. "Non-money income and the elderly: the case of 'tweeters'." *Journal of Policy Analysis and Management, 5,* 704–724.

———. 1990. "Economic Status of the Elderly." In R.H. Binstock & L.K. George (Eds.), *Handbook of Aging and the Social Sciences.* Third edition (pp. 362–381). San Diego: Academic Press.

Stevens, B. 1988. "Blurring the Boundaries: How the Federal Government Has Influenced Welfare Benefits in the Private Sector." In M. Weir, A.S. Orloff, & T. Skopol (Eds.), *The Politics of Social Policy in the United States* (pp. 123–148). Princeton: Princeton University Press.

Stoesz, D. 1989. Policy gambit: Conservative think tanks take on the welfare state. *Journal of Sociology and Social Welfare, XVI,* 73–86.

Streib, G. & Schneider, C.J. 1971. *Retirement in American Society.* Ithaca, NY: Cornell University Press.

Struyk, R.J. & Soldo, B.J. 1980. *Improving the Elderly's Housing: A Key to Preserving the Nation's Housing Stock and Neighborhoods.* Cambridge, MA: Ballinge.

Svahn, J.A. & Ross, M. 1983. Social security amendments of 1983: Legislative history and summary of provisions. *Social Security Bulletin, 46,* 7.

Tilove, R. 1976. *Public Employee Pension Funds.* New York: Columbia University Press, A Twentieth Century Fund Report.

Torczyner, J. 1987. "The Canadian Welfare State: Retrenchment and Change." In R.R. Friedman, N. Gilbert & M. Sherer (Eds.), *Modern Welfare States* (pp. 264–281). Brighton, U.K.: Wheatsheaf Books.

U.S. Bureau of the Census. 1988a. *Measuring the effect of benefits and taxes on income and poverty: 1986.* Current Populations Reports. Series P-60, No. 164–RD-1. Washington, DC: U.S. Government Printing Office.

U.S. Bureau of the Census. 1988b. *Money income and poverty status in the United States, 1987.* Current Populations Reports. Series P-60, No. 16. Washington, DC: U.S. Government Printing Office.

U.S. Bureau of the Census. 1984. *Money income and poverty status of families and persons in the United States: 1984,* Current Population Reports, Series P-60, No. 145. Washington, DC: U.S. Government Printing Office.

U.S. House Select Committee on Aging. 1975. *Government's response to the elderly.* 94th Congress, 1st session, Washington, DC: U.S. Government Printing Office.

U.S. Department of Labor. 1975. Labor Management Services Division, Employee Retirement Income Security Act, Report to Congress.

U.S. Senate Special Committee on Aging. 1981. *Developments in Aging.* 97th Congress, 2nd session, Report No. 97–314, 2, 43–45.

U.S. Senate Special Committee on Aging. 1988. *Developments in Aging 1987.* Vol. 1, 100–291.

Weir, M., Orloff, A.S. & Skopol, T. 1988. *The Politics of Social Policy in the Welfare State.* Princeton: Princeton University Press.

Wheeler, R. 1986. "Housing Policy and Elderly People." In C. Phillipson & A. Walker (Eds.), *Aging and Social Policy: A Critical Assessment* (pp. 217–336). Brookfield, VT: Gower.

Wilensky, H. 1976. *The "New Corporatism." Centralization and the Welfare State.* London: Sage.

Winnick, A.J. 1988. "The changing distribution of income and wealth in the United States 1960–1985: An examination of the movement toward two societies, 'separate and unequal'." In P. Voydanoff & L.C. Majka (Eds.), *Families and Economic Distress* (pp. 232–260). Newbury Park, CA: Sage.

Witte, E. 1962. *The Development of the Social Security Act.* Madison: University of Wisconsin Press.

Ycas, M.A. & Grad, S. 1987. Income of retired persons in the United States. *Social Security Bulletin, 50,* 5–14.

CHAPTER 9

Retirement Planning Services

Abraham Monk

Introduction: Questions Middle-Aged Workers Ask

Middle-aged workers are often concerned about their job security and wonder whether their present employment will carry them safely until reaching the age of full retirement. With plant closing, corporate mergers, and the introduction of new technologies, these middle-agers are likely victims of downsizing trends in the workforce. Their chances for reemployment are, however, statistically only half of those available to younger workers. They are, as often voiced by the media, "too young to retire but too old to find another job."

The fact is that nearly half of all career jobs end in this country at or before age 60 but few, perhaps only one in every ten workers, can financially afford to retire at that age. To make ends meet they take one of several paths: some accept part-time or occasional work, some others rely on a spouse's income, a few others may be eligible for disability or unemployment insurance, and some give up altogether, ceasing to look for employment. The latter are the discouraged workers no longer recorded in unemployment statistics. Many of those who persist have no alternative but to take the so called "bridge" jobs, usually at less pay and in positions or fields unrelated to their expertise or previous experience. They simply hang on to whatever they can find until qualifying for the legal option of early retirement which becomes available at age 62. Early retirement entails, however, a 20 percent lifetime reduction in Social Security benefits but at least it assures a permanent, even if meager, source of income. Moreover, it does not carry the stigma of a welfare hand-out.

There are numerous mid-life job terminations in the United States and the most likely candidates for the resulting "bridge" jobs at substantially reduced wages used to be unskilled workers, ethnic minorities, and women. Not anymore. Job displacement and employment insecurity have made inroads in the executive and professional suites as well. They are not limited to middle-aged and older workers either.

The second question most frequently raised by middle-aged workers concerns the adequacy of the benefits they will receive following their retirement. They accept the inevitable prospects of a reduction of income and standard of living, but they wonder whether they will not end up outliving their resources. A particular concern is whether they will be able to meet their health care costs, specially if they or their spouses are struck by protracted chronic illnesses. They are aware that nursing home bills can whip out life-long savings and assets in a matter of months.

It should be borne in mind that more than half—54 percent—of the American workforce is not covered by private or company financed pension plans and that the overwhelming majority of the pension schemes, actually 75 percent of them, are not adjusted for inflation. Pension coverage is actually declining from an all time high of 48 percent in 1983 to 46 percent in 1988 (SSA, 1989), and the trend is to replace "defined benefit" plans, which guarantee a certain level of income, with financially more risky but cheaper to operate "defined contribution" plans (Uchitelle, 1990). Social Security is pegged to the cost of living index and offers consequently a better protection against inflation, but its earnings replacing ratio—that is, the portion of recent wages for which the Social Security monthly check substitutes—is one of the lowest among the western industrialized nations. With the prospect of an extended life span, older workers are often haunted by the fear that much more than Social

Security, a private pension, and even additional savings may be needed to carry them through their post-retirement years.

The intimidating prospect of income insecurity is in the center stage of people anticipating their retirement, but it is not their only concern. They also seek answers to a host of additional, perplexing questions: how to juggle the conflicting responsibilities of work on one hand, and caring for dependent and chronically sick parents on the other; how to take care of a spouse afflicted with senile dementia; how to find part-time or even full-time work, as a way of tapering off before retirement or to compensate for the painful loss of income, especially when they still have to pay for their children's college bills and home mortgage expenses, etc. The list of questions could be extended *ad infinitum.* Preretirement programs were historically conceived to precisely address those questions in a systematic and speedy way. In the process these programs also generated an awareness about retirement among workers in all levels of employment.

Who Offers Preretirement Programs?

Retirement preparation programs became, in the words of Montana (1985), "one of the hottest topics in the human resources field." Interest in these programs was stimulated by the passage of the Employee Retirement Income Security Act of 1974 (ERISA), which not only regulated the private pensions field but also required that employers keep beneficiaries better informed about their pension rights and benefits. In addition the 1978 Amendments to the Age Discrimination in Employment Act (ADEA) extended mandatory retirement from age 65 to 70 and made it far more difficult to lay off or force the retirement of older workers, just on the basis of age. Early retirement inducements in preretirement programs had to underscore the non-punitive and voluntary nature of such choice.

Although interest in preretirement counseling and information has been apparently high, the number of employers actually offering such programs has remained disappointingly low and stagnant. Optimistic projections that these programs would continue expanding did not materialize.

A survey by Morrison and Jedrziewski (1988) found that no more than 40 percent of the companies they approached reported having become familiar with and administered or conducted such programs. The majority of the survey participants argued that they could not offer these programs because of costs and time factors. They also invoked the lack of specialized personnel to run such programs and the fact that employees have shown little interest in them. Furthermore, only one-third of the employers involved with such programs resort to a formal, full-fledged set of activities such as seminars and individual counseling. The majority limit themselves to the occasional distribution of printed information, or a single annual event where the company's employee benefits are reviewed and explained. Siegel (1986) evaluated in 1984 the status of preretirement programs in Fortune 500 companies and compared the results with those of a study completed in 1977 utilizing the same survey instrument. Less than one-third of the companies responded to both surveys. The first indicators were deceivingly auspicious: 51 percent stated that they were offering programs in 1984, as compared to only 29 percent in the preceding 1977 survey. The level of participation by eligible employees decreased, however, from 85 percent to 50 percent and the length of customized individual counseling had also shrunk.

Culling the data from several surveys, Migliaccio (1990) estimates that probably no more than 35 percent of all corporations sponsor or offer preretirement programs. It must be borne in mind, however, that most of the surveys inquiring whether employers offer a preretirement program obtained rather low response rates. It is conceivable that employers who do offer preretirement programs are more motivated to respond, and as a consequence the overall results may show an affirmative bias, thus inflating the estimated number of companies with programs in place.

Reasons for Offering Preretirement Programs

The reasons why some employers offer preretirement programs are complex. Some of the causes are self-serving, as they enhance the company's reputation. Others are more altruistic in nature and aim to satisfy employees' demands. More specifically, corporations assume these programs will enable them to: 1) project a caring and socially responsible image; 2) Foster greater employees' loyalty and identification with the company; 3) stimulate higher productivity; 4) reduce turn-over rates; 5) deliver information needed by employees to make judicious retirement decisions; 6) help employees to define a lifestyle better suited for their post-retirement years.

A central theme and justification of preretirement programs during the decades of the 60s and 70s was that they helped neutralized the alleged trauma or shock caused by the sudden termination of paid employment. Preretirement programs were then legitimized in mental health terms because it was claimed they facilitated a better adjustment to a leisured stage of life and restored a sense of personal identity no longer associated with the occupational role. The ultimate expectation was that they may lead to a renewed sense of purpose and life satisfaction (Monk, 1990).

There are two arguments of more recent vintage favoring the promotion of preretirement programs. The first affirms that the retirement decision is affected by a host of employer-provided benefits and public entitlements of increasing complexity, and that even the most sophisticated and best informed employees require professional assistance to understand, let alone to claim and utilize, the benefits accruing to them at the time of retirement. Furthermore, each individual has a different set of personal circumstances—health, family life, dependents, financial obligations, savings, investments, etc.—and may need help to figure out how he or she will fare in retirement given the resources at hand.

The second argument stems from the realization that given the prospects of longer life expectancy and the fact that mandatory retirement is on its way out, employers will have to rely on an increasingly older work force. Preretirement planning is viewed, in this context, not as a free-standing service, but as part of the overall personnel management strategy addressed to the changing age composition of the American work force.

Employers wonder what to do with senior workers who are poor performers. It is estimated that one in six workers fall behind and do not keep up with technological changes. Some of them reach a career plateau, lose interest in their job, and experience low morale. Management, on the other hand, wishes also to reward and retain senior workers who are good performers.

It is conceivable then, from a systemic human resources perspective, that preretirement programs may address separately the two issues enunciated above. They may offer poor performers the incentives for voluntarily leaving the workforce, and they may also create the proper contractual framework and conditions for retooling and retaining the good performers.

In reality, and notwithstanding the realization that the workforce is aging, employers have not shown a special interest in keeping older workers. A survey conducted by the Daniel Yankelovich Group for the American Association of Retired Persons (AARP), found a pronounced reduction in senior management's commitment to older employees, from 33 percent as reported in a previous 1985 study to 25 percent in 1989 (AARP, 1989). Despite the almost unanimous praise of older workers' reliability and quality of performance, punctuality and loyalty, employers worry about the ever increasing health insurance and pension costs they must outlay for their older employees. As a consequence, these companies have begun putting into effect early retirement programs aimed at creating a "lean" corporate structure and reducing the total bill for wages and fringe benefits. In 1985 44 percent of companies with 1000 or more employees had already instituted or were contemplating the adoption of early retirement programs. Five years later, by 1989, the proportion of such employers climbed to 55 percent. Preretirement programs were a favored counseling mechanism used to persuade older employees that they should collect their benefits and leave permanently.

Early Retirement Policies

The adoption and implementation of early retirement policies gave new impetus to preretirement planning programs.

According to Taplin (1989), nearly 40 percent of all employers with ongoing preretirement programs also offer special counseling associated with early retirement incentives. A survey of early retirement incentive programs conducted by the Department of Labor's Bureau of Labor Statistics (1988) established that 14 percent of all workers were in firms that offered at least one early retirement program during the period 1983–1988. Early retirement is usually utilized by employers as a more palatable alternative to mandatory layoffs, especially when they must reduce the size of their workforce or restructure corporate operations. In order to obtain a high acceptance rate, employers may offer an assortment of inducements or "sweeteners," including: 1) cash severance payments, which may consist of a flat amount, a percentage of one year's wages, or one or two weeks' salary for each year of service; 2) adding years of service, usually the difference between age 65 and the actual age of retirement, to the computation of benefits and making supplemental contributions to the pension fund for that number of years; 3) continuation of health insurance; and 4) group health coverage may be continued for a fixed number of years, for life, or until age 65 when the retiree becomes eligible for Medicare benefits.

Early retirement programs, far from producing economies, may actually be financially detrimental to employers. A study of Fortune 100 employers by the National Foundation for Occupational and Environmental Health Research found that cash bonuses tend to be so expensive that they are not offset by lower future wages costs. When comparing the costs of early retire ment versus the retention of employees, the retirement of workers aged between 55 and 64 years of age is 33.5 percent more costly than laying off workers between ages 40 to 54 (Morrison and Jedrziewski, 1988).

Early retirement is part of an expedient pattern of manpower development. When market demands for specific product lines decrease, or established methods of production are re placed by new technologies, it is customary in the United States to let go the older workforce and hire in its place a new and younger one. The American workplace thus renews by generational substitution rather than by retooling and recycling its senior workers. After all, the chronic rate of unemployment which wavers around a 7 percent level assures an abundant supply of replacements. Older workers are, in effect, treated as a dispensable and throw-away commodity. Little consideration is given to the psychological consequences involved, as older workers face the stigma of obsolescence, insecurity and economic demotion, years before reaching the modal age of retirement. Preretirement counseling in early retirement is dominated, however, by financial planning considerations. It seeks to determine how feasible is it to take leave at a younger age, and how to take advantage of periodic or occasional "windows" of sweeteners offered by their employers. These programs seldom include consideration of the possible attack on the workers' sense of self esteem, of their perplexity about what to do in the years ahead, and eventually, how to update their skills in consonance with new market demands.

Poorly prepared, early retirees often take any job that will help them earn some additional income; they moonlight, barter services, accept payment in kind and volunteer wherever they can get a few freebies, meals included. They take part-time and temporary jobs at minimum wage levels and with few or no benefits. Not surprisingly, they are satisfied with such meager arrangements because they can supplement their fixed income, they meet people, they feel useful and they feel they are back in the mainstream.

Employers have become more cautious in launching early retirement incentive plans because many such plans were found to be in violation of the Federal Age Discrimination in Employment Act of 1967 (ADEA).

Early retirement incentives cannot be offered selectively to specific individuals but must be made to an entire company or corporate division. The company runs then the risk of losing employees it actually wishes to retain, while finding that those it would prefer to leave cling to their jobs. Finally, no preretirement package may constitute a veiled form of coercion, nor can an employee be forced to choose between early retirement and severance benefits.

The Format of Preretirement Programs

There are no standardized or generic forms of preretirement programs. An inventory of such programs will find a wide range of formats, lengths, methods of delivery and topical areas. Some programs are a misnomer because they may consist of a single film, newsletter, pamphlet or lecture. Others are instead truly comprehensive in scope and are delivered through intensive seminars or courses, concentrated in a weekend or extended over weeks and even months. Some programs limit themselves to factual information, while other are what Eckerdt (1989) called "hortatory," because they resort to normative guidelines intended to lead to a better adjustment or a happier life in retirement.

Programs differ also according to their level of individualization. Most operate according to a lecture and questions and answers format. They may add workbooks and training materials that enable participants to relate the general information to their individual circumstances. Some programs proceed, however, to add individual counseling, on a one-to-one basis with expert advisors, in a number of topical areas. This customized approach is very expensive indeed, and to be effective may require regular monitoring and follow-up sessions.

Although the range of topics is wide, it is safe to assume that most, if not all, programs rely on a similar core, consisting of: company provided benefits, public entitlements, financial planning, health and mental health, estate planning, leisure and life style. Not all topics carry the same weight, and Condron (1985) recommends that financial planning constitute 60 percent of the total package. It is unusual for a single counselor to cover the entire range of topics. Program organizers act as conveners and discussion leaders and, when affordable, they put together a team of speakers and advisors that may include physicians, dieticians, attorneys, estate planners, etc. They also resort to specialized resources and didactic guides and tools produced by voluntary organizations such as the American Association of Retired Persons and the National Council on Aging, or commercial outfits such as Retirement Advisors, Inc., 50 Plus, etc.

A program may begin by calling attention to the meaning of retirement. It then invites participants to inventory their financial resources: private pensions, IRAs, Social Security, income tax liabilities, savings and other income producing assets. Financial planners assume that retirees need between 70 and 80 percent of their previous employment income in order to maintain the same life style and standard of living. The logical next step is, then, to come up with an annual budget and ascertain whether the expected retirement income will suffice to meet those projected annual expenses. In the eventuality that the income may fall short and not cover the estimated budget, preretirement counselors guide participants in revising the budget, trimming some expenditure categories, modifying and scaling down their life style aspirations, considering relocation to a lower cost area, and finding part-time employment to bridge the budgetary gap. In addition counselors may caution about several pitfalls that are characteristic of this stage: 1) not factoring in the rate of inflation; 2) underestimating tax liabilities; 3) underbudgeting for leisure amenities; 4) overestimating the job benefits carried into retirement; 5) similarly assuming that Medicare will pay most if not all the medical costs; 6) Moving to another geographical area without having tried it out first; 7) underestimating the costs of maintenance of a home and of the eventual replacement of the household equipment.

The Social Work Role in Preretirement Programs

Social workers rarely step in and double as financial counselors. They may, however, have a role to play in that first stage, whenever the person's life objectives in retirement are financially unattainable. Social workers can facilitate both reaching a better sense of reality and designing alternative life style scenarios that are more feasible and yet consistent with a person's background and aspirations. They may help by moving the person into a more flexible posture and conversely overcoming the risk of obsessive entrenchment into a rigid and irreducible objective.

The second stage of the retirement preparation process centers around the shaping of a retirement life style, and it is here where social workers could make the most effective use of their professional skills. This is the point where program participants, after realizing that they are leaving behind their lifelong occupational roles, face their futures and take stock of their inner strengths and unfinished agendas: What interests and activities would they like to pursue? Are these interests a continuation of life-long endeavors and occupational routines, or do they constitute a drastic new incursion into unchartered waters? In the latter case, how realistic are these aspirations? Are they affordable, in the context of the person's financial resources and family circumstances? Are they feasible, in light of the person's functional capacity and health? Are they congruent with the spouse's own interests and expectations? Will the person be able to establish new schedules and persevere to master these new interests? Will such an accomplishment translate itself into a greater sense of life satisfaction?

A social worker-counselor assists program participants to deal with these questions and, in the process, helps them to make the transition into retirement. For some this constitutes a major and difficult change, tantamount to a fresh start where the person forges and tests out a new identity. Preretirement counseling is, in this sense, another version of mid-life reassessment. A social worker facilitates refocusing a person's goals and identifying life options or alternatives for that particular stage of life.

The fact remains that most participants just want to know how they will fare financially in retirement. They would be content with an answer to the single question: "Will I be able to make it?", and they put off or ignore issues of a psychosocial nature. A social worker or counselor could help to rectify that imbalance and also bring attention to the impact of retirement on each person's emotional, familial, and interpersonal life.

Elder Care

There are new issues permeating into the preretirement programs of the 1980s and 1990s. One of them is elder care. More retirees still have parents alive, and it is a matter of time before they will have more living parents than children. It is estimated that more than one in four workers in large corporations are already caring for older relatives. It is not a surprise therefore that "elder care" has emerged as a contractual issue both in employment relations and in preretirement planning.

The 1982 National Long Term Care survey revealed that about one-third of the adults caring for an older relative were in the labor force, but that 20 percent of those employed had to either reduce work or rearrange their work schedules. Many have no choice but to take time off without pay. About one-third of those currently employed had to diminish their work hours. Furthermore, over one-third of caregivers who were recently employed left their job within the preceding year of the study because of the exhausting and time consuming demands of the helping tasks they perform (U.S. Senate Special Committee on Aging, 1989).

Employers are fully aware that the stress and fatigue involved in caregiving ultimately causes absenteeism, tardiness, and high turnover rates as well as lower productivity. A few pioneering corporations have begun assisting their employees by linking them to community services, organizing information fairs and seminars, operating adult day care centers and sponsoring support groups. IBM established in 1988 an elder care consultation and referral service, modeled after its Child Care Resource and Referral Service. It operates as a single access point for counseling and information and it includes the following program elements: 1) personalized telephone consultation to employees and retirees and their spouses; 2) review of service options in the caregivers' communities; 3) individualized referrals to services; and 4) consumer education aimed at selecting the most appropriate care (Piktialis, 1990). The referral and consultation service helps employees to select from medical services, homemaker and home health services, congregate housing, nursing homes, specialized transportation, multiservice senior centers, Medicare, medigap, and Medicaid entitlements and insurance, and case management services that can assess the condition of the elder dependent relative, evaluate his or her needs, make recommendations and/or negotiate the provision of specific services. Elder care programs have begun branching off into the provision of flexible work arrangements. Adolf (1988) mentions, to this effect, that some of the work schedules developed by companies offering eldercare programs include: flexible work hours; job sharing by two or more employees; compressed work in fewer days each week but with longer hours each day and even the option of working at home, whenever feasible.

Elder care has the potential of becoming a new major employee benefit. Not surprisingly, employers worry about its potential price tag. There is concern that future additional age-related taxes, which may include a long-term care insurance program, would be too onerous to bear and would contribute to further erode the competitive edge of American producers in world markets. Participants in preretirement programs inquire, in turn, where they should turn for help when caring for chronically dependent relatives. Those working for companies with elder care programs in place request the extension of these benefits after retirement. Both these questions and requests inevitably surface in the course of preretirement counseling.

Reentering the Labor Force

Preretirement programs were created to assist people with the termination of their work careers. A new, incipient trend consists in doing just the opposite, that is, helping people to reenter the labor force. Preretirement programs are thus beginning to include a career development component aimed at facilitating the launching of a second career. When engaged in this task, preretirement counselors follow several steps: first, they identify the workers who are interested in pursuing a new career. Some of these workers may wish to continue in their habitual occupations and professions. Others may also wish to continue in the same line of work but require updating and refurbishing their skills. There are, finally, those who want a break with the past and are ready to undergo the necessary training which will lead them to a new career. In all instances a thorough assessment of their vocational interests is in order. Many companies provide career planning and will assist with the tuition costs for older employees learning new skills.

The *second* step involves determining the receptivity of the occupational market for the workers' new and/or current skills.

Special attention is given to occupational opportunities for part-time or flexible employment. Employers of older workers have been experimenting with diverse time scheduling options, such as part-day, part-week, and part-year assignments; job redesigning which alters the pace, intensity, and physical demands of some of the tasks; job sharing among two or more workers; seasonal leaves, etc.

The *third* and last step entails positioning the older workers in the labor market and facilitating their search for employment. Sommerstein (1985) alludes to the need of older workers for help with the basics of resume writing, interviewing skills, and researching the potential sources of employment. The search is facilitated in many instances by employers willing to hire their own retirees as independent contractors, especially when facing seasonal or temporary increases in demand and/or shortages of labor supply.

The inclusion of second careers counseling in preretirement programs responds to the emerging needs of a segment of the older workforce. It should be borne in mind, however, that there is no universal outcry for work after retirement; only a small fraction of older workers may be interested to return to the labor market and, if given the opportunities, they would mostly prefer part-time employment.

New Directions

Preretirement preparation programs were historically initiated as part of a package of employee benefits but they were also part of the employers' strategies aimed at renewing their personnel cadres, reorganizing the enterprise, and increasing profits. It is not surprising therefore that preretirement programs have been occasionally viewed as a manipulative tool of management. The reluctance of many corporations to launch such programs has been similarly explained on grounds that they do not wish to be labelled as paternalistic and controlling. They do not want to intrude into the privacy of their employees and tell them what to do with their lives.

Preretirement planning should not be the exclusive preserve of the corporate sector. There is no reason why employees who refuse to become dependent on their employer's guidance should not be able to find help elsewhere. There are other options. Preretirement programs are also offered by unions, community colleges, adult education programs, financial planning and actuarial firms, accountants, banks, public libraries, clubs and community centers, etc. There is also an abundant bibliography easily accessible and there is a growing number of computer assisted software programs, such as Discover, created by ACT (American College Testing, 1990), and the Friendly Retirement Data Base, a product of Employee Benefit Systems, Inc. described by Pyrnne (1987–88).

Ultimately, the effectiveness of any preretirement preparation program is contingent on the personal motivation and interest of each participant. No matter how well a program has customized and responded to a range of individual circumstances, it will not do much good unless the individuals themselves take charge of their destiny, internalize the information, reflect and act upon it. A guidance counselor or social worker could play a critical role in helping rally the personal motivation and provide feedback in the decision making process.

REFERENCES

Adolf, B. 1988. How to minimize disruption caused by employees taking care of elderly relatives. *Journal of Compensation and Benefits,* March/April, 291–294.

American Association of Retired Persons (AARP). 1989. *Business and older workers: Current perceptions and new directions for the 1990s.* Washington, DC: Author.

American College Testing. 1990. *Discover, Retirement Planning Software.* Iowa City, IA: Author.

Condron, C.M. 1985. Anatomy of a successful preretirement planning program. *Retirement Planning,* Spring 6–7 and 11–13.

Department of Labor, Bureau of Labor Statistics. 1988. *Employee Benefits in Medium and Large Firms* (Bulletin 2336). Washington, DC: Superintendent of Documents, U.S. Government Printing Office.

Eckerdt, D.J. 1989. "Retirement Preparation." In M.P. Lawton, ed., *Annual Review of Gerontology and Geriatrics, 9,* 321–356. New York: Springer.

Migliaccio, J. 1990. *Corporate Sponsored Assistance for Senior Employees: the Unfulfilled Promise.* New York: Retirement Advisors Division, Hearst Business Corporation.

Monk, A. 1990. "Preretirement Planning Programs." In A. Monk, ed., *Handbook of Gerontological Services* (400–419). New York: Columbia University Press.

Montana, P.J. (1985). *Retirement Programs: How to Develop and Implement Them.* Englewood Cliffs, NJ: Prentice Hall.

Morrison, M.H. and Jedrziewski, K. 1988. Retirement planning: Everybody's benefits. *Personnel Administrator, 33,* 74–80.

Piktialis, D.S. 1990. Employers and elder care: a model corporate program. *Pride Institute Journal of Long Term Home Health Care, 9,* 26–31.

Pyrnne, T.A. 1987–88. Using the computer as an interactive tool in retirement planning: FRED revisited. *Retirement Planning,* Winter, 6–7.

Siegel, S.R. 1986. Preretirement programs in the 80s. *Personnel Administrator, 31,* 77–83.

Social Security Administration (SSA). 1989. Pension coverage among private wage and salary workers: Preliminary findings from the 1988 survey of employee benefits. *Social Security Bulletin, 52.*

Sommerstein, J.C. 1985. A second careers component for preretirement programs. *Retirement Planning,* Winter, 12, 19.

Taplin, P.T. 1989. Spencer Survey of preretirement counseling: Ongoing, early retirement program described. *Employee Benefit Plan Review,* August, 14–18.

Uchitelle, L. 1990. "Company financed pensions are failing to fulfill promise." *The New York Times,* May 29, Al and D5.

U.S. Senate Special Committee on Aging. 1989. *Aging America: Trends and Projections.* Washington, DC: U.S. Government Printing Office.

RESOURCES

American Association of Retired Persons Worker Equity Department
1909 K Street, NW
Washington, DC 20049

Andrus Gerontology Center
Preretirement Program
Leonard Davis School of Gerontology
University of Southern California
University Park
Los Angeles, CA 90089–0191

50 Plus (Preretirement Services)
850 Third Avenue
New York, NY 10022

Mercer-Meidinger-Hansen, Inc.
Social Security Division
1500 Meidinger Tower
Louisville, Galleria, KY 40202

The National Council on the Aging, Inc.
600 Maryland Avenue, SW
Washington, DC 20024

Retirement Advisors, Inc. (RAI)
555 West 57th Street, 17th FL.
New York, NY 10019

Friendly Retirement Database (FRED)
Employee Benefit Systems, Inc.
P.O. Box 11485
Columbia, SC 29211

International Association for Financial Planning
Two Concourse Parkway
Atlanta, GA 30328

Institute of Certified Financial Planners
Two Denver Highlands
100 65 East Harvard Avenue, Suite 320
Denver, CO 80231

Social Security Administration
709 East Lomsard Street
Baltimore, MD 21202

(For questions on pension plans)
Department of Labor's Division of
Technological Assistance and Inquiries
Division of Public Information, Room N-5666
U.S. Dept. of Labor
200 Constitution Avenue, NW
Washington, DC 20210

CHAPTER 10

Housing Services

Lenard W. Kaye

The need for adequate shelter constitutes a pivotal concern in an individual's life. For older persons the characteristics of their housing can assume particularly significant proportions given the many changes that occur in their physical, functional, mental, social, and economic status over time. While the majority of older people continue to live in independent, free-standing housing throughout their lives, advancing age is inevitably accompanied by the increased likelihood that an individual will benefit from an enriched supportive living environment. Such supports can range from limited functional additions to a person's apartment or house to intense structural and service enhancements integrated into an institutional long-term care facility. This chapter will delineate the range of non-institutional needs and problems that older adults present in terms of their housing environment. An overview of the range of established and emerging types of housing programs and services for elders will be provided, including a detailed discussion of the wide variety of roles and functions that are assumed by gerontological social workers in such settings. Comparisons will by made between elder housing initiatives in the United States and those in selected other countries. Finally, problems and prospects for the future of elder housing will be considered. This chapter will limit its attention to those elder housing programs that are considered non-institutional. Institutional long-term care settings, such as nursing homes and homes for the aged, are dealt with elsewhere in this volume.

The Housing Environment of Older Adults

The interrelationship between older persons and their housing environment is crucial. Many would agree that the impact of environment is particularly powerful on older persons given the increased frequency of occurrence of physical, mental, and sensory deficits among this population. As older people age there is inevitable decline in their speed, agility, strength, and visual acuity. Chronic disorders such as arthritis surface with increased frequency. Mastery over the environment, usually expressed in terms of one's capacity to perform various activities of daily living (i.e., shopping, climbing stairs, cleaning, cooking), becomes more challenging. Research supports the notion of reduced home upkeep with advancing years. The reduction is attributable to three trends that accompany increasing age: fewer household members engage in upkeep, the number of tasks undertaken by those who continue upkeep decreases, and the average size of the tasks declines (Reschovsky and Newman, 1991).

Housing Needs and Problems of the Elderly

The housing needs and problems of the elderly result from a combination of forces reflective of the human aging process itself and the aging of much of the housing stock and the communities in which a large proportion of the elderly find themselves living. Both private owners and public landlords in rural areas and large cities are increasingly beset with expanding inventories of older, poorly suited housing. In addition, we find that the elderly as a group are less mobile than younger cohorts and tend to remain in the same community housing accommodations for increasingly extended periods of time as they pass into the later decades of life (Struyk and Soldo, 1980). Indeed, given the choice, older adults choose to "age in place." Even when neighborhoods deteriorate significantly most older people resist uprooting themselves and would prefer to remain where they are. But, as noted by Tilson and Fahey (1990), relatively few people understand the complex social and economic implications and potential consequences of that decision. It is, in large part, the consequences of the "aging in place" phenomenon that translate into the range of housing problems and needs expressed by the elderly.

Complicating the "aging in place" phenomenon is the reality that housing stock in this country for the most part was never designed to respond to the emergent social and health support needs of residents living into their seventies, eighties, nineties, and beyond. Elderly tenants of today, more likely than not, moved into their current housing at a point in their lives when they were active, healthy, and independent in terms of their ability to cope with the demands of daily life. However, advances in life expectancy and increments in the number of older people suffering from chronic, functional disabilities have created increasingly a serious mismatch between the needs of many elderly tenants and the offerings of the community and the particular dwelling units in which they reside. The lack of fit between communities, independent housing, and the needs of the elderly results in a series of classic issues of concern.

Housing problems of the aged may be categorized according to the point in time in which they occur. Thus we can identify problems and needs which arise prior to relocation from independent to planned housing and those which surface during and subsequent to relocation from independent to planned housing.

Elder Needs and Problems in Independent Housing

The problems associated with tenancy in independent housing include: (a) Coping with the condition of physical/cognitive frailty and functional limitation; (b) The state of being inadequately housed; (c) The pain of loneliness and social isolation; (d) The cost of home maintenance; and (e) The consequences of changing neighborhoods.

A statewide survey of older people's interests in service-assisted housing found the top seven reasons (in the order of their popularity) for considering the move to planned housing to be:

1) problems with home maintenance;
2) one's own poor health;
3) death of a spouse or significant other;
4) financial hardship;
5) spouse's or other's poor health;
6) an unsafe neighborhood; and
7) poor transportation.

Almost all those persons indicating some degree of housing dissatisfaction cited multiple reasons for being dissatisfied with their current housing (Matrix Research Institute, 1990; Granger and Kaye, 1991). Data collected on why approximately 500 residents had moved to seven life-care facilities in the southeast, midwest, and northeast serve to confirm the importance of the issues cited in the Matrix study. Parr, Green, and Behncke (1989) found the primary factors leading to the decision to move into a life care facility to be the need for access to needed health care, the desire to live somewhere for the rest of their lives, desirability of location, and the need for safety and security.

The decision to move is obviously a complex one which will be influenced ultimately by a variety of factors including those that might be expected to inhibit the move decision. The Matrix Institute study found that five factors would serve to delay or stall an older person's decision to move to service-assisted housing. These inhibiting factors (in the order of their importance) were:

1) interest in retaining one's possessions;
2) familiarity with the neighborhood;
3) proximity of family members;
4) the general disruption caused by moving;
5) the difficulty anticipated in selling a home; and
6) the overall costs associated with moving.

Physical and Cognitive Decline

The likelihood of physical and cognitive frailty increases with age. When such frailties interfere with performing such basic functions as reaching into cabinets, climbing stairs, opening and closing windows, and standing on stepladders, the point is quickly reached where one's capacity to maintain a home independently is questioned.

Mismatches between the demands of independent home maintenance and an older person's functional capacity increase over time. The more infirm the individual, the tighter that individual's "microenvironment" or immediate personal environment becomes. Of course personal decline in health may be experienced by one or more members of an older household. Decline in health and functional capacity of more than one member of the household can be expected to lead to pressures for making earlier rather than later decisions about obtaining assistance with home maintenance or relocating to planned housing.

Inadequate Housing

Independent housing in which the elderly live tends to be increasingly inadequate as their needs change over time. Barrow (1986) suggests four broad reasons for dissatisfaction with present housing situations: personal reasons, increasing maintenance, rising cost of living, and urban blight.

Personal reasons arise when there is a discrepancy between the resident's needs and the features of the housing setting. As families dwindle due to "empty nests" and death, the remaining resident may find the dwelling unnecessarily large and, therefore, too burdensome to maintain. Studies confirm that large proportions of older homeowners live in housing that is too large for their current needs (United States Conference of Mayors, 1986).

With the reduction in family members and withdrawal from the labor force comes a decrease in income and financial resources, making the cost of maintaining housing difficult. And older homeowners are concentrated at the lowest income levels. Indeed, many elderly are considered "house-rich" and "cash-poor" due to their financial resources being tied up in the house in which they reside (United States Conference of Mayors, 1986). The elderly spend a larger proportion of their budget on housing (primarily maintenance and major repairs) than younger age groups, and those most dependent on Social

Security have the highest rates of inadequate maintenance and facilities (National Conference on Social Welfare, 1981; Turner, Schreter, and Zetnick, 1982).

The inaccessibility of transportation due to financial inability to own a vehicle, a decrease in driving ability, lack of convenient mass transit, and/or physical difficulty utilizing public transportation can result in social isolation. Further, lack of transportation can serve as a barrier to medical care, shopping, and other critical services.

The quality of America's housing stock has improved significantly over the past 40 years in terms of physical quality and size, especially among owner-occupied units. Yet those persons who are poor remain significantly more likely to live in physically deficient units (Struyk, Turner, and Ueno, 1988). Typically, older persons reside in older homes, the two having aged together over the years. Unfortunately this results in increasing maintenance concurrent with decreasing abilities to manage the demands of upkeep. As a result of this and other phenomena, approximately 20 percent of the elderly live in substandard housing, with a higher concentration among residents of rural areas and rental housing (Barrow, 1986).

As the cost of living rises so do rents, property taxes, and utilities. The income of a retiree on a fixed budget generally does not keep pace with these increasing financial demands. Consequently many renters and homeowners are forced to move to less costly quarters (Kaye, Monk, and Diamond, 1985).

Finally there is the issue of urban blight. What may have been a desirable and safe neighborhood when a house was bought or apartment rented may now be a deteriorating and crime-ridden community. Elders, who are threatened on their neighborhood streets or even fearful within the confines of their own homes, may have no other choice but to seek housing elsewhere.

Types of Housing Service Programs

The traditional and simplistic dichotomy between independent living and long-term institutional care is gradually losing its popularity. A variety of programs have emerged which subscribe to the increasingly popular philosophy that health and social services can successfully be attached to non-institutional housing stock. The growing convergence of philosophies influencing the structural design of housing environments and the satisfaction of the service needs of residents has resulted in a series of alternative (albeit largely *ad hoc*) forms of intermediate housing residences, programs, entitlements, and policies geared to the older adult. Taken together, they constitute a *de facto* continuum that aims to respond to the changing physical, cognitive, functional, social and familial needs of the elderly as they grow older (Monk and Kaye, 1991).

Intermediate Housing Models

Congregate Housing

Congregate housing, designed for persons requiring only minimal support, offers individual apartment units with limited services for older adults or couples. Services vary across housing programs, but may include: building security; transportation to shopping areas and/or medical appointments; social/recreational activities or facilities; social services; nutritional programs; and emergency call systems for medical crises.

Congregate care may be under private or public auspices. In the former case, it is often sponsored by a religious or social organization and may be part of a larger geriatric center which includes facilities such as a nursing home and home health care. Congregate housing may be subsidized by government programs such as Section Eight of the Federal Housing Authority. Regardless of auspice, there are often income guidelines and tenants may live in these apartments for approximately 30 percent of their income, including rent, utilities, and services. Other congregate care facilities cater to the more well-to-do aged and the costs may run much higher (Kraus, 1986).

Congregate housing is often the appropriate option for the individual who wants to maintain independent living but needs or desires the social and functional supports afforded by such facilities. For the lower-income aged, subsidized housing also provides financial reprieve from the expenses of home ownership or escalating rental costs. There is evidence to suggest that this type of housing can help prolong independence, provide companionship, develop a sense of community, reduce isolation, and increase opportunities for socialization among its residents (Kaye, Monk, and Diamond, 1985). Such housing has also displayed substantial cost savings compared to nursing home care (Heumann, 1991). A national survey of 1,500 adults aged 55 years and older sponsored by the American Association of Retired Persons (1990) found that almost one in three said they would consider moving into a congregate housing facility. This same survey found that seven percent of the elderly respondents had already moved into a congregate apartment house or were seriously considering doing so.

Public Housing

The U.S. Department of Housing and Urban Development (HUD) administers the financing for public housing for low-income persons of all ages. Low-income persons age 62 and older, or the spouse of a person at least 62, are eligible for public housing designed for older persons. Rent is considerably lower than comparable private housing and determined by a sliding scale (Hancock, 1990).

Section 202 Housing

The Section 202 Direct Loan Program of the Housing Act of 1959 provides subsidies for suppliers of housing to assist them in selling or renting units for less than the going market rate. The program is intended to benefit moderate-income elderly and handicapped whose incomes are above eligibility levels for public housing but too low to afford adequate housing on the open market. Section 202 housing programs are developed by nonprofit corporations or nonprofit consumer cooperatives (Hooyman and Kiyak, 1988).

Life Care Communities

Life care communities, also referred to as continuing care retirement communities (CCRCs), are planned communities that offer some or all types of housing along the continuum of care: independent living, assisted living, and nursing home care. Life care communities are privately sponsored and, because of the cost, cater primarily to the middle- and upper-income aged population. Although cost structures vary across communities, many require a significant up-front fee in addition to monthly payments. In exchange, the resident is guaranteed nursing care in the future should it become necessary (Sherwood, Ruchlin, and Sherwood, 1990). To assure long-term financial solvency of the community, new residents are accepted into the independent living quarters only. The more resource-intensive nursing facilities are usually reserved for residents whose condition has deteriorated following admission. Given the recent evolution of this category of elder housing, a number of political, social, and financial issues surrounding their development have yet to be resolved. While encouraged in some regions, CCRCs have been discouraged in others (Morrison, et al., 1986).

Boarding Homes

Boarding homes, as opposed to personal care boarding homes, provide a housing alternative for those who are alert and independent enough to manage without constant supervision. Such homes may be under the auspice of a religious, social, or professional organization, a philanthropic trust, or a private, for-profit group. In some cases the cost of care may be subsidized by the parent organization. Regardless of auspice, boarding homes offer room and board, heavy cleaning, and monitoring. Some may also offer any or all of the following: linens, maid service, light personal assistance, laundry service, social/recreational activities, and transportation.

Although there is nothing intrinsically inferior about boarding homes as a living alternative for older adults, those operations which offer substandard care have given such housing a bad name. Boarding homes must meet labor and industry inspections as well as state licensing requirements (Kraus, 1986).

SROs/Transient Hotels

Single room occupancy (SRO) or transient hotels are a common feature of most urban landscapes, although they may be found elsewhere as well. Such facilities are hotels that provide daily, weekly, or monthly rooms with few of the amenities offered by other types of hotels. In exchange for the low rates, tenants are provided with one room, perhaps with some bathroom facilities (more often bathrooms serve a hallway or floor). Extra charges are often imposed for linen service. Their residents are often low-income persons of all ages, the aged, recent immigrants, deinstitutionalized mental patients, and various transients.

According to Barrow (1986), SROs are inhabited by the most marginal and poor aged. These elderly are generally "loners," having traditionally lived alone, have an over-representation of drug and alcohol abuse, and frequently have physical and emotional handicaps.

Granny Flats

Introduced in Victoria, Australia in 1974 under the name "granny flats," this elder housing alternative is often referred to as ECHO housing (Elder Cottage Housing Opportunity). The concept was developed in response to the desire of many older adults and their families to live close to, but not with, each other. Granny flats are self-contained housing units designed for temporary installation on the same property as an adult child's home. In Australia the Victoria Ministry of Housing installs and rents such units and removes them when they are no longer needed (Lazarowich, 1990). A few private manufacturers in the U.S. make reusable ECHO homes.

The benefits of granny flats are numerous and include: continued independence for the older adult without sacrificing support; mutual support between households; intergenerational contact; and affordable senior housing. There are, however, obstacles as well in the U.S., as very few municipalities' zoning codes permit granny flats, and public attitudes frequently discourage modifications to such regulations (American Association of Retired Person, 1984).

Group Homes

Sponsored by a non-profit, for-profit, private, or public agency, a group home is a residence for anywhere from two to about ten aged individuals. Each resident is furnished with a bedroom and shares the remainder of the home's facilities as a traditional family would. In exchange for a rental fee, each resident receives basic household services: shopping, meal preparation, maintenance of the grounds, housekeeping, laundry service, transportation, and household financial management.

Because of the absence of hands-on assistance, residents must be fully independent. In addition to the financial benefits of living in a group home, this environment affords its residents a homelike atmosphere, social companionship, and freedom from household management activities (Kraus, 1986).

Naturally Occurring Retirement Communities

Given the powerful inclination of older people not to move from the familiar surroundings of their long-term residences and neighborhoods, it may not be surprising to find that such settings may gradually take on some of the characteristics of planned, supportive housing. The term "naturally occurring retirement Communities" or NORCs has been used to describe this phenomenon (Hunt and Gunter-Hunt, 1985). In some respects NORCs may be considered similar to various forms of planned private retirement environments. The latter have been classified previously as retirement new towns, villages, subdivisions, residences, and continuing care retirement centers, depending on the scale of the community, characteristics of the population, the kinds and amounts of services offered, and sponsorship or auspice under which the community was constructed (Hunt, et al., 1984).

Unplanned retirement communities or NORCs are usually situated in apartment buildings or housing complexes in particular parts of town that have remained desirable places to live (Hooyman and Kiyak, 1990). Initially occupied by individuals varying considerably in age, such settings are resided in increasingly by older residents who are often widowed but continue to be surrounded by a substantial network of close friends and neighbors.

NORCs by their very nature offer security, stability, and both a familiar and attractive setting in which to live. NORCs are likely to be characterized as much by a substantial constellation of informally-organized services as they are by the importation of a series of formal, organizationally based programs. Frequently residents band together in NORCs and develop on a voluntary basis needed service supports including escort and shopping services, home and community watch projects, transportation programs, emergency help, and respite assistance. Because such housing was not built originally for the purpose of serving the needs of elderly tenants, it may be able to avoid more easily the stigma that can be associated with such initiatives.

Housing Service Programs

Home Repair Programs

Because of the high cost of home repairs and the popularity of security features such as locks and window grates, and the addition of items such as ramps and grab bars for the physically compromised aged, many home repair programs have emerged. These services, often subsidized by Older Americans Act, Title III funds, offer such repairs and additions at little or no cost to the low-income elderly (Hancock, 1990).

Shared Housing

The concept of shared housing for the elderly is not a new one. Many older people with the need and desire to share financial and functional responsibilities have either opened their homes to an unrelated "roommate" or "boarder" or have arranged to move into another person's home. What is new about shared housing is that within the last decade many home-matching services have emerged to coordinate such arrangements and serve, in a sense, as a broker.

While shared housing situations may vary greatly, most share certain characteristics. Two or more unrelated persons, each having his or her own private bedroom, will share the common areas of a house or apartment. Most frequently the arrangement is between two or more older adults, but there are many examples of intergenerational home sharing. Rents vary depending upon the extent of task-sharing that is agreed upon, but the compensation received by the owner is always rental income and assistance with functional responsibilities. The end result is a reduction in housing expense and/or home-related tasks for both parties (American Association of Retired Persons, 1984).

While the financial benefits are clear, there are other advantages which may result from such an arrangement. Home sharing frequently defers a move to congregate housing through planned interdependence; it also reduces social isolation and provides companionship and can offer increased security as well as, in certain situations, provide an important intergenerational experience (American Association of Retired Persons, 1984).

Although home sharing can be a mutually satisfying arrangement, it is not without potential pitfalls. Streib (1984) has described shared living households as "social experiments in creating families." It is predictable that any effort at creating a primary group environment could expect to face challenges. Since both home owner and "tenant" share common areas and, often, responsibilities, a high degree of personal compatibility is required. Therefore, in addition to coordinating the terms of the home sharing agreement and accommodating the desired demographic profiles for both parties, the home sharing program must try to match personalities. Not surprisingly, this is no small task. It is not uncommon to find that, although both parties are generally compatible, issues of "turf" arise when a newcomer is introduced to the owner's domain. Jaffe and Howe (1989) find that case management is an important service in helping homesharers obtain skills for guiding the development of a successful match.

Energy Assistance and Weatherization Programs

Increasing energy costs in recent years have significantly reduced the purchasing power of many older adults. Supported by federal funds, the Low Income Energy Assistance Program (LIEAP) provides assistance to low-income households to meet their fuel bills. The program routinely supplements heating costs of eligible households and provides special assistance in weather crisis situations. Persons of all ages may qualify if household income does not exceed 125 percent of the current federal poverty guidelines.

The same eligibility requirements apply to the federally-sponsored Weatherization Assistance Program which helps qualifying households decrease consumption of energy (Hancock, 1990).

Tax Relief/Circuit Breaker Programs

A variety of state programs, referred to as tax relief/circuit breaker, and homestead exemption, among other titles, provide eligible homeowners with a deferral of, reduction in, or exemption from property and, in some cases, state and local taxes.

Among the most common tax relief programs is the circuit breaker, which entitles eligible homeowners to annual rebates on property taxes and renters to annual rental rebates. These programs, supported by public funds, target low-income households of persons of all ages (Council of State Housing Agencies and National Association of State Units on Aging, 1986).

Other Housing-Related Programs

Home Equity Conversion

Home equity conversion plans, also known as home equity liquefying plans (HELP), enable homeowners to use the equity they have built in their home to receive income without selling or moving. There are six major forms home equity conversion can take, most of which are available in selected states only:

1. Deferred-payment loans for property taxes permit homeowners to postpone payment of taxes until the house is sold or the owner dies;
2. Deferred-payment home improvement loans, usually geared to low-income homeowners, are also repaid after sale of the property or death of the owner. Until the time of repayment, a lien is placed on the property;

3. A "reverse mortgage" is a deferred payment general purpose loan with no annuity. Using the home as collateral, these fixed-term renewable loans are repayable at the end of the loan period;
4. A "reverse annuity mortgage" is similar to a reverse mortgage, but with an annuity. The loan is based on the value of the home equity and the anticipated longevity of the homeowner. Because it is designed to provide lifetime income, it is repayable upon the death of the homeowner or sale of the property;
5. "Sale-leaseback" plan entitles the owner to a lifetime lease and occupancy in exchange for sale of the home to an investor; and
6. "Sale-of-remainder-interest" allows the homeowner to retain lifetime ownership and occupancy by selling only the "remainder interest," or the ownership of the property after death (Chen, 1987).

International Perspectives

Specialized housing for the aged is a relatively recent phenomenon, growing in popularity and numbers only since World War II. Furthermore, this development has occurred almost exclusively in the most developed countries (Lawton, 1982).

Housing in developed countries other than the United States has tended to receive more public support. Additionally, many of the initiatives in planned housing in this country, such as granny flats, were tested and developed at earlier points in time in many other countries.

The level of sophistication of housing policy, or lack thereof, is often a reflection of a country's demographic composition or how recently it has become an "aging nation." However, there remain great variations across countries that transcend age composition. One measure of adequacy of housing policy is how well it can postpone or prevent nursing home placement. While in the U.S. nursing home admission rates have been rising in recent years, comparable figures for Sweden reflect a decline. Furthermore, the average age for nursing home entrants in Britain is two years greater than that of their American counterparts (Hokenstad, 1988).

There are also marked differences in policies mandating support for the frail aged to remain in their own homes. Sweden, The Netherlands, Great Britain, the Federal Republic of Germany, and other European nations have established national systems of service provision. Although each is quite different in both its structure and flaws, all share the perspective that services should be universally available and easily accessible. Not all such services are available without cost to the recipient, but they are viewed as a citizen's right and no means-testing stigma is attached (Nusberg, 1984). For example, in Britain publicly-funded housing is provided for a full one-third of its elder population (Hooyman and Kiyak, 1988) as compared to the 3 percent of older Americans who live in federally assisted housing (Lawton, 1982).

In the United States and elsewhere the majority of specialized housing units are age-segregated, despite the fact that the majority of the aged prefer an age-integrated environment. In France developers of large projects are required to designate 20 percent of their units as senior dwellings as part of a national plan to integrate the elderly into the larger community (Lawton, 1982).

What is commonly referred to as a "continuum of care" for the older adult is often not a continuum at all. Unfortunately, the road from complete independence to institutionalization is often wrought with gaping holes in available housing services. The absence of intermediary housing options or the lack of coordination of continuum of care can result in premature nursing home placement. In the Federal Republic of Germany, for example, there are several levels of "homes" for the aged, each responding to a slightly different level of need. Boarding homes for the aged are apartments within or adjacent to nursing homes designed for the independent dweller. All of the facilities of the nursing home are available to residents if and when they have a need. The next step along the housing continuum are the "homes" or "asylums" for the old. Such facilities cater to the needs of those who are no longer able to maintain their own residences but do not necessarily require nursing care. These homes are generally equipped with a medical ward for temporary illness. Social workers provide a range of services in both housing settings including information and referral, program planning, counseling, and management (Schumann, 1988).

A similar concept is reflected in Great Britain's public housing structure which has three basic types of housing corresponding to three levels of independence or frailty. Category I dwellings are designed for the relatively self-sufficient and active aged. Category II, also referred to as "sheltered housing," is composed of groups of adjacent apartments with a manager for emergencies. "Residential homes" or "Part III homes," financed and managed by local government, house approximately 40 to 60 senior residents who require limited nursing and assisted care (Streib, 1984).

Social Workers' Role

The multiplicity of social work roles in housing settings and services is not surprising given the range of programs and concomitant experiences for the older persons involved. Although the specific roles may vary from one setting or service to another, there are several that figure prominently across programs.

Psychosocial Intervention

A home is more than a physical habitat to most anyone, but perhaps more so to an older adult. The elder's residence is representative of a lifetime of activities carried out within its walls, of family and other significant persons, of achievements, and, perhaps, of a permanency not granted to one's own life. Each item in the home and its deliberate placement is a critical piece of the picture. The home's significance is magnified as the life it reflects changes and fades. Any disruption, due to the introduction of a roommate, having repairs or structural changes made, or moving out, can have a significant impact on an individual.

A social worker, in such a situation, will frequently need to deal with issues of disruption and loss. At a time in life when there may be loss of family and friends to death, loss of functionality, loss of financial security, and loss of role, the additional loss of home, familiar surroundings, and neighborhood must be addressed. Clients can be assisted with recognizing and coping with the feelings associated with displacement and relocation through social work intervention.

Upon relocation to planned housing, the aged client may experience the "halo effect" characterized by an initial positive response followed by a period of upset and depression in the face of an unfamiliar environment (Hooyman and Kiyak, 1990). Awareness of this potential reaction can help the social worker prepare the client for a possible emotional downturn before symptoms actually manifest themselves.

One of the potential sources of disturbance in relocation to planned housing is the adjustment to cohabitation. The elder who had lived alone or with immediate family is suddenly thrust into a semi-communal environment, sharing common areas or perhaps a living unit. Similarly, moving in with family members or having a caregiver or roommate move in can give rise to issues of cohabitation and interdependence. Individual, group, and family counseling can be employed to ease the transition.

Social workers may need to address the needs arising from prolonged home ownership rather than those related to relocation (Hooyman and Kiyak, 1990). Such needs may include the increasing burden of home maintenance and repair as well as the expense associated with these activities. Intervention may include many of the concrete roles addressed elsewhere in this section which reinforce the elder's efforts to remain an independent homeowner or renter.

It is critical that social workers be aware of and, when appropriate, utilize resources that can prevent or defer a client's relocation to planned or supportive housing. A case plan, developed in conjunction with the client, should take shape only after there has been a thorough investigation of all available alternatives.

Whether in planned housing or receiving support at home, the older person who prides himself on having always been independent and self-sufficient may respond to the need for assistance with lowered self-esteem, a sense of inadequacy, and, possibly, depression. The professional working with the elder applying for or receiving services must understand the significance of "taking a handout" or asking for help for a person who grew up in an era when only the truly indigent received public subsidies or other assistance.

The social work role can be enhanced by the availability of other resources. Specifically, the availability of peers, family members, and other informal supports provides an opportunity to develop new and solidify existing critical peer groups and social networks. The key role of informal supports and interpersonal relations in the later years is well documented. Relationships with family members, neighbors, friends, and even casual acquaintances have been shown to reduce the adverse effects of stressful life events (Hooyman and Kiyak, 1988). By encouraging and supporting informal relationships through counseling, the social worker is able to help the aged client achieve greater life satisfaction and reduced stress through increased independence. As Golant (1984) notes, intervention should be a combination of both individual- and client-oriented strategies which, in proper proportions, result in the improved quality of daily life for the client.

Concrete Services

Social work intervention in housing settings and services is frequently a combination of psychosocial and concrete support. The provision of a meaningful network of concrete services often requires both accessing services external to the organization and offering internal programs. Concrete services may include any or all of the following.

Outreach

Social work responsibility involves identifying potential service recipients and making them aware of service availability, service features, and eligibility requirements. This is frequently accomplished through outreach efforts and other marketing strategies. A poor marketing strategy could result in the permanent alienation of an elder from a useful service, as older adults frequently make decisions regarding service usage based upon the first exposure to marketing information (Kaye and Reisman, 1991).

Screening and Intake

Almost all services and certainly all planned housing settings have a mandatory application or intake process. The screening and intake role is often a social work responsibility and, if handled appropriately, requires professional skill. Given the applicant's likely feelings about needing and requesting help, as well as the anticipation of changes which will accompany service provision, it is incumbent upon the social worker to address those issues which extend beyond the simple task of application or registration.

Information and Referral

A primary social work role requires that the professional develop a data base of programs and benefits available to clients and build linkages with other organizations serving the aged. Whan called upon to assist a client with acquiring a needed support, the resources should be easily accessible (Settlement Housing Fund, 1986).

Consumer Education

Informing a client of the existence of a program or service often is not enough. To ensure that the provision of information to the elder service consumer results in a meaningful match between service provider and beneficiary, the social worker should provide consumer education. Information on how to evaluate services and make informed decisions can often be found in printed form. For example, *The Right Place at the Right Time: A Guide to Long-Term Care Choices* (American Association of Retired Persons, 1985), a how-to handbook, offers advice on how to make intelligent choices regarding long-term care. Other guides provide easy-to-understand reviews of senior housing options including advantages and cautions (see, for example, *Housing Options for Older Americans,* American Association of Retired Persons, 1984).

Program Planning

In housing settings, staff may be involved in the development and support of recreational, social, and educational programs to enhance the quality of life for residents. Programs such as transportation to shopping areas, medical appointments, and banks may be the only alternative to costly private service.

The tenants themselves may be the building's greatest resource, often bringing with them skills such as craftwork and gardening. These individuals are often eager volunteers for classes and lectures (Settlement Housing Fund, 1986).

Community Liaison

To enhance the image of the housing program or service in the community, the social worker can play an important role by attending interagency council meetings, community board meetings, and other neighborhood activities. Particularly in the case of planned housing, which is not always received warmly by the surrounding community, the worker can reduce the negative image and help integrate the housing into the life of the community. Each public appearance presents an opportunity for marketing services as well.

Advocate

A crucial role for the social worker requires some degree of political activism. The advocacy role, serving as champion on the group or individual level, is a primary method for effecting change.

On the group level, advocacy may entail introducing or supporting the passage of local, city, regional, state, and/or federal elderly housing policy. Of equal importance is advocacy on behalf of a particular client who may be denied sorely need services.

Social workers should remain abreast of current regulations pertaining to housing in their state. The *AARP Housing*

Report, for example, is an excellent guide for keeping community activists informed of new studies, housing initiatives, and policy developments in elder housing. Advocates should also be aware that several committees of Congress (Select Committee on Aging of the House and the Special Committee on Aging of the Senate) periodically hold hearings on issues pertaining to the elderly and their personal circumstances. Hearings on the federal, state, and local levels provide potential opportunities for social workers and other advocates to express their opinions and convey their experiences working with the elderly. Those interested in this type of activity should keep abreast of hearing schedules in their areas of interest and concern.

Problems and Prospects for the Future of Elder Housing

Pressure for change in housing for the elderly will be significant in the future. In large part change will be sought in terms of increased levels of demand for housing stock which is explicitly designed to satisfy the specialized needs of the older tenant. A 1990 study of the need and demand for service assisted living environments in the Commonwealth of Pennsylvania discovered the potential market for this type of housing option to be much greater than expected. Fully 23 percent of persons over the age of 60, or approximately 550,000 persons across the state, indicated interest in service assisted housing options (Granger and Kaye, 1991). Similar levels of interest in other states are not inconceivable.

Much of the change in housing demand will be dictated by the imperatives of demographic change. The proportion of older persons in American society will continue to increase for the foreseeable future at a rapid rate. Households composed of elderly persons are expected to grow very rapidly over the next 90 years and are projected to constitute at least 20 percent of all households in the early part of the next century (Struyk, Turner, and Ueno, 1988). Specifically, increases in the number of women (widows in particular), single-parent households, those who are very old (85 years and older), and minorities are anticipated. Elderly and middle-aged persons who live alone or with non-relatives will grow in number at a particularly rapid rate. And while households generally will continue to decline in size, the size of elderly households is expected to increase as more married couples survive into old age (Katsura, Struyk, and Newman, 1988). Such households are expected in particular to place heavy demand on smaller housing units which can provide an increasingly wide array of ancillary services (Struyk, Turner, and Ueno, 1988). In addition it is likely that demand will be voiced for more effective linkages between community housing and the kinds of intensive health care services that are offered through the long-term care sector.

Fluctuating migration patterns of older adults who are relocating and especially rapid increases in the number of older suburban residents may also prove to be significant in influencing the level of need and demand for particular categories of elder housing (American Association of Retired Persons, 1985; Lawton and Hoover, 1981; Longino, 1979; Newman, 1985).

In addition it is important to remember that the elderly are subject to increasing losses in their social and family networks. As persons live longer, such networks of informal support inevitably weaken. Furthermore, families, friends, and neighbors—those individuals who have traditionally performed the lion's share of the elder support function in the community—may be inevitably reaching their absorptive capacity (Kaye and Applegate, 1990). Increases in dual income, highly mobile families have served to both place greater burden on and decrease the availability of such informal supports for the elderly (Brody, 1981).

Finally, it is essential to remember that the aging-in phenomenon in community housing is going to continue on its present course. This inevitable progression of persons growing increasingly frail and unable to care for themselves as they grow older, while not a significant problem for all older persons, does present itself as a factor of growing significance.

Taken together, the demographic transformation of the older population presents a sobering agenda for housing policymakers, planners and practitioners alike. Gerontological social workers who engage in work with or on behalf of older persons residing in non-institutional settings must be counted among those who will be pressed to help shape the elder housing environment of the future. Advocating for forward-looking housing policy, developing creative programs which aim to enrich the living environments of older environments, promoting flexible and accommodating elder housing, and maximizing residential choice for this cohort are challenging yet essential responsibilities of human service professionals in this field of practice. Whether one provides direct services to elderly residents within a single housing facility or performs housing policy analysis in a government bureau or community research institute, there is much to be done. Taken together, the performance of these professional obligations ensures that the elderly, frail and able alike, will remain in housing and communities of their choice for as long as is feasible.

REFERENCES

American Association of Retired Persons (AARP). 1984. *Housing options for older Americans.* Washington, DC: Author.

American Association of Retired Persons (AARP). 1985. *The right place at the right time: A guide to long-term care choices.* Washington, DC: Author.

American Association of Retired Persons (AARP). 1990. *AARP's 1990 housing survey shows more older people want to age in place. AARP Housing Report 1.* Washington, DC: Author.

Barrow, G.M. 1986. *Aging, the Individual, and Society*. St. Paul, MN: West Publishing Company.

Brody, E.M. 1981. Women in the middle and family help to older people. *The Gerontologist, 21,* 471–480.

Chen, Y.P. 1987. "Home Equity Conversion." In G.L. Maddox, ed., *The Encyclopedia of Aging*. New York: Springer.

Council of State Housing Agencies and National Association of State Units on Aging. 1986. *State initiatives in elderly housing: What's new, what's tried and true*. Washington, DC: CSHA and NASUA.

Golant, S.M. 1984. *A Place to Grow Old: The Meaning of Environment and Old Age*. New York: Columbia University Press.

Granger, B. & Kaye, L.W. 1991. "Assessing Consumer Need and Demand for Service-Assisted Housing in Pennsylvania." In L.W. Kaye and A. Monk, eds., *Congregate Housing for the Elderly: Theoretical, Policy and Programmatic Perspectives*. New York: The Haworth Press.

Hancock, B.L. 1990. *Social Work with Older People*. Englewood Cliffs, NJ: Prentice-Hall.

Heumann, L.F. 1991. "A cost comparison of congregate housing and long term care facilities for elderly residents with comparable support needs in 1985 and 1990." In L.W. Kaye and A. Monk, eds., *Congregate Housing for the Elderly: Theoretical, Policy and Programmatic Perspectives*. New York: The Haworth Press.

Hokenstad, M.C. 1988. Cross-national trends and issues in social service provision and social work practice for the elderly. *Journal of Gerontological Social Work, 12*, 1–15.

Hooyman, N.R. and Kiyak, H.A. 1988. *Social Gerontology: A Multidisciplinary Perspective*. Boston: Allyn and Bacon.

Hunt, M.E.; Feldt, A.G.; Marans, R.W.; Pastalan, L.A.; and Vakalo, K.L. 1984. *Retirement Communities: An American Original*. New York: The Haworth Press.

Hunt, M.E. and Gunter-Hunt, G. 1985. Naturally occurring retirement communities. *Journal of Housing for the Elderly, 3*, 3–21.

Jaffe, D.J. and Howe, E. 1989. Case management for home sharing. *Journal of Gerontological Social Work, 14*, 91–109.

Katsura, H.M.; Struyk, R.J.; and Newman, S.J. 1988. *Housing for the Elderly in 2010: Projections and Policy Options*. Washington, DC: The Urban Institute.

Kaye, L.W.; Monk, A.; and Diamond, B.E. 1985. *The Enrichment of Residential Housing Stock for Elderly Tenants: A National Analysis and Case Feasibility Study*. New York: Columbia University Press.

Kaye, L.W. and Applegate, J. 1990. *Men as Caregivers to the Elderly: Understanding and Aiding Unrecognized Family Support*. Lexington, MA: Lexington Books.

Kaye, L.W. and Reisman, S.I. 1991. *A comparative analysis of marketing strategies in health and social services for the elderly: provider and consumer perspectives*. (Final Report to the AARP Andrus Foundation). Bryn Mawr, PA: Bryn Mawr College.

Kraus, A.S. 1986. *A Guide to Supportive Living Arrangements for Older Citizens*. Wallingford, PA: Geriatric Planning Services.

Lawton, M.P. 1982. "Environments and Living Arrangements." In R.H. Binstock, W.S. Chow, and J.H. Schulz, eds., *International Perspectives on Aging: Population and Policy Challenges*. New York: United Nations Fund for Population Activities.

Lawton, M.P. and Hoover, S.L. 1981. *Community Housing Choices for Older Americans*. New York: Springer.

Lazarowich, N.M. 1990. A review of the Victoria, Australia granny flat program. *The Gerontologist, 30*, 171–177.

Longino, C. 1979. Going home: Aged return migration in the U.S.: 1965–1970. *Journal of Gerontology, 34*, 736–745.

Matrix Research Institute. 1990. *The need for service assisted housing by older Pennsylvanians: Results of a statewide survey*. (Pennsylvania Department of Aging, Contract No. 887003). Philadelphia, PA: MRI.

Monk, M. and Kaye, L.W. 1991. "Congregate Housing for the Elderly; Its Need, Function, and Perspectives." In L.W. Kaye and A. Monk, eds., *Congregate Housing for the Elderly: Theoretical, Policy and Programmatic Perspectives*, New York: The Haworth Press.

Morrison, I.A.; Bennett, R.; Frisch, S.; and Gurland, B.J., eds. 1986. *Continuing Care Retirement Communities: Political, Social and Financial Issues*. New York: The Haworth Press.

National Conference on Social Welfare. 1981. *Long-Term Care: In Search of Solutions*. Washington, DC: Author.

Newman, S. 1985. The shape of things to come. *Generations, 9*, 14–17.

Nusberg, C. 1984. *Innovative Aging Programs Abroad: Implications for the United States*. Westport, CT: Greenwood.

Parr, J.; Green, S.; and Behncke, C. 1989. "What people want, why they move, and what happens after they move: A summary of research in retirement housing." In L.A. Pastalan and M.E. Cowart, eds., *Lifestyles and Housing of Older Adults: The Florida Experience*. New York: The Haworth Press.

Reschovsky, J.D. and Newman, S.J. 1991. Home upkeep and housing quality of older homeowners. *The Journal of Gerontology, 46*, S288–S297.

Settlement Housing Fund, Inc. 1986. *Tenants Aging-In: The Challenge for Staff in Housing for the Elderly.* New York: Author.

Sherwood, S.; Ruchlin, H.S.; and Sherwood, C.C. 1990. "CCRCs: An Option for Aging in Place." In D. Tilson, ed., *Aging in Place: Supporting the Frail Elderly in Residential Environments.* Glenview, IL: Scott, Foresman.

Schumann, J. 1988. Social services and social work practice with the elderly in the Federal Republic of Germany. *Journal of Gerontological Social Work, 12,* 61–76.

Streib, G.F. 1984. "Introduction." In G.F. Streib, W.E. Folts, and M.A. Hilker, eds., *Old Homes—New Families: Shared Living for the Elderly.* New York: Columbia University Press.

Struyk, R.J.; Turner, M.A.; and Ueno, M. 1988. *Future U.S. Housing Policy: Meeting the Demographic Challenge.* Washington, DC: The Urban Institute Press.

Struyk, R.J. & Soldo, B.J. 1980. *Improving the Elderly's Housing: A Key to Preserving the Nation's Housing Stock and Neighborhood.* Cambridge, MA: Ballinger Publishing Company.

Tilson, D. & Fahey, C.J. 1990. "Introduction." In D. Tilson, ed., *Aging in Place: Supporting the Frail Elderly in Residential Environments.* Glenview, IL: Scott, Foresman.

Turner, L.; Schreter, C.; & Zetnick, B. 1982. *Housing options for the community resident elderly.* Bryn Mawr, PA: Bryn Mawr College.

United States Conference of Mayors. 1986. *Assessing elderly housing: A planning guide for mayors, local officials, and housing advocates.* Washington, DC: Author.

CHAPTER 11

Health Service Policies and Programs for the Elders

Donna L. Yee

Introduction

Being old is not the same as being sick, but among the fastest growing cohort of elders (those 85 and older), the likelihood of having difficulty with at least three activities of daily living due to poor health is more than four times greater than for elders who are under 70. For African Americans, the likelihood of having difficulty with at least three activities of daily living is twice that of whites (U.S. Senate Special Committee on Aging, American Association of Retired Persons, Federal Council on Aging, and U.S. Administration on Aging, 1991). National costs for health care for elders are higher than for any other age group, and among the oldest old the combination of impoverishment and declining informal care resources points to a higher demand for publicly funded formal care (Wethers, Capitman, and Yee, 1992; Yee and Kamikawa, 1992).

Advances in public health, technological advances, lower mortality rates for some groups of infants and youth, and an increased focus on healthier lifestyles for all age groups that result in the prevention or delay of many chronic and terminal diseases, have all contributed to longer life expectancy. Furthermore, patterns of longevity indicate a clear advantage for women over men. In response to the increasing number of elders living longer with greater numbers of chronic conditions, more elders need and use health care than at any time in the country's history (Moon, 1991; U.S. Department of Health and Human Services Public Health Service, 1990). While public policy has mediated some of the problems of inequitable access to health care among some groups of elders, efforts to expand access to and define quality health care in the last two decades may not be adequate as we approach the year 2000. The major issues facing elders related to health care are the *cost* of health care and *access* to care, including adequate health financing.

Yet not all elders can get the care they need. Since 1965 the Medicare program has provided almost universal health insurance; 95 percent of all elders are covered. Medicare is an entitlement health insurance program administered federally. There are two parts to Medicare. Part A, which covers hospital and other inpatient care, is available to all persons who participate in the Social Security program. Part B covers outpatient and related home health services and is an optional insurance that is purchased by most Medicare beneficiaries. Medicare, however, only covers specific kinds and amounts of health care. Unless an elder purchases additional private health insurance such as a medigap policy, those bills not covered by Medicare, including pharmaceutical, permanent nursing home care, dental care, vision and hearing aids become out-of-pocket expenses. For elders who are poor, Medicaid supplements and complements Medicare coverage. Medicaid costs are shared by federal and state taxes and the program is administered by states. It expands access to health care for poor elders, supplementing Medicare coverage for almost one-third of poor elders and almost one-tenth of near poor elders (Kasper, 1988).

This chapter presents issues in health policy and of health service delivery with a particular focus on elders who are the most vulnerable. The key policy issues outlined above, health care cost and access to care, are discussed in the following sections on: (a) differences in health status and service use among the aged; (b) health care costs; (c) the effect of the juxtaposition of acute and long term care services on health care access for the most vulnerable elders; and (d) financing barriers, cost controls, color-blindness, and quality of care as a context for understanding access to health care. The chapter will conclude with a discussion of health policy and service delivery challenges and options.

Health Status and the Most Vulnerable Elders

The median age of elders (persons 65 and over) continues to increase; one-half of the aged will be over 75 in the year 2000—just eight years away—and the proportion of elders to other age groups in the U.S. is estimated to continue to rise. Three significant demographic trends drive health policy decisions in this country: (1) the growing number of elders who are among the oldest old (80 and over) and the growing number of elders with disabilities; (2) the disproportion of women elders; and (3) rapidly increasing cultural diversity among elders.

First, more elders are living longer and living more years of their lives with chronic diseases and attendant disabilities. The paradox of medical progress is that technology and general improvements in the availability of quality medical care have saved more lives but prolonged the years of living with disability in our society. The challenge of chronic care needs for elders and their family members or informal caregivers for as many as twenty years is a mixed blessing.

Second, elders are a female majority, a heterogenous group of survivors who were born between the turn of the century and just prior to the depression. Among those 65 and older, women outnumber men three to two. Among the oldest old (those 80 years and older), women outnumber men three to one. It is likely that as the population in the United States continues to age, women will continue to outnumber men.

Third, cultural diversity has long been a feature of life in the United States, but demographic trends for elders in this country show an even more rapid growth than expected among African-American, Latino, Pacific/Asian-American, Native American, and other elders of color. In this chapter the term "elders of color and Hispanics" is used to include persons who identify as African Americans/Blacks, Hispanics/Latinos, Pacific

Islander/Asians, and American Indian/Native Alaskans and Aleut. This term allows for positive differentiation between persons rather than negative assignment of the absence of "whiteness" as does the term "non-white," while recognizing that the majority of Hispanics are white. Additionally, the term "minority" implies the assignment of marginal social and political status to persons. In some communities ethnic and racial groups collectively make up the majority of the population. As the 60s generation approaches a new century, elders, like the overall population, will become increasingly multicultural, multiracial, and diverse. In the 1980s elders of color and Hispanics accounted for over ten percent of the population over 65. Their rate of growth is expected to increase thirty percent by 2050—over twice the rate of increase expected in the general population.

Among women of color, little is known about the factors that might predict unmet needs for care, particularly among Pacific Islander/Asian-American and American Indian older women. Studies of white, African-American, and Hispanic women indicate a higher need for formal care and provide information about older women's access to and the adequacy of informal care resources. Among all elders:

- one in five white elders 65 and over is poor and lives alone;
- two in five African-American and other "minorities," and one in three Hispanic elders, are poor and live alone;
- women outnumber men in all age groups (or cohorts) of elders, and are twice as likely to live alone compared to men; and
- among the oldest old, women are three times as likely as men to live alone.

Among the poor and near poor, one-third and more than one-fourth respectively have health problems that limit their ability to independently perform activities of daily living such as bathing, dressing, and toileting. Among elders 70 and over who live alone, a third rely on a hired person and over half rely on both paid and unpaid help with at least one important daily task.

Over one-third of African-American elders living alone have no living children to assist them, as compared to about one-fourth of white elders living alone. Compared to all groups of elders, the highest use of community services is among poor elders who are 75 and over and living alone (Kasper, 1988).

As the number and proportion of persons 65 and over rises in the U.S., they are increasingly heterogenous in their health status and care needs. According to national studies in the last decade, those most vulnerable and at risk for needing assistance but using low levels of most services are those who are:

- the oldest old (those 80 and over);
- living alone; and
- persons of color and Hispanics.

Health Service Use and Access

There are differences among elders in access to health and long-term care by gender and race.

- White women tend to make more physician visits than white men and the intervals between the visits are shorter.
- White men tend to use hospital services more than white women.
- When white women use hospitals, however, the length of stay is longer.

Comparable data on women of color are not available, but compared to white elders, women of color are more likely to use hospital services and to have a lower number of physician visits in a given year. Older women of color are more likely to get their regular care from hospital outpatient units and emergency rooms and neighborhood health centers than from private physicians (U.S. Department of Health and Human Services, 1986; U.S. Department of Health and Human Services Public Health Service, 1990; U.S. Senate Special Committee on Aging, et al., 1991).

While it is generally known that women, particularly white older women, are twice as likely to be placed in nursing homes as men (U.S. Senate Special Committee on Aging, et al., 1991), few studies have focused on the use patterns or triggers to admission for elders of color and Hispanics. In a series of recent studies using National Long Term Care Survey and Longitudinal Survey on Aging data, Karon and Capitman (1992) explored Medicare skilled nursing and home health use and informal care effects on home care use with regard to race/ethnicity and gender. It was found that: (1) whites and those living alone had the greatest likelihood of being in nursing homes, and that women generally stayed longer; and (2) women living alone had the highest likelihood of using home health services and using them for longer periods than men or persons with a spouse (Karon and Capitman, 1992). Furthermore, it was found that the likelihood of using paid help because of functional impairments was explained by a complex combination of factors relating to the elder's functional and medical status, the presence of informal supports, financial resources available, race and gender. A review of quantitative studies in the last fifteen years on the use of formal services by race/ethnicity and gender characteristics of elders concurred that little is known that would further explain what aspects of care use can be attributed to the race/ethnicity or gender of the elder and his/her caregivers or the motivations and resources of the service provider. The report concludes that:

1. the dearth of data, primarily due to under-sampling, on Pacific Islander/Asian Americans, American Indians/Native Alaskans and Aleut, and Hispanics/Latinos means that few conclusions can be drawn about white versus elders of color and Hispanic differences or about differences among diverse populations of elders with regard to the use of formal care and the role of informal care resources on service use;
2. there is an urgent need for systematic research on how the practices of provider organizations, including the attitudes and behaviors of individual providers, influence service access and use;

3. more attention is needed on how attitudes, knowledge and preferences toward long term care (LTC) vary by race/ethnicity and gender and how those attitudes affect service use; and
4. more demonstrations and evaluation studies are needed on how to ensure equitable access to LTC for elders of color in the context of national and local reform proposals (Capitman, Wethers, and Sadowsky, 1992).

Access to health care and the use of health services differ among elders when race/ethnicity and gender are considered. Health status can be seen, like income security in old age, as a result of life chances (i.e., differences in educational, occupational, and social opportunities) and differences in cultural values and norms. For the aged, it is also a reflection of how health and illness are understood. First, health status does not confer need as it is perceived by elders. While some may define health in old age as the absence of illness, others are likely to define it as the absence of pain or complaints that limit daily activities. Second, the use of health services is not always related to health status. Access to health care can be as much a function of income and insurance as it is of geographic location, education, race/ethnicity, gender, and other factors. Being assessed and diagnosed does not always result in predictable treatments and costs (Soldo and Manton, 1985; Verbrugge, Lepkowski, and Imanaka, 1989). Finally, the health status of elders is in part an outcome of cumulative effects of access to care and care quality over a lifetime. If persons have not had adequate health care as children or working adults, they are not likely to embrace new approaches to health care or understand some aspects of health care delivery in old age, even if they have useable and affordable insurance.

Health Care Costs for Older Americans

Between 1977 and 1988, personal health care expenditures under Medicare have increased at an average annual rate of 14.4 percent, more than twice the rate of inflation and almost one-fourth faster than the growth in total national personal health care expenditures. Even with savings measures enacted in the 1980s, Medicare is still projected to grow at twice the rate of inflation or more through the end of the decade. (U.S. Senate Special Committee on Aging, et al., 1991). In 1988 Medicare and Medicaid accounted for ten percent of the Federal budget (Office of National Cost Estimates, 1990).

In the last generation, elders have accommodated great change in the delivery of health care. Since 1965, when they became a visible, growing constituency in every political jurisdiction of the country, the Medicare Insurance title of the Social Security Act has represented a movement toward health care as a right rather than as a privilege. In 1989 only one in twenty persons 65 and over did not have Medicare insurance (U.S. Senate Special Committee on Aging, et al., 1991). Practically universal insurance coverage for elders is a remarkable accomplishment in 25 years; it is expected to protect elders and their caregivers from the hazard of the catastrophic cost of illness and care needs and from the hazard of unavailable and inaccessible care. Closer scrutiny of increases in personal health care expenditures among elders, however, reveals an unexpected outcome in the progress toward minimizing cost and access barriers to health care. In 1987 elders spent an average of $2,004 per capita on health care for medigap insurance to supplement the shortfall of Medicare insurance coverage for care, for Medicare part B premium payments, for care in nursing homes, pharmaceuticals, dental care, and other health care not covered by the Medicare program.

Yet the escalating costs of health care are not borne by any one group—neither elders, taxpayers (who fund public sector health programs), nor employers (through high health benefit costs). Efforts to ascribe blame for America's health care crisis to the growing number of elders or their reluctance to shoulder their share of the cost of their care, the opportunism of health care providers, or the inefficiency of government in managing the costs of health care are unconstructive and misleading. These and several more viewpoints portion blame in an attempt to explain why America's health care system needs to be fixed. Most of these attempts portion blame by targeting elders already in the health system and by pointing to the inappropriate allocation of scarce system resources, but such efforts have not yielded solutions for equitable, affordable and accessible health care for all. Many elders still have not benefited from improvements in access to care that were supposed to be afforded by Medicare and Medicaid, or from the proliferation of private insurance products.

Efforts to reform the financing and organization of America's health care system need to address issues of equity, affordability, and accessibility. In the context of the most vulnerable groups of elders, reform of the acute and primary medical care delivery system without commensurate reform of the long term care delivery system, and linkage of the systems in ways that assure continuity and quality care, are necessary parts of the overall debate on health care reform.

Acute and Long-Term Care Service Delivery

There is a hierarchy among health services; the most costly are generally the most highly valued. High tech care (e.g., Magnetic Resonance Imagery, CAT Scans, and organ transplantation) is generally associated with the high cost of better care, while low tech care is generally associated with low or no cost caring—the kinds of procedures and tasks that any caring person can do for another person. Studies show that men need the most valued or costly kind of care, while women need the least valued or costly kind of care in the short term (U.S. Department of Health and Human Services Public Health Service, 1990; U.S. Senate Special Committee on Aging, et al., 1991). Greater levels of morbidity and co-morbidity among older women and persons of color and Hispanics, however, mean that over the long term the cost of acute and chronic care for older women may be higher (Verbrugge, et al., 1989). When help from informal caregivers for functional and cognitive impairments is not enough to help elders remain in community settings, the immediate or inevitable burden on public resources to pay for that care necessitates public policy strategies that mediate and control public sector costs.

The *separation of primary health and long term care* (LTC) is an example of a pattern in which health services are defined and financed to maximize institutional interests, an agenda that fosters the fragmentation and lack of service continuity that endangers every person's quality of care. LTC is a generic group of services and care approaches that respond to the chronic care needs of elders and persons with disabilities; it is defined as less than acute care. LTC as a concept is a residual of the primary medical care and acute hospital care parts of health care service delivery.

When the cost of convalescence in acute care beds for persons still uncured and in transition to "custodial" care became costly and caused a bed shortage in acute hospitals, the government, through Medicare and Medicaid, fostered the construction of rehabilitation and skilled nursing units and the proliferation of freestanding skilled nursing units (not attached to licensed acute hospitals). When skilled nursing facility costs grew because more people still uncured needed nursing care, without necessarily needing the interventions of a registered nurse, intermediate care facilities were created. When nursing home costs overall threatened to unbalance state budgets, efforts to establish community-based long term care services as "alternatives" to nursing home care were emphasized at the federal and state levels (California Health and Welfare Agency, 1988; Callahan and Wallack, 1981; Capitman, 1990).

Concurrently, however, as technology to improve morbidity and chronic disease outcomes developed (e.g., kidney dialysis, intravenous therapies and tube feeding in the home, outpatient pre-surgery diagnostic procedures, and ventilator care in non-acute facilities), the high cost, high technology interventions pushed the line separating acute and LTC. Step-down care and subacute care units in hospitals, and under special licensing conditions in nursing homes and in patients' homes, became new classifications of care that provided targeted reimbursement for specialty areas of chronic care but not LTC in general. As reimbursement for greater numbers of high tech procedures in LTC settings becomes available, traditional LTC providers gravitate toward those services. These trends benefit providers and their concern about their financial viability, but they do little to change the public's general perceptions or way of valuing low technology (i.e., high touch) LTC services or the need for such care.

While high tech approaches improve diagnostic capability and treatment for specified chronic conditions, they do not necessarily improve the low tech caring needed by elders and the disabled with uncured and increasingly debilitating ailments as they age. In the last decade before the year 2000 LTC continues to be the low technology end of the health care system. As procedures, new drugs, and machines decrease rates of mortality, they often increase rates of morbidity—namely, the number of years people can live with disability. When science leaves off, human caregiving—assistance getting in and out of bed, with bathing, with grooming, with dressing, with meal preparation, with feeding, with toileting, with getting out of the house, with maintaining a household—all fall into a low tech group of services, an undifferentiated chasm called LTC. Family and other informal caregivers provide most of the LTC needed by growing numbers of elders, and as more women enter the work force there is also an increasing use of formal caregivers to supplement and complement family caregiving efforts.

Caregiving (both paid and unpaid) for the elder and family means making tradeoffs—between the affordability of skilled and less skilled practitioners, between finding a person who cares about the elder's preferences in how care is provided and just having someone there, and between someone who is available and a person who is trained. Caregiving is in part about having a caring heart, but it also about having skills that, as they say in medicine, "do no harm." Caregiving is about empathy and motivation as well as about physical care; it is about providing assistance with safe transfers (in and out of a tub, in and out of bed, on and off a toilet), preparing meals that limit salt or sugar intake, or providing consistent supervision during periods of combativeness, depression, or anxious confusion. No matter how society pays for or recognizes it, low tech care is not unimportant—it is the high touch care, and care that requires both caring and knowledge about providing assistance.

The growing number of elders with chronic care needs and the resulting demand for adequate and acceptable LTC services will continue, in the context of the need, to require that cost control issues at all service delivery levels be addressed. Even efforts such as the 1987 Omnibus Budget Reconciliation Act which instituted nursing home reform have had limited short-term effects. On the one hand, major shifts in the scope of licensing and certification reviews of facilities in every State have refocused concerns on the enforcement of standards of care and the quality of care provided in nursing homes, but little has been accomplished to control institutional costs. The establishment of alternative, community-based long term care (CLTC) services has not been less costly, although it has slowed the construction of institutional beds and enabled the most able elders to remain in the community with supportive nursing and health care rather than be inappropriately placed in institutions.

Additionally, the Prospective Payment Assessment Commission (ProPAC), formed to control Medicare costs through the use of diagnostic related groups, has in the short term, done little to control overall Medicare acute care costs. Its impact on providers of post-acute care, particularly home health agencies, home care and other aging and LTC service providers, has contributed to a substantial increase of skilled and high technology care in home and post-acute care settings (Dobson et al., 1991) and a trickling down of complex and skilled care responsibilities to informal caregivers and formal CLTC providers.

The dividing line between primary/acute health care and long term care is a function of financing mechanisms for kinds of care and the adequacy of the reimbursement. Care that includes little technology has always been part of long term care. As long as levels of reimbursement and financing mechanisms define the societal importance and value of kinds of care, long term care will continue to be a burden that society tries to ignore, tries to accommodate without developing policy or the political will to define a system that is integrated as part of the overall health care system, and that is validated as part of the society's vision of optimal health and quality of life in old age.

Access to Care

As primary health and long term care providers and patients compete for scarce resources to access adequate quality care, issues of access to care have been more clearly and broadly defined. Access to care refers to the ability of a patient to get into a care system as well as to access appropriate care once assessed and diagnosed. Access is not just "getting through the front door"; it includes how individuals and classes of patients get treated once they have found the clinic or gotten into the doctor's office. In this section, financial access barriers to care, system design barriers, color-blindness and provider beliefs/behaviors, and quality of care are discussed as part of the larger issue of access to care.

Financial Access Barriers

Even with universal insurance coverage, many elders can not afford to use Medicare; the cost of premiums, deductibles and co-payments make the insurance unusable (Yee, 1992). Only one in three poor elders have Medicaid to supplement and enable them to use their Medicare insurance coverage. Of the near-poor (those with incomes at less than 200 percent of the poverty level), only one in ten have Medigap insurance (U.S. Senate Special Committee on Aging, et al., 1991). The lack of funds to purchase additional insurance, to cover the attendant costs of using insurance, and to pay for care not covered by Medicare makes access to health care (including long term care) an ongoing problem for elders.

Two policy dilemmas related to access to care in the context of health services organization are: (1) how to promote and enforce standards of care; and (2) how to assure availability of a comprehensive array of services while fostering autonomy and promoting local initiatives and innovations that respond to specific needs of diverse populations. Global policies that define outreach strategies for all geographic regions and all target populations are likely to be too limiting and too general to effectively assure adequate and equitable levels of program access or participation. An approach used in many existing federal laws such as the Medicaid or Social Services Block Grants is the distinction between "mandatory" and "optional" services. Mandatory services provide a basic framework for health or social services, allowing and sometimes motivating states to invest in a richer service mix or intensity for targeted populations (the poor, adults, or children).

According to a recent American Association of Retired Persons publication, the range of personal health costs per capita in 1990 was from $1,689 in South Carolina to $3,031 in Massachusetts, and the range of Medicaid payment per recipient in fiscal year 1989 was from $79.93 in Mississippi to $4,523 in New York. The average personal health cost per capita across all states was $2,425, and for Medicaid payment per recipient in fiscal year 1989 was $2,318 (Raetzman, 1991). The variation across states is striking, and it underscores the need to bring programs for the poor "up to the poverty line". As the national safety net for access to health care, Medicaid reaches only 59 percent of the poor in need of care. Variation across states can be beneficial in motivating local governments to be innovative and responsive, but it can also condone inequities in federal attempts to assure accessible and adequate health care for everyone.

As noted in the conclusion of a study by Pendleton, et al. (1990) on the capacity of states to provide CLTC, the main barrier in state infrastructures is the absence of centralized management of CLTC programs that have multiple funding sources. Only one in five states was found to have a core management and administrative structure to integrate services. There were inequities across states in the availability of a range of CLTC services for frail elders, and inequities within states (e.g., service programs not offered on a statewide basis). Even when offered through existing state policy, the core CLTC services (home health, personal care, adult day care, and transportation) were rarely available statewide. Furthermore, states that had developed systems for long-term care across Medicaid, Older Americans Act, Social Service Block Grant, state funded services, and/or Medicare differed in the way services were organized and administrated and in service pathways. This diversity stems from the absence of a national policy or uniform program and from the historical differences among the states in the evaluation of state and local management and service systems. Differences in markets for services and available technology also contribute to observed differences in state regulatory approaches and practice (Pendleton, et al., 1990). Differences across states and within service systems particularly affect elders at the margin of those service programs. For frail elders who are the most vulnerable, the oldest old, those living alone, and elders of color and Hispanics, such differences also define barriers to getting into and appropriately using services.

Cost Controls as Access Barriers to Service Systems

Aside from rationing care, or limiting access to health care by economic status of those needing care, several strategies have been used by states to manage access to care and health care utilization among the poor. While cost control efforts may appear to be a benign approach to rationing resources, they may limit access to care for the most vulnerable populations.

In the 1970s and 1980s California and other states had, for example, "presumptive eligibility" as part of the authorization process for Medicaid services. For persons who appeared to meet eligibility criteria for a service (e.g., if a person was edentulous and poorly nourished, and had a Medicaid identification card), a provider was not required to obtain prior authorization from Medicaid before providing care. Providers could confidently provide care and be reimbursed when they submitted a bill. Few states in the 1990s continue the practice, not because the needs of Medicaid patients have changed, but because it is a way to control the flow of Medicaid expenses by delaying the provision of care, constraining the conditions under which authorization is granted, and by limiting the level of reimbursement for discrete procedures. While such policies at the local level may not be life threatening, they do affect the individual's ability to manage self-care adequately (appropriate and adequate nutrition in this case). Few providers are willing to spend the time and effort, and few elders have the confidence to self-advocate for needs through a lengthy administrative or grievance procedure in order to have authorization decisions reconsidered. Furthermore, health care providers become less willing to accept patients with Medicaid and Medicare insurance—patients who are more troublesome and time consuming, and whose care may not be adequately reimbursed.

Another example of ways programs control costs is to change the scope of discrete benefits or the amounts of care. This is not always done by statute or regulation and is sometimes done by intermediary review practices. Studies demonstrate that the average number of visits authorized for discrete home health services under Medicare differed by region, and these differences were explained by Medicare professional peer review organization practices and performance, not by provider behavior or the needs of beneficiaries (Rak, 1991; Rak, 1992). With this approach the most vulnerable elders are less likely to file a grievance when they disagree with a fiscal intermediary's decision to discontinue coverage for a service, and the poor are often less successfully linked/referred to other follow-up care. For those who are not cured, needing a "lower level of care" is still needing care.

Yet another method of controlling access to care is state moratoria on facility construction—the control of the capacity of the system to provide nursing home, acute, or rehabilitation inpatient care. This affects elders in several ways: it may increase the price of care for those paying "out-of-pocket"; it may make care geographically less accessible because facilities are primarily located in urban areas; or it may make care less available to the poor because they must compete with privately insured persons who need the same care.

The extent to which states regulate or require private health insurance carriers to provide a comprehensive range of services, or require a standard definition of benefits or amounts of care covered, also affects access to care. On the one hand states that do little regulation leave the insured individual at risk, often finding out what the insurance did not cover when the bills arrive. States that heavily regulate insurance companies and set standards for comprehensive products with strong consumer protection provisions, on the other hand, often have fewer affordable products available to employers and individuals. The government and providers of care affect access to care through the organization of the health care delivery system, and through incentives that skew the availability of obtainable care.

Color Blindness and Provider Beliefs and Behaviors

Treating people the same is not necessarily the same as treating people equitably. Service providers since the civil rights era of the 60s have worked hard not to talk about responding to individual differences. Treating everyone as a "human being" and not "seeing differences" is a credo for non-discriminatory care in many parts of the country. Color-blindness, however, denies the differences that do exist.

As a service delivery policy, color-blindness denies differences in people's life chances and experiences with service systems. It also denies differences in individuals' ability to speak understandable English and places the burden of language access on the patient and not the provider. It also implies that it makes little difference that an elder's understanding of health and illness in old age differs from that of younger adults or from America's mainstream high tech culture. Practitioners are taught rather linear diagnostic and treatment protocols in their health disciplines; each step is a direct result of a yes/no response to a diagnostic possibility of treatment result. Color-blind approaches to care do not work, for example, when:

- one group of elders expects symptomatic relief and another group expects curative action (by medical or supernatural intervention); or
- a 72-year-old has a lower priority to obtain a hip replacement compared to a 50-year-old who has more active years ahead; or
- elders believe that traditional and "modern" or "Western" medicine are both needed to treat a condition; or
- elders insist that family members convene and the eldest son decide on the advanced directives and choose between aggressive or palliative care.

When service providers and service systems insist on an undifferentiated response to the patient needs and the health beliefs of individuals and groups, poor and inadequate care is provided in the terms and expectations of the patient/consumer. In these examples, provider beliefs and behavior affect access to care and the quality of care.

As a result of a series of focus groups convened around the country that involved aging and long term care service providers, community advocates, and administrators/program monitors, to focus on how the service system is responding to the growing diversity of elders and the growing diversity of the work force providing care to elders, a number of recommendations was made that provider groups and large service organizations conduct Diversity Assessments (Capitman, Hernandez, and Yee, 1990; Capitman, Hernandez-Gallegos, and Yee, 1992; Capitman, Hernandez-Gallegos, Yee and Madzimoyo, 1991). Such assessments would involve service providers in addressing issues of diversity at the level of: (a) direct service approaches (including outreach and the process of service provision); (b) the organization of services (including how services are accessed and how delivery is monitored); and (c) how organizations can incorporate the perspectives of diverse populations in their decision-making (including governance, inter-agency care planning mechanisms, and supervisory practices).

In general, recipes for action, i.e. approaches that help direct service staff to become more sensitive by learning about the foods and holidays of specific racial/ethnic groups, or learning to identify the differences between Tagalog, Cantonese and Korean, or learning about the differences in the refugee experiences of El Salvadorans, Russians, and Vietnamese elders, or the differences in expectations of immigrant elders who have been in the urban U.S. for forty years as opposed to five years, are helpful, but the information is not always helpful in improving the responsiveness of service or caregiving approaches. By conducting diversity assessments, organizations and local service systems can develop and monitor ongoing efforts to respond appropriately to the diversity of their communities.

New Dimensions for Considering Quality of Care

Access to care—getting into the service system as well as appropriately using services—needs to be incorporated in plans to improve quality in service approaches and service delivery systems. If timely and appropriate access to health care in managed care systems is as difficult for the most vulnerable elders as it has been in fee-for-service care, savings will not be achieved. Elders may relearn how to get timely care from an emergency room instead of getting routine care in a more appropriate service setting. Having identification cards for a health maintenance organization and cards for Medicare and Medicaid are not enough to assure timely and appropriate care. In some communities care is still denied or care provided is inadequate. Service systems and service providers need to understand how elders perceive and understand their needs and the purposes and resources of the health care delivery system in order for new services such as ambulatory surgery, urgent care, and high tech home care to be acceptable. In a home or hotel room with no running water or unreliable electricity, plans for wound care or the use of electricity-powered respiratory equipment may be as inappropriate as care plans for active and uncomfortable range of motion exercises for an elder with contracture who believes she will die soon and wants to be left in peace. Judgments about the quality of care provided to elders, especially the most vulnerable, need to explicitly reflect the ways in which elders and the service system/service providers negotiate the provision of care.

Challenges and Opportunities

If the most vulnerable elders who use a large proportion of some of the costliest health care in the country cannot access adequate care, then health care reforms that reorganize care and control the cost of care will have been unsuccessful. After providing an overview of the major issues in health care for elders, this chapter discussed access to care as a broad array of issues that encompassed getting into the system and obtaining appropriate care once in the system. Several steps can be taken to address the challenges presented to improve access to care:

First, define new outcomes in health care for elders, particularly older women and elders of color. More data and information are needed on how diverse populations of elders age, access care, and benefit from care received. Particular attention to understanding health status, health care needs, and service use among Pacific Islander/Asian-American as well as Hispanic elders is warranted. The 1990 Census indicates that these groups are the fastest growing populations in the U.S. Additionally, adequate samples of the oldest old women and elders of color and Hispanics need to be included in national and small area studies on the aging and aged in biomedical and health services research.

Second, conduct cross-national studies of models of successful health and long term care service approaches in multiethnic countries, such as Singapore, to provide practitioners with a better understanding of how a society can accommodate multicultural approaches in understanding: (a) health, illness and old age among diverse populations; (b) how services can be organized to meet the needs of diverse cultural and religious populations; and (c) how public policy can promote access among diverse populations.

Third, create a human resource agenda for health and long term care. This would include the recruitment, training, and retention of a diverse work force at all levels of the health care system, and developing service approaches that accommodate diverse populations.

Fourth, conduct diversity assessments as part of organizational responses to the increasing diversity of those who will use health service and those who will provide care.

REFERENCES

California Health and Welfare Agency. 1988. *A study of California's publicly funded long-term care programs*. Report of the California Health and Welfare Agency to the Legislature. Sacramento, CA: Author.

Callahan, J.J. & Wallack, S. 1981. *Reforming the Long-Term Care System*. Lexington, MA: Lexington Books.

Capitman, J.A. 1990. "Policy and Program Options in Community-Oriented Long-Term Care." In M.P. Lawton, ed., *Annual Review of Gerontology and Geriatrics* (pp. 357–388). New York: Springer.

Capitman, J.A.; Hernandez, W.; & Yee, D.L. 1990. *Cultural Diversity and the Aging Network: An Exploratory Study*. National Aging Resource Center Long-Term Care. Waltham, MA: Brandeis University Heller School of Social Welfare.

Capitman, J.A.; Hernandez-Gallegos, W.; & Yee, D.L. 1992. Diversity assessments. *Generations, 15*, 73–76.

Capitman, J.A.; Hernandez-Gallegos, W.; Yee, D.L.; & Madzimoyo, W. 1991. *Diversity Assessment Handbook*. National Aging Resource Center Long Term Care. Waltham, MA: Brandeis University Heller School of Social Welfare.

Capitman, J.A.; Wethers, B.; & Sadowsky, E. 1992. *Use of formal long term care services: Evidence for the roles of race/ethnicity, gender, and informal care*. Prepared for the American Association of Retired Persons. Waltham, MA: Brandeis University Heller School of Social Welfare.

Dobson, A.; Spaw, N.; Hearle, K.; & McGowen, M. 1991. *An examination of winners and losers under Medicare's prospective payment system: A synthesis of the evidence*. Report to Congress, Technical Report Series Extramural Report 1–91–06, prepared by Lewin/ICF for the Prospective Payment Assessment Commission.

Karon, S.L. & Capitman, J.A. 1992. *Race, gender and informal care effects on formal long term care use of elders with chronic health needs*. Prepared for the American Association of Retired Persons. Waltham, MA: Brandeis University Heller School of Social Welfare.

Kasper, J.D. 1988. *Aging Alone: Profiles and Projections*. New York: The Commonwealth Fund Commission on Elderly People Living Alone.

Moon, M. 1991. The economic status of older Americans. *Aging Network News* (September), p. 1, 4.

Office of National Cost Estimates. 1990. National health expenditures 1988. *Health Care Financing Review, 11,* 1–41.

Pendleton, S.; Capitman, J.; Leutz, W.; & Omata, R. 1990. *State Infrastructure for Long Term Care: A National Study of State Systems 1989*. Waltham, MA: Brandies University Heller School of Social Welfare.

Raetzman, S.O. 1991. *Reforming the health care system: State profiles 1990.* Washington, DC: American Association of Retired Persons Public Policy Institute.

Rak, K. 1991. Home health industry prepared stronger anti-sampling measure for Senate. *Home Health Line* (September 18), 345–346.

———. 1992. Spending for home health care climbed by 440 percent. *Home Health* Line (March 18), 126.

Soldo, B.J. & Manton, K. 1985. Health status and service needs of the oldest old: Current patterns and future trends. *The Millbank Memorial Fund Quarterly, 63,* 286–319.

U.S. Department of Health and Human Services. 1986. *Health status of the disadvantaged: Chartbook 1986*. Washington, DC: Public Health Service, Bureau of Health Professionals.

U.S. Department of Health and Human Services: Public Health Service. 1990. *Healthy people 2000: National health promotion and disease prevention objectives.* Summary Report No. (PHS) 91–50213. Washington, DC: U.S. Department of Health and Human Services, Public Health Service.

U.S. Senate Special Committee on Aging, American Association of Retired Persons, Federal Council on Aging, & U.S. Administration on Aging. 1991. *Aging America: Trends and Projections.* DHHS Publication (FCoA)91280001. Washington, DC: U.S. Department of Health and Human Services.

Verbrugge, L.M.; Lepkowski, J.M. & Imanaka, Y. 1989. Co-morbidity and its impact on disability. *The Gerontologist, 67,* 450–484.

Wethers, B.; Capitman, J.A.; & Yee, D.L. 1992. *Health Status and Access to Health Care for Older Women.* Prepared for the National Eldercare Institute on Older Women, the National Council for Negro Women. Waltham, MA: Brandeis University Heller School of Social Welfare.

Yee, D.L. 1992. Health care access and advocacy for immigrant and other underserved elders. *Journal of Health Care for the Poor and Underserved*, 2, 448–464.

Yee, D.L. & Kamikawa, L.M. 1992. *Caregiving: Challenging complexity*. Prepared for the National Eldercare Institute on Older Women, the National Council for Negro Women. Waltham, MA: Brandeis University Heller School of Social Welfare.

Note

The author expresses appreciation to John A. Capitman, Ph.D. for his comments and assistance.

CHAPTER 12

Mental Health and Mental Health Services

Mary S. Harper

Although the advances of recent years in the field of health and particularly in mental health and aging have been unprecedented, we are having trouble coping with success. People are living longer and we have more "walking wounded"; their lives are not necessarily better. To accommodate the changing needs of an increasingly older society, we must broaden the traditional goals of health—curing disease and preventing its occurrence—to include preventing the ill from becoming disabled, helping the disabled live with the disabilities, and preventing excessive disability.

Caring for persons who are disabled must include dealing with the consequences of the disease (stigma, social isolation, lack of access to affordable, quality care) because we are living in a time which we not only fear failure, we fear success. For with success comes additional responsibilities, demands, and opportunity for failure.

As we read in chapter 1, the United States is a graying society. About 6,000 persons celebrated their 65th birthdays per day in 1990, or about 2.2 million persons celebrated their 65th birthdays in 1990. The older population (persons 65 years of age and above) numbered 31.2 million in 1990. They represented 12.7 percent of the U.S. population or about one in eight Americans. By the year 2000, persons 65 and over are expected to represent 13 percent of the population, and this percentage will increase to 21.2 percent by 2030. In 1990, African-American elderly represented 18 percent of the population 65 and over; about 3 percent are other ethnic or racial groups, (including Native Americans, Eskimos, Aleut, Asian and Pacific Islanders). Persons of Hispanic origin represented 4 percent of the older population (AARP 1991). By 2025, 15 percent of the elderly population will be nonwhite and by 2050, 20 percent are likely to be nonwhite (Harper, 1990).

Currently there are nearly 50,000 centenarians (per 100 years old and above); twice the number of five years ago. By the year 2000, the number is expected to double. The fastest growing group of elderly are the 85 and over group (Johns Hopkins Medical Letter, 1991). This group is 24 times larger than it was in 1900. Despite the image of illness, disability, and impending death that our society has given to old age, the majority of community-dwelling elderly report themselves to be in good health. They describe themselves as healthy even though over 80 percent admit to at least one chronic medical condition, and 50 percent to 70 percent are diagnosed as having physical illness (LaRue, Bank, and Jarvik, 1979).

The Incidence and Prevalence of Psychiatric Disorders

The elderly suffer disproportionately from psychiatric disorders. Incidences of suicide and functional disorders, notably depression and paranoid states, increase with age. Organic brain disease increases after 60, and the suicide rate is highest in elderly white males (Butler, 1975; NCHS, 1987; Wasylenki, 1982).

Kay, Beamish, and Roth (1964) found a 31 percent prevalence of functional psychiatric disorder among the over-sixty-five population living in Newcastle, England. Other studies have found roughly a 30 percent prevalence of diagnosable psychiatric disorder in the over-sixty-five population with about 15 percent likely to be severely disabled. In general, it is estimated that 18 percent to 25 percent of the elderly in the United States have significant psychopathology (Talbott, 1989).

The American Psychological Association (1991) and the National Alliance for the Mentally Ill (1991) reported that 28 million adults have a serious mental disorder other than substance abuse. One in five Americans will suffer from mental illness at some point in their lives, and only 20 percent of them will receive professional care. According to Regier (1988), there is a 22.1 percent lifetime prevalence of mental disorders in the U.S. population and a 12.6 percent one month prevalence.

Almost four million people, including one-third of the nation's 600,000 homeless persons are now suffering from severe mental illness. These mental illnesses cost society an estimated $129.3 billion annually, about half of which is attributed to at least productivity loss in the work place (Bevilacque, 1991).

By severe mental illness, I am referring to persistent mental or emotional disorders (including but not limited to schizophrenia, schizo-affective disorders, mood disorders, and severe personality disorders), that significantly interfere with a person's ability to carry out such primary aspects of daily life as self care, household management, interpersonal relationships, and work or school. Mental illness, including depression, can be as functionally disabling as a serious heart condition and more disabling than other chronic physical illnesses such as lung or gastro-intestinal problems, angina, hypertension, and even diabetes (Wells, 1989). Sixty percent of all health-care visits are by people with no physical problems. This figure rises from 80 percent to 90 percent when stress-related illnesses (e.g., peptic ulcers, ulcerative colitis, hypertension, etc.) are also included. Stigma surrounding mental disorders and ageism rob from the elderly with mental illness their ability-willingness to seek assessment, diagnosis and treatment.

"Health" among the elderly has been defined as the ability to live and function effectively in society and to exercise self-reliance and autonomy to the maximum extent feasible. This does not necessarily mean the total absence of disease. Mental illness can occur at a time when a cluster of behavioral signs and symptoms come together and disrupt the individual's ability to function effectively within the mainstream of the family, work, or community setting.

Mental health and the older adult is a complex area of study because mental illnesses can be the result of physical, emotional, social or mental disorders. The following points will provide examples of how physical and mental illness interface:

1. Physical health problems with emotional, social and mental disorders sequelae (e.g., confusion, anxiety, depression, delusions, memory disturbance, dehydration, and electrolyte disturbances, hypothermia and severe pain) may cause confusion, depression and fecal impaction.
2. Psychiatric factors that precipitate physical health problems (e.g., depression) may create weight loss, dehydration, or electrolyte disturbance.
3. Psychosocial factors might influence the course of a medical problem (e.g., living alone and/or never being married, might precipitate nursing home placement after the amputation of the right leg of a 90-year-old man). Bereavement and emotional factors have been associated with decreased immunologic reactivity and hospitalization for congestive heart failure.
4. Concurrent mental and physical health problems influencing the course of another (e.g., paranoid state and congestive heart failure [CHF]) might make a patient think his prescribed medicines are poisons. The resulting paranoia might ultimately interfere with the proper medical management for CHF.
5. Mental or physical health problems resulting from the toxic side effects of drugs (e.g., digitalis, steroids, anti-diabetic agents, anti-hypertensive agents as well as tri-cyclic antidepressants) may produce delirious states of disorientation, memory loss, confusion and personality changes. Several studies indicate that up to 25 percent of individuals 65 and older admitted to health care facilities are due to drug-interactions or drug-food interactions.

The elderly do not have high prevalence of severe mental illness such as schizophrenia, manic depressive psychosis, etc. According to the NIMH (National Institute of Mental Health), the elderly in the community had the lowest rates of all groups with the eight disorders studied. The eight disorders included affective disorders, panic-obsessive compulsive disorders, substance abuse dependence, somatization disorders, antisocial personality disorders, schizophrenia, phobia, and cognitive impairment. The NIMH study found mild cognitive impairment in 14 percent of adult males and females, and severe impairment in 5.6 percent in older men and 3 percent in older women.

The most common behavioral, emotional and mental disorders of the elderly representing medical illness include:

- depression
- cognitive impairment
- dementia
- anxiety
- agitation/restlessness
- confusion (delirium)
- sleep disorders
- feelings of unworthiness, hopelessness
- suicide/suicide ideation
- substance abuse
- loneliness

Atypical and Nonspecific Presentation of Disease in the Elderly

The elderly will often present their illnesses in one or more nonspecific ways (i.e., disabilities) that rapidly results in functional impairment. The early signs of disease and/or functional impairment in the elderly frequently include:

- change in appetite, cessation of eating or drinking
- disturbance of gait
- dizziness upon standing
- new onset of urinary incontinence
- constipation or diarrhea
- apathy/withdrawal
- crying spells
- impaired ability to concentrate for long periods
- restlessness/agitation
- confusion
- insomnia
- headaches
- fatigue

It is estimated that 30 percent of the elderly have problems with sleeping, including insomnia (problems initiating and maintaining sleep, often associated with psychiatric disorders such as depression, anxiety and drug toxicity). The elderly may also have problems with sleep walking, sleep terror, sleep-related epileptic seizures, or irregular waking (Miles, 1984).

Symptoms such as fatigue, insomnia, apathy, confusion, anorexia, as well as headache, abdominal and other more diffuse pains in the elderly may represent a human reactivity to psychological disorders as well as physical illness. In the elderly patient, in whom chronic and acute medical conditions may produce a myriad of symptoms, it can be a formidable task to distinguish psychological from physical symptoms. Several studies have shown a close relationship between physical symptoms and psychopathology in the elderly (Ouslander, 1982). Pfeiffer and Busse (1973) noted that 33 percent of the elderly in the community have an anxious preoccupation with bodily functions. Salzman and Shader (1978) found 64 percent of the elderly individuals hospitalized for depression, had physically unadjusted bodily complaints, most frequently involving the gastrointestinal tract, the head, or the cardiovascular system.

Any medical condition that is associated with systemic involvement and metabolic disturbances can have profound effects on mental function in acutely ill elderly patients (Habot and Lebow, 1980; Jarvik and Perl, 1981). The most common among these are fever, dehydration, decreased cardiac output, electrolyte disturbances, and hypoxia. The elderly have to be frequently reminded to take fluids. They have a different thirst level from persons under 65 years of age.

Cancer of the pancreas combined with anxiety and depression can present in addition to anorexia, weight loss and back pain in up to 75 percent of patients (Fras, Litin and Pearson, 1967). These patients often lack the feelings of guilt, agitation, delusions, memory impairment, and suicidal thoughts that are commonly seen in psychiatric depression in later years (Blinder, 1966). Eight to 90 percent of hypothyroid patients manifest psychomotor retardation, irritability and depression (Brown, 1975; Ouslander, 1982).

The most common atypical findings of diabetes mellitus in the elderly is an alteration in mentation. This may present as an acute confusional state, delirium or dementia. In a recent study of mental illness among the elderly in noninstitutional settings, one nurse described a clinic for diabetics as a clinic for depressives. They noticed that 85 percent of the 75 diabetic patients were depressed elderly people using the DSM III criteria for depression. This is an observation which should be studied. Because 38 percent of all people with diabetes mellitus are over 65 years of age, it is essential that all health care providers and family caregivers have a thorough understanding of the signs and symptoms of diabetes mellitus and its diagnoses in order to distinguish it from age-related changes or glucose tolerance (Gambert, 1990a; Gambert, 1990b).

Most health care providers, such as physicians, social workers, nurses and nurse aides, and have seen elderly persons who have fecal impactions in a state of confusion and delirium; myocardial infarction commonly present with a shortness of breath without chest pain; hyperthyroidism may be present with apathy and cachexia; diabetes is no exception and also has a myriad of atypical symptoms in later life. Pneumonia may be present with confusion and dehydration instead of a high temperature (Keating and Lubin, 1990).

Perioperative Psychiatric Considerations in the Elderly

About 190 surgical procedures per 100,000 population are performed yearly on patients aged 65 years or older, as compared with 136 procedures per 100,000 in the age group aged 45 to 64 (Keating and Lubin, 1990). As both surgical techniques and technology, and the general health of the elderly improve, this rate of intervention is likely to increase. Some common psychiatric problems encountered in this surgical elderly population include:

- postoperative agitation
- delirium/confusion
- alterations of cognitive
- alcohol withdrawal
- depression
- anxiety (Keating and Lubin, 1990; Hogstel and Taylor, 1988).

Some illnesses present with violent behavior include: amphetamine-induced psychosis, temporal lobe epilepsy, delirium tremens, homosexual panic, and alcoholic paranoia (Slaby, 1986). Some illnesses present with depression include: Alzheimer's disease, barbiturate intoxication, multiple sclerosis, diabetes mellitus, hepatitis, steroid and digitalis toxicities (Slaby, 1986; Baker, Jones, and Lavizzo-Mourey, 1990).

Psychiatric Emergencies

Many of the elderly do not have a regular family physician, and therefore they use emergency care (Reynolds,1988; Hogstel, 1990). The emergency department serves the elderly in three ways:

1. as a primary care provider
2. as a place for receiving urgent and emergent care
3. as an entry into the acute or long term care health system

Elderly with poor family support or no regular physician will use the emergency caregiving system 7 to 30 times per year. In some emergency rooms, 20 percent to 30 percent of their patients are over 65 years of age. Therefore, in cross training of staff, the emergency room personnel should be given organized instruction in aging and mental health. Some of the reasons the elderly use the emergency room include: vascular problems which alter behavior, confusion, anxiety, depression, accident, acute disturbance of thought, mood or social relationship, drug-drug interactions side-effects. Psychiatric emergency has been defined as an acute disturbance of thought, mood, behavior, social relationship) that requires an immediate intervention as defined by the patient, family or the community (Satloff and Worby, 1970).

Most small hospitals do not have a staff gero-psychiatrist, therefore, it may be helpful if they have a psychiatric liaison, consultant psychiatrist or gero-psychiatric nurse practitioners. Because many of the elderly who use the emergency room are racial and ethnic minorities, this service should have a bicultural and bilingual staff person on each tour of duty.

It must be remembered that some of the elderly experience many losses: loss of roles, serious visual loss, loss of income, loss of work, loss of ability to drive and a loss of good friends and family. On many occasions, these losses make the elderly vulnerable to behavioral, emotional and social breakdowns.

Mental Illness in Nursing Homes

It has been reported that more than 50 percent of the nursing home patients have some type of mental illness (Hogstel, 1990; Harper and Lebowitz, 1986). In many nursing homes the use of restraints and psychotropic drugs are misused.

Some of the reasons for referring the elderly to a nursing home include: depression, disruptive behavior, wandering, paranoid behavior, general confusion and disruptive behavior (physical, verbal, or sexual), and assaultiveness (Hogstel, 1990). Most of the reasons for transfer or referral of the elderly to the nursing home are for behavioral reasons or incontinence, and therefore nursing home staff must be trained, and there should be an individual care plan on each patient. According to OBRA (Omnibus Budget Reconciliation Act) of 1987, a MDSF (Minimum Data Set Forum) should be prepared on each patient and used for care planning and actions. The federal register (1989) includes the definition for active psychiatric treatment, as well as the requirement for training nurse aides. In OBRA Pre-admission Screening/Annual Resident Review (PASARR) is required on all admissions followed by periodic screening. There are over 325 rules, regulations, guidelines or policies governing medicare, medicaid eligible nursing homes. The health care provider should become familiar with the regulations, comment on them during the NPRM (Notice of Proposed Rule Making) period. These regulations are drawn upon to improve the quality of care and to regulate cost.

In the delivery of mental health services, one must be concerned with long-term care facilities such as nursing homes, boarding care homes, assisted living, adult day care, acute medical institution, home health-care agencies, shelters and nursing for the elderly who are homeless, and homes for the aged. Ninety-five percent of the elderly live in the community and only 5 percent are in institutions.

Mental health services must be extended to the shelters and missions for the elderly who are homeless and mentally ill. At any given time, there are approximately 600,000 homeless people in America. It is estimated that 200,000 homeless persons suffer from severe mental disorders. Rossi and Wright (1987) estimated that 19.4 percent of his study group were elderly, while Lamb (1984) and his task force estimated that 70 percent of the adult homeless had a mental disorder. The mental health services for the homeless elderly are fragmented and lack continuity (Tessler and Dennis, 1989). Some of the shelters report 40 percent to 50 percent of their residents are over age 55 (Harper, in press).

Resources for funding research in this area are available from NIMH and the Health Resources and Health Administration. There is an Interagency Council on the Homeless in Washington, DC (Task Force on Homelessness and Severe Mental Illness, 1992). Another resource is the National Resource Center on Homelessness and Mental Illness. The task force report includes several guidelines and recommendations for implementing a program for the homeless. It is imperative that aging and mental health agencies build ties and collaborate with each other. They must identify the elements of coalition building so as to minimize the fragmentation of mental health services to the elderly (York, 1977).

Guidelines for Clinical Practices

The Institute of Medicine and the Agency for Health Care Programs and Research (AHCPR) have developed guidelines for clinical practice. The AHCPR has established 12 panels of experts to develop clinical guidelines, in such areas as pain, incontinence and so on. Of special interest to the mental health worker, will be guidelines on depression, pain, and Alzheimer's disease. These guidelines are not available at the time of this writing. Nonetheless, the guidelines are aimed at bringing about consistency and improving the quality of care. In order to improve the quality of care, we must study the processes, structure and outcomes as proposed by Donabedian (1980).

Assessment

The selection of the instrument for assessment is very important. Many instruments have not been normed on the elderly. Few instruments have been normed on the minority elderly. One of the most common problems in the care of the elderly is misdiagnosis, and such a mistake is contributed more often than not by the use of an instrument with low validity of reliability for the sample.

Burgess (1992) has developed a mental status examination which can be used to assess four major mental disorders (depression, schizophrenia, personality disorder, and bipolar disorder). Ashford et al. (1992) have developed a scale to assess the severity of dementia. Diagnoses of dementia need to be complemented by precise determination of disease severity across the broad spectrum of disease progression. Ashford and his associates modified the Mini-Mental Status Exam (MMSE), the Activities of Daily Living Assessment (ADL) and the Clinical Dementia Rating Scale (CDRS) for direct comparability, and administered these exams to 112 outpatients and 45 nursing home residents. Nonetheless, the scales that showed the highest correlation for the probable Alzheimer's disease patient group were the Global Assessment of Dementia (GAD) and the

Extended Mini-Mental Assessment (EMA). They found high correlations and correspondence among these scales, and subsequently demonstrated their reliability, validity and utility in the assessment of dementia severity. Moreover, Hasegawa (1983) and Hasegawa, Inoue, and Mariya (1974) have developed a dementia rating scale for the Japanese elderly. Kawai et al. (1992) are using the Hosegawa scale to develop a comparable scale for the Chinese.

Summary

Mental health services to the elderly should add life to the later years by assuring all older people independence, community participation, care, self-fulfillment, and dignity. It must be remembered that 75 percent of mental health services to the elderly are provided by members of the family and family physicians; namely, nonpsychiatrist. All caregivers, informal and formal, need cross training (Brodaty & Peters, 1992).

REFERENCES

AARP (American Association of Retired Persons). 1991. *A profile of older Americans.* Washington, DC: Author.

American Psychological Association. 1991. *Mental health benefits: Needs and cost effectiveness.* Washington, DC: Author.

Ashford, J.W.; Kuman, V.; Barringer, M.; Bocker, M.; Bice, J.; Ryan, N; Vicari, S. 1992. Assessing Alzheimer severity with a global clinical scale. *International Psychogeriatrics*, 4, 55–74.

Baker, F.M.; Jones, B.E.; & Lavizzo-Mourey. 1990. "Acute Care of the African American Elder." In S.P. Jonas and M.J. Mellor, eds., *Geriatric Psychiatry for African Americans* (pp. 22–37), New York, NY: the Hunter Mt. Sinai Geriatric Education Center.

Bevilacque, J.J. 1991. *Mental Illness in America: A Series of Public Hearings.* Testimony presented at the National Advisory Mental Health

Council and the National Mental Health Leadership Forum Hearing on Severe Mental Illness and Homelessness in Chicago, Illinois.

Blinder, M.S. 1966. The pragmatic classification of depression. *American Journal of Psychiatry, 123,* 259–269.

Brodaty, H. & Peters, K.E. 1992. Cost effectiveness of a training program for dementia carers. *International Psychogeriatrics, 3,* 11–22.

Brown, G.M. 1975. Psychiatric and neurologic aspects of endocrine disease. *Hospital Practice, 10,* 71–79.

Burgess, J.W. 1992. A standardized mental status examination discriminating four major mental disorders. *Hospital and Community Psychiatry, 43,* 937–939.

Butler, R.N. 1975. Psychiatry and the elderly: An overview. *American Journal of Psychiatry, 132,* 893–900.

Donabedian, A. 1980. *The Definition of Quality and Approaches to its Assessment*. Ann Arbor, MI: University of Michigan Health Administration Press.

Fras, I.; Litin, E.M.; & Pearson, J.S. 1967. "Comparison of psychiatric symptoms in carcinoma of the pancreas with those in some other intra-abdominal neoplasm." *American Journal of Psychiatry, 123,* 1555–1556.

Gambert, S.R. 1990a. "When to Treat: Glucose Intolerance Versus Diabetes Mellitus." In G.R. Gambert, ed., *Diabetes Mellitus in the Elderly: A Practical Guide.* New York, NY: Raven Press.

———. 1990b. "Atypical Presentation of Diabetes Mellitus in the Elderly." In J. From, ed., *Diabetes Mellitus in the Elderly.* Philadelphia, PA: W.B. Saunders.

Habot, B. & Lebow, L.S. 1980. "The Interrelationship of Mental and Physical Status and Its Assessment in Older Adult: Mind-Body Introduction." In J.E. Birren & R.B. Sloane, eds., *Handbook of Mental Health and Aging*. Englewood Cliffs, NJ: Prentice Hall.

Harper, M.S. 1990. "Introduction." In M.S. Harper, ed., *Minority Aging: Essential Curricula Content for Selected Health and Allied Health Professional* (p. 323), Washington, DC: U.S. Government Printing Office.

Harper, M.S. & Lebowitz, B.O. 1986. *Mental Illness in Nursing Homes: Agenda for Research.* Rockville, MD: National Institute of Mental Health.

Harper, M.S. (in press). Mental health services to the elderly who are homeless. *The ABNF Journal.*

Hasegawa, K. 1983. "The Clinical Assessment of Dementia in the Aged: A Dementia Screening Scale for Psychogeriatric Patients." In M. Bergenes, U. Lehr, E. Lang, & R. Schmits-Schnerzer, eds., *Aging in the Eighties and Beyond* (pp. 207–218), New York, NY: Springer Publishing Co.

Hasegawa, K.; Inoue, K.; & Mariya, K. 1974. An investigation of dementia rating scale for the elderly (In Japanese). *Clinical Psychiatry, 16,* 965–969.

Hogstel, M.O. & Taylor, M. 1988. "Perioperative Care." In M.O. Hogstel, ed., *Geropsychiatric Nursing* (pp. 335–353), St. Louis, MO: C.V. Mosby.

Hogstel, M.O. 1990. "Mental Illness in the Nursing Home." In M.O. Hogstel, ed., *Geropsychiatric Nursing* (pp. 260–282), St. Louis, MO: C.V. Mosby.

Johns Hopkins Medical Letter. 1991. *Health after 50.* Baltimore, MD: Johns Hopkins University.

Jarvik, L.F. & Perl, M. 1981. "Overview of Psychological Dysfunction and the Production of Psychiatric Problems in the Elderly." In A. Levenson & R.C. Hall, eds., *Psychiatric Management of Physical Disease in the Elderly.* New York, NY: Raven Press.

Kay, D.W.; Beamish, E.; & Roth, W. 1964. Old age mental disorders in Newcastle upon Tyne, *British Journal of Psychiatry, 110,* 146–158.

Kawai, M.J.; Sumazaki, K.; Miyamoto, M.; Miyamoto, Y.; & Miyamoto, K. 1992. Relationships among the symptoms of the elderly as revealed by multivariate analyses: A preliminary study. *International Psychogeriatrics, 4,* 75–89.

Keating, H.J. & Lubin, M.F. 1990. "Perioperative responsibilities of the physicians/geriatrician." In H.J. Keating, ed., *Perioperative Care of the Older Patient* (pp. 459–467), Philadelphia, PA: W.B. Saunders Co.

Lamb, H.R. 1984. *The Homeless Mentally Ill.* Washington, DC: American Psychiatry Association.

LaRue, A.; Bank, L.; Jarvik, L. 1979. Health in old age: How do physicians' rating and self rating compare. *Journal of Gerontology, 34,* 687–691.

Miles, L.A. 1984. "The Diagnosis and Evaluation of Sleep-Wake Disorders in Elderly Patients." In D.J. Kupfer & T. Crook, eds., *Physicians Guide to the Recognition and Treatment of Sleep Disorders in The Elderly.* New Canaan, CT: Mark Poewley Associates, Inc.

NCHS (National Center for Health Statistics). 1987. Health statistics of older persons in the United States. *Vital and Health Statistics, 25* (Series 3).

Ouslander, J.G. 1982. Illness and psychopathology in the elderly. *Psychiatric Clinic of North America, 5,* 145–158.

Pfeiffer, E. & Busse, E.W. 1973. "Affective Disorders." In W.E. Busse & E. Pfeiffer, eds., *Mental Illness in Late Life.* Washington, DC: American Psychiatric Association.

Regier, D.A. 1988. One month prevalence of mental disorders in the United States. *Archives of General Psychiatry, 45,* 977–986.

Reynolds, C.A. 1988. "Emergency Care." In M.O. Hogstel, ed., *Nursing Care of the Older Adult* (pp. 313–333), New York, NY: John Wiley & Sons.

Rossi, P.H. & Wright, J.D. 1987. The determinants of homelessness. *Health Affairs Bulletin, 6,* 19–31.

Salzman, C. & Shader, R.L. 1978. Depression in the elderly: Relationship between depression, psychologic defense mechanisms, and physical illness. *Journal of the American Geriatric Society, 26,* 253–260.

Satloff, A. & Warby, C.M. 1970. The psychiatric emergency service: A mirror of change. *American Journal of Psychiatry, 12,* 1628–1632.

Slaby, A.E. 1986. *Definitions and Conceptual Framework of Psychiatric Emergencies.* New York, NY: The Haworth Press.

Talbot, J.A. 1989. Clinical and policy issues. *New York Academy of Medicine Bulletin, 61,* 445–646.

Task Force on Homelessness and Severe Mental Illness Report. 1992. *Outcast on Main Street.* Rockville, MD: NIMH.

Tessler, R.C. & Dennis, D.L. 1989. *A synthesis of NIMH-funded research concerning persons who are homeless and mentally ill.* Rockville, MD: NIMH.

Wasylenki, D. 1982. The psychogeriatric problem. *Canada's Mental Health, 12,* 16–19.

Wells, K.B. 1989. The functioning and well-being of depressed patients: Results from the medical outcomes study. *Journal of the American Medical Association, 262,* 914–919.

York, J.L. 1977. *Community mental health centers and nursing homes: Guidelines for cooperative programs.* Columbus, OH: St. Lawrence Hospital.

PART IV

Conclusion

CHAPTER 13

A Service Model for the Aging and Aged
An International Perspective

Paul K.H. Kim

A pandemic phenomenon, that is the "graying world," has been well recognized by concerned scholars, human service professionals, and politicians worldwide. In the developed countries the number of older citizens will be doubled within 25 to 30 years. During the same period Chinese elders are estimated to be tripled; and the Singaporean, Malaysian, and South Korean elderly will quadruple within the same time (United Nations, 1988). Such a global wonder can be attributed to medical and other scientific technologies that have brought to humanity a healthier and more convenient lifestyle than ever before, resulting in longevity, while also achieving low fertility rates through a successful worldwide campaign.

The results of such changes in life expectancy and in the birth rate have consequently created other social problems for the world. For example, the issue of changing labor forces in the respective countries: The Japanese and U.S. governments are being forced to legislate and implement a variety of immigration and/or foreign laborer policies that are most attractive to younger work forces that are available in a number of countries, i.e., those in the Southeast Asia, Middle East, South and Central America, and the African regions. The United States, in order to maintain its economic stability, may have to immigrate annually as many as 400,000 persons from the above-mentioned areas of the world. Japan, which once was and perhaps still is the country that vehemently opposed the philosophy of xenogenesis, now grants foreign laborers the right to enter into the country for employment and also reluctantly accepts interracial marriages. Moreover, the Japanese government conceived and attempted to implement what was called the "Silver Columbia Plan," by which the rich and older Japanese were encouraged to retire in a number of the world's resort areas (Martin, 1989).

Moreover, Japan emphasizes pro-natalism and implements national policies relevant to fertility (Kojima, 1990). The Singaporean government has developed and set in motion a national fertility award system that provides tax advantages for those mothers who give birth to the second child before age 29 and for those who have 3 or more children; in addition, working mothers receive a tax break of 15% more than the normal tax allowance (Fawcett and Khoo, 1980).

To alleviate a future human disaster on the globe, which is positively in the making, countless numbers of innovative gerontological human service policies have been conceived and implemented to date. Those strategies can be characterized by four major categories: (1) extension of retirement age; (2) increased pension programs; (3) better social and health insurance programs; and (4) the mobilization of informal supports. Olson (1993) has compiled the gerontological human services in one volume, titled *The Graying of the World*, which promotes mutual understanding and learning of a variety of policies and service programs that are being implemented in the respective nations. This book is designed to share the service experiences in selected countries in order for others to learn and hopefully modify practices that will fit into their own social, cultural, and political spectrum. For example, Olson and her associates discuss: the U.S. model of privatization and the two classism of geriatric care; Swedish family-like "rehabilitative geriatric institutions"; Finland's communal support; Israel's service network model; British community-based care package system; Canadian integrated long term care; France's need coordination model; Germany's "Sozialstationen" for family care and in-home services; family and morality based care model in China and Japan; and competitive public choice (self-management) model in Yugoslavia.

The purpose of this concluding chapter is to briefly describe three seemingly effective gerontological service modalities and to conceptually integrate them into one model that could suggest a pragmatic venture in alleviating the plights facing the aging and aged in many countries. The three models are: the Central Provident Fund in Singapore, Community Care Project in England, and Modified Privatization of Services in the United States.

Central Provident Fund in Singapore

The country of Singapore, known as a city-nation or a nation of a small island, provides a higher quality of life to about three million people whose life expectancy is the second highest in Asia. About 160,000 Singaporean elders enjoy the country's natural and economic resources. Moreover, this nation is being well respected for her national policy which is based on a Confucian teaching, the filiation. Singapore may be the only country where a morality has become legislated and implemented nationally.

A unique nature of Central Provident Fund (CPF), which is a form of Singaporean national social insurance programs, is to cultivate a human morality, i.e., caring for the aged parents, and encourage middle-aged children to establish a savings account for their parents. It is designed to grant tax exemption for the children who contribute to the account up to the specified limit per annum; subsequently, the respective parents withdraw the savings upon their retirement. Parents may use the accumulated fund for other personal causes such as purchasing a retirement living quarter or initiating a small business that they would like to run after retirement. The fund can be used to pay monthly premiums for additional health insurance (i.e. U.S. medigap policies), as well as for supplementing their limited income. Thus those parents would have a higher level of income security by having incomes both from their own employment pension programs and from a CPF account.

Community Care Project (CCP) in England

The first CCP was established in May, 1977 in the City of East Kent of Canterbury, England, and implemented by two social workers. Today the CCP model is highly respected by concerned gerontologists throughout the world. The model has been imported by interested countries and is being implemented with or without modifications.

This service model is designed to maximize existing social and health resources, as well as to develop service programs for the elderly; to minimize any bureaucratic dysfunctional management procedures in the provision of services; and to enable social workers to provide services, which are autonomously and professionally devised (Challis and Davies, 1980; 1985). In other words, the CCP can be characterized by (1) program flexibility and (2) autonomous decentralization, by which the unique needs of the individual elderly can be met with a series of "personalized" services developed by professional social workers. The first principle, program flexibility, is based on the fact that needs of the elderly are different form individual to individual; and the second, autonomous decentralization, is on the premise that professional social workers, who maintain close contact with the elderly in need, have better understanding of the problems and means to solve them most efficiently and effectively.

The universal means of service delivery used by professional social workers is what is called "case management" structure and "service package," which are developed by the worker based on his/her assessment of the client's needs as well as on the availability of community resources. Should there be no resources in the community, the worker is expected to reach out to the community, including neighboring ones, with an intent either to develop the resources needed or to utilize resources found within other communities. In addition the worker, who is serving about 20 to 30 elderly clients as his/her caseload, dispenses cash promptly as needed; establishes service contract with vendors; recruits and trains unpaid volunteers and paid helpers, including informal network members of the elderly clientele; "matches" the elderly client with volunteer(s) and/or helper(s); and most of all, monitors service routines through the case management system. Thus, the elderly clients can live in their own familiar surroundings, i.e., their homes, friends and neighbors in their respective community. They are under the constant CCP supervision beginning from as early as 7 A.M. till 10 P.M.

Modified Privatization of Services in the United States

Based on political and cultural needs, all levels of the U.S. government have been electing to utilize private service industries by establishing a series of governmental service contracts with social and health care facilities, and to directly or indirectly reimburse such vendors. For the older citizens, the government institutes health care contracts with hospitals, nursing homes, boarding homes, home health care agencies, social service agencies, insurance companies, etc. This policy was originally conceived in the hope of minimizing dysfunctional bureaucratic federal and state management problems, and as an effort of maximizing effectiveness of services at the local level.

Nonetheless, the American long term care system is unwittingly becoming a two-class system (see Olson, 1993)—a tug at war between the public bureaucrats and private entrepreneurs. In such a dual scheme, economically disadvantaged elderly are primarily cared for by a number of public entitlement service programs and apt to be institutionalized more than their rich counterparts. On the other hand, the rich elderly, who are financially capable of purchasing services available in their community, will be able to maintain themselves in their own homes. They promote profit making motives in the minds of the business sectors of the community. Consequently, the American privatization plan and its implementation certainly have created a welfare quagmire; i.e., a variety of geriatric services programs, a series of subsequent confusions in the minds of the clientele, duplication of services, counter productive competitions, and questionable effectiveness in the minds of the concerned public over the welfare entrepreneurs.

Triadic Approach to Gerontological Human Services: An Integration of Three Models

The triadic approach to gerontological human services herein proposed is an integration of the three models discussed above; namely, it is a joint venture of (1) family members of the elderly (CPF program); (2) community where the elderly reside (CCP program); and (3) government that effectively facilitates privatization of human services. As graphically depicted below in Figure 1, the center where the three models intersect is called "Triadic Model," which is a combination of only the unique qualities of the three models.

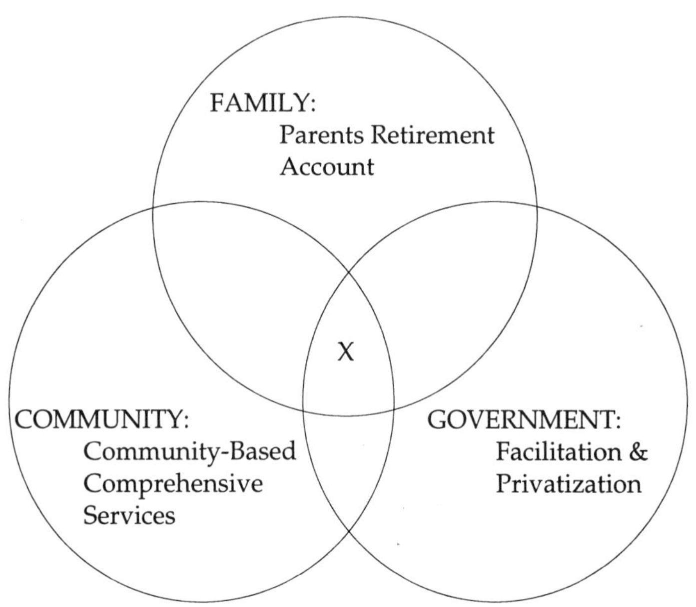

X=INTEGRATED GERONTOLOGICAL SOCIAL WORK

Figure 1. A Triadic Approach to Gerontological Social Services

To make this model work, some relevant functions of the respective actors are listed as follows:

Family

It is said in an adage that "As parent crows fed their baby chicks, grown-up babies feed their parents." This is a lesson from the world of nature as well as from teachings of morality that is more than appropriate for mankind. Human children are expected to and should take care of their elderly parents as their parents once did for them, though the debt of the parental love is never paid off by the children. Nonetheless, children of American families should exercise the following filial responsibilities and duties to make the model work:

1. The spirit of competition among siblings in taking care of their older parents:

No one was born out of a blue sky, but through his/her parents. And thus every sibling is responsible for his/her parents—not only the oldest son or sons, daughters, or those who happen to live nearer to the parents, but all of them. This further implies children's commitment to the parents for their physical, emotional, and spiritual needs. Children should realize the fact that as they take care of their parents today, they will be taken care of by their own children tomorrow. Namely, children today should understand the fact that their endurance in parental care is indeed for themselves tomorrow.

2. Advocacy for and participation in the Parents Retirement Account (PRA):

The PRA policy is being suggested to be an American version of the Singaporean CPF. Unlike the American IRA (Individual Retirement Account) that only protects the individual who contributed during his/her adult years, PRA is to financially benefit the parents upon their retirement. Children are expected and should advocate not only for legislation of PRA but also should participate in the program in accordance with their financial capability. The American public should educate children today to set aside some funds for their parents through a thrifty life style. American children should be helped to understand that there is no limit in spending to satisfy any degree of human greed.

3. Gerontological human services beginning from younger age cohorts, before the magic age of 60 or 65:

A broader concept of gerontological human services includes younger age cohorts. In fact it starts with individuals of all ages, simply because children today will be the elderly of tomorrow. The American public should be provided information on the aging process as they grow older in American societies, as well as the types of service programs available to them such as public entitlement. Moreover, children today should be encouraged to be active participants in the creation of a better world to live in for themselves in the near future.

Community

As an Asian adage saying that "it is definitely lighter if two persons together hold a sheet of paper," the family with elderly members alone may not be able to cope with problems associated with human aging. It requires formal and informal assistance external to their family system, called "community." The community in which the elderly reside is called upon to help older constituents by participating in the following activities:

1. Mobilization of philanthropists:

Irrefutably, America (USA) is still beautiful, in that she is a country of giving people. More than fifty billion dollars a year have been donated by Americans for a number of good causes, including human service programs. Therefore each community should be responsible for identifying local philanthropists and working with them for the welfare of older citizens. On the other hand, communities should encourage their constituents to become "Good Samaritans" who actively participate in helping the underprivileged in their respective communities.

2. Development of a CCP program appropriate for the community:

The elderly in the community deserve quality services that are delivered through an effective case management system, which is to be implemented under the flexible and autonomous service delivery structure. This should be an "A to Z" program that is to be constantly monitored by the community volunteers and helpers.

3. Education, training, and mobilization of community volunteers and helpers:

The success of the model is dependent upon the community's readiness in being responsive to the human service needs of its elderly population, and such an arrangement can only be made possible when the community recruits and trains volunteers and helpers. The cadre of such individuals should be established in each community and relied upon in the time of need.

4. Public education and forums:

A representative body of the respective voluntary agencies in the community should plan, develop, and implement a series of community forums to inform the public about community needs, as well as to solicit public opinions about problem solving strategies for the elderly.

5. Voluntary or not-for-profit organizations:

A variety of forms and structures are essential elements for the model proposed here. Such organizations should be maintained in the community where the elderly reside. Some of their functions, which are certainly inter-related with those of the various governmental bodies, are:

a. Contributions to the community of knowledge through research and planning:

Voluntary agencies should be involved in maintaining a series of dialogues among service providers, conducting needs assessments and program evaluations, and finally in taking proactive roles in the promotion of effective and adequate service programs.

b. *Creation/promotion of an environment that is free from competitive mentality against other agencies:*

Constructive competitions that presage positive effects include continuous sharing of information about how to be programmatically efficient and effective, and frequent discussions among service providers. Unlike business and competitive research industries, human services enterprises are to be enhanced through a wide-open system. And thus mutual help is the key to the success in human services.

Government

All levels of government, the federal in particular, must take leadership roles in the development and implementation of the integrated model. Some of their functions include:

1. Government support for a minimum of one professional social worker employed by local governments (township, city and/or county/parish) to serve the elderly. The number of such professionals may increase in accordance to the scope of the local needs of the elderly. Each social worker will provide direct services to an average of no more than 30 intensive cases. Social workers should perform autonomous professional activities, including the formulation and utilization of community resources.
2. The legislative branch of the federal government enacting public law(s) that promotes the PRA program to be a national public movement by granting specific tax exemptions to those children who establish an account and/or who support parents' medigap insurance premium programs. Details of the PRA act should include the following: the maximum/minimum amount of contribution by the children to the account, parents' age of maturity, privileges and rights of the parents over the account, etc.

3. A Presidential Office of Aging is to be established and operated under the direct supervision of the White House. This office should be placed at a cabinet level charged with consolidating all national entitlement programs designed to serve the aging and aged that are currently being administered through a number of (if not all) administrative departments. Moreover, the secretary of this office is responsible for the following functions: the development of a national budget for the older Americans; dispensing the budget directly to local governments; program planning and monitoring (including formative, experimental and evaluation research, as well as manpower training); and involvement in national advocacy activities (including public education), etc.
4. In consultation with local governments, the Office of Aging grants service funds to not-for-profit private social and health service agencies that are responsive to the local needs of the elderly. Secretary is charged to examine the local needs, avoid undue duplication and competition of services, and to promote mutual cooperation.

Roles of Local Professionals Concerned with the Welfare of the Elderly

In order to make the model functionally realistic, it is imperative to effectively mobilize local professional volunteers, who are sincerely concerned about the total welfare of the community elderly. These professionals and concerned citizens constitute a group, perhaps a structured board, to whom the following advisory roles are charged:

1. Public education for local citizens, philanthropists in particular, in order for them to be involved in the activities that would enhance the welfare of older neighbors.
2. Utilization of community resources, i.e., institutions of higher education, to conduct locally relevant research projects and intensify service programs for the elderly

beginning from the time of intake of the client to the post care planning.

3. This group of concerned citizens advocates for the elderly through the political arena at local, regional, and national levels.
4. This group of experts works closely with local social worker(s) and is involved in training of local helpers and volunteers, who can provide services required by the elderly.
5. This professional body translates the state-of-the-art scientific knowledge for the public and subse quently prevents problems of the elderly from being insurmountable.

Conclusion

Although the provisions under the PRA entitlement could/should be specified in terms of its limitations, it should further require some stipulations relative to both parties (parents and children) of the account. This is necessary because the American life style (as well as the life style prevailing in many countries of the world today) consists of the phenomenon of divorce and multiple or frequent marriages. Thus the following questions need to be carefully considered in depth and appropriate answers formulated:

1. *Ownership of the PRA fund*: Who is the owner of the PRA in case of divorced or separated parents? Father? Mother? or children? If children, who should be responsible and how is it to be managed? If a divorced parent remarries, does each take one-half of the account balance irrespective of the cause of separation? Should a judicial system be involved in this case?
2. *Elderly singles or the couple without children*: How does PRA benefit elderly couples without children? How about the single elderly? Does the PRA entitlement allow children to institute and contribute to PRA of the elderly *relatives* who have no dependents? Does the law permit

rich children to support their elderly relatives who are poor and/or whose children are unable to contribute to their parent's support?

3. *Compulsory and/or Participatory*: As part of the Social Security Trust Fund, should the PRA entitlement be made compulsory and/or participatory? Or should it be implemented strictly on a voluntary basis?

Services to the aging and aged, including public policies, rely on the imagination, creativity, commitment, and ingenuity of the professionals who are trained to be gerontological human service workers. And thus human services in theories and practices could be unlimited. Nonetheless, from a programmatic point of view, certain limitations imposed by societal and cultural circumstances are unavoidable. Implementation strategies may be situational and relative, though service ideologies, i.e., philosophies and ethics toward the welfare of the elderly, are universal and thus transferrable.

In conclusion, the nucleus of the matter in the field of American gerontological human services is not the availability of resources but the lack of public decision to appropriately attend and systematically alleviate the plights facing the aging and aged today and tomorrow. Let us think and proact on this matter, for that is our responsibility today.

REFERENCES

Central Provident Fund. 1991. *Central Provident Fund (CPF)*. Singapore: Author.

Challis, D. & Davies, B. 1985. Long term care for the elderly. *British Journal of Social Work, 15*, 563–579.

Challis, D. & Davies, B. 1980. A new approach to community care for the elderly. *British Journal of Social Work, 10*, 1–17.

Fawcett, J. & Khoo, S.E. 1980. *Population Development Review, 6*, 549.

Kojima, H. 1990. *Attitudes toward population trends and policy in Japan.* Paper presented at the annual meeting of the American Sociological Association, Washington.

Martin, L.G. 1989. *Population Bulletin, 44.*

Olson, L. ed. 1993. *The Graying of the World*. New York: Haworth Press.

United Nations. 1988. *World Population Prospects*. New York: Author.

Contributing Authors

Martha Baum
Professor, School of Social Work, University of Pittsburgh

David E. Biegel
Henry L. Zucker Professor of Social Work Practice, Professor of Sociology, Mandel School of Applied Social Sciences, Case Western Reserve University

Jerome L. Blakemore
Assistant Professor of Social Work, School of Social Work, University of Wisconsin at Milwaukee

Robert H. Binstock
Professor of Aging, Health, and Society, Department of Epidemiology and Biostatistics, School of Medicine, Case Western Reserve University

Kathleen J. Farkas
Associate Professor, Mandel School of Applied Social Sciences, Case Western Reserve University

Mary S. Harper
Co-Chair, Health Care Reform, Mental Health-Public Sector, Coordinator of Long Term Care Program, NIMH Mental Disorders of Aging Research

Robert B. Hudson
Professor and Chair, Department of Social Welfare Policy, School of Social Work, Boston University

Lenard W. Kaye
Professor of Social Work, School of Social Work and Social Research, Bryn Mawr College

Paul K.H. Kim
Professor of Social Work, School of Social Work, Louisiana State University

Rosemary McCaslin
Professor and Director, Department of Social Work, California State Unviersity, San Bernardino

R.L. McNeely
Professor of Social Work, School of Social Work, University of Wisconsin at Milwaukee

Abraham Monk
Professor of Gerontology and Social Work, School of Social Work, Columbia University

Laura Katz Olson
Professor of Government, Lehigh University

Jon Pynoos
Director for the National Elder Care Institute on Housing and Supportive Services; United Parcel Services Foundation Associate Professor of Gerontology, Public Policy, and Urban Planning, Andreus Gerontology Center, University of Southern California

Nancy Wadsworth
Geriatric Education Center, Case Western Reserve University

Robert O. Washington
Professor, College of Urban and Public Affairs, University of New Orleans

Donna L. Yee
Senior Research Associate, Institute for Health Policy, Heller School for Advanced Studies in Social Welfare, Brandeis University

Index